RADICAL THEOLOGY

INDIANA SERIES IN THE PHILOSOPHY OF RELIGION

Merold Westphal, *editor*

RADICAL THEOLOGY

A VISION FOR CHANGE

JEFFREY W. ROBBINS

Indiana University Press
Bloomington and Indianapolis

This book is a publication of

Indiana University Press
Office of Scholarly Publishing
Herman B Wells Library 350
1320 East 10th Street
Bloomington, Indiana 47405 USA

iupress.indiana.edu

The paper used in this publication meets the minimum requirements
of the American National Standard for Information Sciences—Permanence
of Paper for Printed Library Materials, ANSI Z39.48-1992.

Manufactured in the United States of America

Cataloging information is available from the Library of Congress.

ISBN 978-0-253-02202-8 (cloth)
ISBN 978-0-253-02212-7 (ebook)

1 2 3 4 5 21 20 19 18 17 16

For my friend and colleague
John Hinshaw

CONTENTS

PREFACE

I want to take this opportunity to thank the many readers, critics, and conversation partners I have had through the years who have contributed to the effort put forth in this book. My thanks must begin with a close-knit group of pathbreaking scholars who I first read and met during my years under the tutelage of Charles Winquist at Syracuse University. They include Thomas J. J. Altizer, Carl Raschke, Mark C. Taylor, and Edith Wyschogrod. Individually and collectively they not only contributed to defining radical death-of-God theology for a generation and for the deconstructive postmodern a/theology that followed but also taught me how intimate and personal the scholarly pursuit could be. I mean this in the best possible way. I remember being surprised to discover they were all friends, that arguments were forged and insights gleaned just as often over dinner or drinks as in the privacy of one's study. It was then that I began reading their articles and books as conversations with and commentaries about one another. And it was thereby that, somewhere along the line, I came to be among the initiated.

So as not to give the false impression that this was an exclusive or exclusionary group of scholars, I should add that it was during the same period and among those same conversation partners that I was introduced to such inspirational figures as the great historians of religion Huston Smith, Charles Long, and David Chidester. I remember how each in his own way pressed us graduate students, who were under the thrall of postmodern theory, to consider more fully questions of historicity, materiality, and economics. Their personal challenge, along with the rigor of their methodology, has remained with me just as assuredly as the pronouncements of the radical theologians, both old and new. If this book achieves its goal of reactivating and expanding the tradition of radical theology, then that is the fruit of the seeds first planted by them.

In the decade since, the scholarly dialogues have developed into enduring friendships. The closest circle includes my colleagues at Lebanon Valley College (LVC), a dedicated and innovative group of professionals with whom I'm constantly impressed because of their genuine commitment to students. To avoid the risk of leaving a name out, I will just say thank you en masse to the LVC transdisciplinary collective. You know who you are, and I am most grateful to you all for mustering the courage to say "yes" to our collective vision to excite and empower students, to collaborate and innovate, and to risk the reenvisioning of a liberal arts education. The book is dedicated to John Hinshaw, who is part of that collective whether he wants to be or not. Although no theologian himself, John is a different sort of radical—LVC's resident stalwart supporter of the AAUP, committed to collective action; a keen observer of both local and global politics; and the sort of loyal friend with whom you can just as well argue as laugh, and always at a feverish pitch. This book marks the ten-year anniversary of the "Radical Reading Group" we conducted together with a group of students. The reading group was empowered by the radical pedagogy of Paulo Freire. Back then, Jordan Miller was a rabble-rousing, ring-leading undergraduate student. He has since become a first-rate radical theologian in his own right, finding original ways to read, apply, and affirm the lineage in concert with contemporary scholarship and current events. Much of the argumentation in this book was forged by my conversations with him in regard to his own developing research.

There are many others, of course, who are constant touchstones for me. The influence of John Caputo and Catherine Malabou should be clear to readers of this book. They serve not only as the two main interlocutors who provide the book's organizational structure but also as friends and role models. Catherine Keller is more an unspoken point of reference throughout the book. I regard her as the most creative and important theologian of our time, and I have appreciated the ways she has gently chided and instructed me through the years. Her legion of students and circle of friends provide direction and inspiration for all of us working at the intersections of religion, philosophy, politics, and critical theory. To Sharon Baker, Ward Blanton, Karen Bray, J. Kameron Carter, Clayton Crockett, Creston Davis, Bo Eberle, Gavin Hyman, Katharine Sarah Moody, Elias Ortega, Hollis Phelps, Elijah Prewitt, Keith Putt, Joshua Ramey, Alan Richard, Chris Rodkey, Mary-Jane Rubenstein, George Schmidt, Phil Snider, and Santiago Zabala—I look forward to our next email exchange; to your next article, book, or talk; or to the next conference or occasion at which the passion will run deeper than the ridicule.

Working with Indiana University Press on this publication has been a real privilege and pleasure. Most especially, I appreciate the critical and constructive feedback I received from the series editor, Merold Westphal, and the sage advice from Dee Mortensen for making the manuscript into a better book. I owe a special thanks as well to Gretchen Otto for her masterful job preparing the manuscript for publication, and to Victoria Gluszko for her assistance with the index.

And, as always, I owe my deepest gratitude to my wife, Noëlle Vahanian. Even if our time and conversations are largely consumed with the mundane, I know how lucky I am to have someone with whom to share this intellectual journey. She is my soul mate, and her encouragement and support mean more than anything to me.

Material from this book has been presented and published in revised form elsewhere. Permissions for republication have been granted. Chapter 1 is adapted from an article first delivered at the Annual Meeting of the American Academy of Religion and subsequently published in *Aquinas* (vol. 48, no. 3). Chapter 2 was first delivered at a summer meeting of the International Institute for Hermeneutics at Mount Allison University and subsequently published in a special issue of *Analecta Hermeneutica* (vol. 2). Chapter 3 is adapted from a forthcoming chapter solicited for a volume of collected essays, titled *Weakening Communism Through Hermeneutics* and edited by Silvia Mazzini and Owen Glyn-Williams (Springer). Chapter 4 is adapted from a chapter for a volume of collected essays titled *The Radical Tillich*, edited by Russell Re Manning (Palgrave Macmillan, 2015). Chapters 6 and 7 combine material from a series of review essays written for the *Journal for Cultural and Religious Theory*, *Expositions*, and *The Global Spiral*. Chapter 8 is adapted from a paper first presented at the University of Central Arkansas and subsequently published in the edited volume by Donna Bowman and Clayton Crockett, *Cosmology, Ecology, and the Energy of God* (Fordham University Press, 2011). Chapter 9 is adapted from a presentation first given at Salve Regina University and subsequently published in the edited volume by Mike Grimshaw, *The Counter-Narratives of Radical Theology and Popular Music* (Palgrave Macmillan, 2014).

RADICAL THEOLOGY

Radical Theology Come of Age

In one of the most stirring images in cinematic history, from the 1962 classic *Lawrence of Arabia*, we see T. E. Lawrence taunt God and nature alike in a daring attempt to save the life of Gasim, who was left for dead in the desert. Braving near-certain death himself, Lawrence defies the command of the more experienced, desert-dwelling Sherif Ali to backtrack into the heart of the desert only an hour before the break of day and the rise of the scorching sun. Without water, without a guide, and at the point of utter exhaustion, Lawrence is nevertheless undeterred. The words exchanged are as telling as they are well remembered: Sherif tells Lawrence that "in God's name," he must not go back, that if he does, he will surely die. Sherif also tells Lawrence "in God's name" that Gasim's time has come, that "it is written." Lawrence's response as he departs is that "nothing is written." As he rides away on camelback, Sherif yells out, implores, and condemns: "Go back then. What did you bring us here for with your blasphemous conceit?" He then adds insult to the accusation with a tone of righteous outrage, disappointment, and despair, not only telling Lawrence that he would never reach their destination in Akaba, but also, invoking the unmistakable colonial overtones, calling him an "English blasphemer." With wounded pride and defiance, Lawrence responds again, "I shall be at Akaba." Then, pointing to his head, he adds with blasphemous emphasis, "That is written in here."

From there, the scene goes quiet. We see the great, open expanse of the desert, and we hear a faint drumbeat. We cut to Gasim alone in the desert, stripping himself of his sword and his empty canteen and stumbling from footstep to footstep. Then we see a lone boy on a camel facing left, keeping a lookout for Lawrence's return. The desert now fills the entire screen, from top to bottom, without even a sliver of blue sky. It is dry, it is hot, and it is empty. The scene then cuts from the desert to the radiating sun as the drumbeat gets louder and faster. There is now a ringing sound reminiscent of a mind's delirium, and then the melody starts slowly and quietly, as we cut back from the desert to the sun. The drumbeat gets faster and the ringing louder. Gasim takes his final, disoriented step and then collapses into the sand. The ringing delirium stops, and we hear again the lilting melody as we return to the lookout, who takes a few halting steps on the camel as a tiny speck appears on the horizon. The camel begins to trot and then breaks into a full gallop. The melody is now full throated as we see the sprinting camel move from the right of the screen to the left to meet the slow and steady pace of Lawrence, entering the screen from the left. He is now carrying Gasim on his camel's back, and the caravan welcomes Lawrence as a conquering hero. He had cheated death in a heroic rescue. He had defied God and lived to tell the tale. If initially the people had followed him reluctantly into the desert out of duty, now they believed with him that anything was possible, that nothing is written. And thus, East meets West—a traditional religiosity predicated on unquestioning submission meets a modern anthropology predicated on freedom and autonomy. One man's blasphemy is another's belief in the sacred dignity of every human life. One man's callous indifference is another's resolve and respect for nature's elements.

Of course, this scene is as fanciful as it is stirring. Although the film is historically based, primarily drawn from the romanticized, conflicted, and self-aggrandizing accounts of the Arab Revolt of 1916–1918 as told by Lawrence himself, it shows the picture-book version of Orientalism, replete with the myth of the white male redeemer, as exposed by Edward Said. The underpinnings for colonialism are easy enough to detect. But less obvious, perhaps, is the fact that Lawrence is forging a guerrilla army of Arab nationalists. Throughout the film the strategic importance of water is made clear. Indeed, we are introduced to Sherif as he shoots dead Lawrence's Arab friend and guide for the mere act of drinking from his well. But, as a British military officer, Lawrence was not sent to Arabia to protect its water wells. Think of him instead as a pioneer for oil, staking a claim on a land and its people and resources while backroom negotiators were literally redrawing the region's maps as the rise of the Arab national identity was marshaled to feed off the dying carcass of the Ottoman Empire.

It is with this geopolitical context in mind that we must return to the scene from the film. When Sherif says, "It is written," and Lawrence responds that "nothing is written," who is right and who is wrong? As we are swept up into the film the answer appears obvious. Lawrence dared God and cheated death, and with his triumphant return proved that anything was possible for those who recognized that their fate was in their own hands. Especially as played by Peter O'Toole, Lawrence's bravado had an almost sensual appeal. He skirted along the razor's edge of the forbidden, and he dared others to follow him. But even as he helped to inspire and lead the successful attack against the Turkish defenders in the Jordanian port of Akaba, the moment that marked the triumph of the Arab uprising was still in service to the British World War I military strategy. The Arab revolt had done the impossible, but the people's political fate had already been written.

I did not open with this scene to simply recount the standard postcolonialist script. Instead, I am genuinely interested in the theatrics of it all. We are made to identify with Lawrence and his devil-may-care attitude. We are made to see him as an example of one who defied the odds, crossed cultural boundaries, and persisted to the point of changing history. As T. E. Lawrence's biographer Scott Anderson makes clear, there was no doubt he was driven as much by love and solidarity as he was by ambition.[1] But what are we to make of the cinematic image of the man with the extreme naïveté to declare that "nothing is written"? He who chafed at the military bureaucracy? He who would go on to write of the wonders of the ancient Bedouin culture in a literary masterpiece that Winston Churchill once identified as ranking with "the greatest books ever written in the English language."[2] He was a military adventurer who forcibly, if charismatically, wrote himself into a people's history; he was a rebel in search of a cause—or, if one prefers, a cultural imperialist who courageously did the bidding of government technocrats for the sake of his own vainglory. A hero and a pawn.

But most significantly for my purposes we must consider the nature of his blasphemy. Lawrence's stubborn defiance put not only himself but the entire mission at risk. Sherif accused him of "blasphemous conceit" not simply because Lawrence had the effrontery to proclaim that nothing is written—a religious offense bordering on nihilism—but because, by playing to the lone-ranger-hero type, he betrayed his true motivations and the superficiality of his professed solidarity. Sherif and his compatriots who were willing to follow Lawrence into the desert were then in a position to see the death wish behind the daring. And when Lawrence responded to Sherif by proclaiming that their fate was written in Lawrence's own head, he showed his blasphemous conceit not so much as nihilism but as idolatry. Lawrence *played God* just as certainly as his own military and political taskmasters played sovereign to the rising Arab nationalist cause that they exploited for their neocolonialist designs. And so, in this dramatized meeting between East and West, we have the inevitable confrontation between a will to submission hardened by, if not respect, an awareness at least as much for nature's elements as for imperialistic hubris laid bare and a will to self-actualization that is the presumed entitlement of Western man come of age after the death of God.

More Radical Than Rebellious

This book begins with the brief meditation on this classic scene from *Lawrence of Arabia* in order to declare at the outset what radical theology is *not to be.* Becoming radical must mean more than merely being defiant or rebellious, especially when that defiance or rebellion is for its own sake. A radical theological method must be aware of its own Oedipus complex, just as it must admit its own provenance as largely a Western and Christian discourse. And a theology after the death of God must not delude itself into thinking that its emancipation is complete, that the theopolitical logic of sovereignty is not still operative, or that the desire for God does not outlive the death of God. By taking Lawrence's story as a cautionary tale, we must take into consideration the intervening century. *First, Western Christian man takes the world as his entitlement. Second, after the nearly wholly colonized world erupts into near-total war, radical theology begins as Western post-Christian man announces a world come of age after the death of God. Third and contemporaneously, only after radical theology learns of its provincialism, by virtue of the liberationist, feminist, ecological, and postcolonialist critiques (among others), and its nearly complete marginalization is it now in a position to come of age by realizing its own long-dormant political, ontological, cultural, and even ecclesiological implications.*

Let me be clear: by articulating this particular history and claiming this potential legacy I do not mean to suggest more for radical theology than is its due. My position is that radical theology has been more ineffectual than it has been complicit and that this is largely to do with its own self-failings and limitations. Thus, the key to not so much the rehabilitation as *the activation of radical theology as a mechanism for change and a voice of relevancy* rests in thinking what this discernible lineage of thought has left largely unthought, specifically in the realms of politics, ontology, and culture. My thesis is that radical theology—specifically as it pertains to politics (by way of its contribution to the burgeoning discourse on political theology), ontology (by way of its engagement with the new materialisms), and culture (by way of its critical intervention in discussions of ecology, race, and performance)—is an identifiable tradition of thought that remains as relevant today as at its high point in the death-of-God movement.

These three spheres of contemporary thought provide the organizational structure for the book as a whole, with the chapters ordered accordingly. First, I evaluate the concept of the political and the basis of political action by way of a critical engagement with phenomenology and hermeneutics. Next is a series of chapters that invoke the work of Catherine Malabou, specifically the way that her reading of being as change provides a metabolic ontology that alters the terrain between the ethical and the political and between the philosophical and the theological. The book then transitions from Malabou to the work of John Caputo, as I show how he has successfully radicalized theology while still positioning himself as a mediating figure whose hermeneutics of the kingdom of God is without contradiction thoroughly deconstructive and biblical at the same time. Chapters 8 and 9 are less expository and more constructive, offering up two snapshots that illustrate the possibilities of a radical theology of culture, first through the issues of energy and ecology and then through the music of Louis Armstrong as a meditation on time. Finally, the book concludes by developing theses on a radical theology of the future.

Uniting these three spheres is my effort to draw on, reactivate, and expand the discernible lineage of thought of radical theology. This lineage of thought is as much a methodology as a sensibility. As such, I want to insist that it is not time bound—or at least not a passing fad, as it is sometimes taken to be. When I speak of radical theological method, what I have in mind specifically is a willingness and commitment to engage in a fundamental theological inquiry that pushes the limits of any given discourse. And so, as I show in the chapters that follow, how a phenomenological philosophy invested in establishing a rigorous methodology actually *becomes theological* even as it seeks to define the borders between philosophy and theology. Likewise, theological thinking, which throughout the modern period has accepted the datum of religion as essentially a private, interior matter of individual conscience, is shown to be *always already political*. Additionally, deconstruction, which is largely seen and accepted as a postmetaphysical endeavor, *develops an ontology of its own*, albeit one defined in terms of plasticity.

The purpose of this book is neither to write a history of radical theology nor to critique it as moribund. It is instead to draw from and apply the tradition where it is most relevant to contemporary concerns, and, in so doing, to reactivate and expand it. My strategy throughout is to engage more with contemporary streams in philosophy, theology, and critical theory, and, rather than rehearsing the "canon" of radical theology, to make connections with liberationist thought, feminist theology, and critical race theory wherever possible. In so doing, I do not mean at all to disparage the lineage of radical theological thinkers. I show throughout the book how my thinking has been inspired and informed by the original generation of death-of-God thinkers (most especially William Hamilton and Thomas J. J. Altizer but also Richard L. Rubenstein and Gabriel Vahanian) as well as by the first generation of postmodern deconstructive theologians (Carl Raschke, Mark C. Taylor, Edith Wyschogrod, and Charles Winquist), many of whom are still contributing pioneering work in religious and cultural theory. As the argument progresses, the reader can see how I describe their collective achievement as a general "secularization of theology," in terms akin to those Gianni Vattimo uses when he describes the historical process of the weakening of being. This secularization of theology, which transforms what it means to think theologically, leads us to the seemingly impossible possibility of a theology after the death of God, between faith and suspicion and stripped bare of its appeal to religion, supernaturalism, and mythology. To be sure, this is a theology unrecognizable to most. But it is precisely where this book begins.

Radical Theology Defined

In the remainder of this introduction, my aim is to defend the claim that radical theology has an identifiable lineage and is a discernible tradition of thought.

In short, radical theology is a postliberal tradition of thought that emerged out of the death-of-God movement of the 1960s. It is neither theistic nor atheistic but still recognizes God as a formulation of extremity that gets *at the root* of thought and opens up pathways for a thinking that *knows no bounds*. In this way, the idea of God and the desire for God outlive the death of God, and thus, although radical theology emerged out of the death-of-God movement, it is no longer bound by that movement.

Each of the elements from the definition above can be parsed further. By describing radical theology as postliberal, I do not mean to identify it with the postliberal school of theology associated with Hans Frei, George Lindbeck, and Stanley Hauerwas, among others. That variant of postliberal theology is a neo-traditional, confessional theology, while radical theology is more critical—or even deconstructive—than it is confessional and takes tradition to task for the ways it tends to domesticate the full, radical implications of faith. Thus, the use of the term *postliberal* for the tradition of radical theology I have in mind is meant to convey a certain critical distance from the liberal Protestant establishment in recognition of radical theology's point of origin in a time of cultural despair and crisis that came to its clearest expression in the death-of-God movement.

The phrase *formulation of extremity* is borrowed from the late Charles Winquist, one of the early pioneers of postmodern theology, who fused radical death-of-God theology with deconstructionism, poststructuralism, and psychoanalytic theory. By identifying theological thinking with a "desire for a thinking which does not disappoint," Winquist recognized the "complex association of meanings" that the word *God* still contained and that the very idea of God was "weighted with a sense of being real and important."[3] At the same time, he recognized that theology as such had largely lost its hold on secular culture's imagination, and so, drawing from Gilles Deleuze and Felix Guattari, he redefined theology "as a minor intensive use of a major language."[4] Borrowing further from Deleuze, we might say that although theology after the death of God is a "science of non-existing entities," it is nevertheless still productive of a series of affects.[5] Theological language is disruptive and often transgressive. Elsewhere, Winquist invokes the work of Julia Kristeva when he identifies theological language as an expression of jouissance or as a gesture of transcendence that gives expression to a longing for the infinite. As a disruption of ordinary discourse, it "introduces uncertainty and undecidability in any discourse by transgressing the boundaries set by reductive rules seeking to secure clarity and distinctness at the price of the loss of force and vivacity." In a particularly arresting image, Winquist compares this theological effect to "the Trojan horse that can slip past the guardians of the law of the father."[6]

What must be noted here is how radical theology thus defined is not so much reflective as creative and constructive, *for the purposes of transformation instead of reformation*. In this way, it is a reversal of the formulation offered up by Martin Heidegger when he defined theology as a positive science of faith that gives systematic coherence and conceptual clarity to that which was already known by revelation. By rendering theology as a positive science, Heidegger believed theology was a closed circle ruled by certainty. Radical theology, by contrast, is a fundamental theology in that it gets at the root of religious meaning. But in so doing, radical theology has had a history not of reifying but of upending, not of functioning as a grounding discourse but of uprooting the cultural safeguards associated with religious practice and meaning—a continuation and extension of the hermeneutics of suspicion. I add to this definition of radical theology the notion that it is a thinking that knows no bounds, because although the hermeneutics of suspicion stops short at its ideological critique of religion as a form of false consciousness, radical theology plunges further with the realization that the desire for God persists even after the death of God, even after the image of God is exposed as an opiate, a psychological projection or a phallogocentric fantasy. Thus, it is a fundamental theology that is also fundamentally open and that must remain open ended.

Renewing Radical Theology

Recently there has been a veritable flood of best-selling books propounding what has come to be termed the new atheism. Collectively the new atheists tell us that religion has been one of the principal causes of human suffering and that it promotes extremism and has led to violence. They say also that the religious mindset thwarts the rationalistic approach to the world and to human problem solving, allowing untestable and unsupported mythological stories to serve as explanations for natural phenomena. And what's more, the new atheists say, when actually examining what religious devotees believe when they attest to their faith in God or in sacred scripture, those beliefs are riddled with contradictions that should either outrage the mind or offend moral sensibilities. Presenting plain facts in the most provocative style, the new atheists seized on the cultural angst known to those who felt left out or beaten down by the cultural warriors on the Right and who worried that the two successive terms of President George W. Bush set the United States on a perilous path toward theocracy.

But when examining the central claims of the new atheists—not to mention the public discussion that surrounded their publications—we must ask whether anyone is really surprised to learn that the historic faiths are guilty of self-contradictions, that religious fanatics are prone to violence, and that all religions have a human origin. These observations are commonplace in the academic study and teaching of religion. And although there was a time when these observations were truly radical and provocative, they have long been established as the starting points for modern liberal theology. By opening itself up to critical inquiry and modern ways of knowing, liberal theology has asked religious devotees not only to learn the truths of their tradition but also to rethink the nature of religious truth. Most (with the exception of fundamentalists) would now concede that religions are *true* not in the same way that science or mathematics is true but in the way a Picasso portrait conveys a *subjective* truth that belies the merely representational. For instance, except for the most literal minded, the Bible is not proven untrue or unreliable because it has two contradictory stories of creation in the first two chapters of the book of Genesis or because it has four different portraits of Christ included in the New Testament. On the contrary, an appreciation of these variances—even contradictions—is essential to understanding the particular nature of truth that belongs to the religious. It is precisely this insight that gives rise to contemporary hermeneutical philosophy, in which the contemporary theorists echo the claim made by Friedrich Nietzsche over a century ago—that there are no facts, only interpretations.[7]

In this sense, the problem that the new atheists have with religion is not with religion per se but with religious literalism. Radical theology's answer to this problem is not to dispense with religion altogether but to think and to invent religion otherwise. The point is that the new atheists do not go far enough in their critique of traditional religion. Put succinctly, *the new atheism is insufficiently radical.* But although the new atheists garner headlines, radical theology seems largely a forgotten or neglected tradition of thought. Yet in recent years there has been a reclamation, if not a renewal, of radical theology. This has taken place most prominently within certain circles of emergent Protestant theologies led by the likes of Peter Rollins, who invokes the work of Caputo and Slavoj Žižek.[8] In a recent book, *The Insistence of God*, Caputo has gone on to define the specific lineage of radical theology with which he is aligned, citing Hegel's dialectical philosophy of religion over Kant's more fideistic formula of faith as a radical unknowing.[9] Caputo's turn to Hegel is an insistence that theology must be thought together with philosophy, that faith must be conceived of as more than that which is factually unknown and structurally unknowable, and that, instead, it is an invocation of thought or a critical philosophy that harbors no sacred datum, nothing safe and secure from critical inquiry and the quest for understanding.

For his part, Žižek has at times been critical of Caputo's appropriation of radical, death-of-God theology. (I discuss this topic in chapter 7.) For Žižek, Caputo's radical theology has been insufficiently radical, as it stops short of a fundamental theological claim on the self-negating nature of the godhead itself. Insofar as Caputo is still operating in a postmetaphysical mode, Žižek views Caputo's Hegelian turn as less radical still than that of Thomas J. J. Altizer, who remains the radical theologian par excellence.[10]

Much more can and should be said about these two possible directions for a contemporary radical theology, and the pages that follow will afford me the opportunity to elaborate on the stakes of this important debate. But, for now, my purposes are much simpler. Before now, radical theology has articulated itself almost exclusively as an expression and outgrowth of the death of God. More directly put, radical theology heretofore has operated within what is essentially a modern, liberal horizon of thought. Its radicality amounts to a radicalization, but still a continuation, of Enlightenment norms. What if, instead, radical theology came into its own not only as postmodern but also as postsecular and postliberal?

Postliberal, with a Difference

The link between radical theology and postmodernism is well established. It began first when Carl Raschke, and later Mark C. Taylor, identified *"deconstruction [as] the 'hermeneutic' of the death of God."*[11] From that point, postmodern a/theology, led by figures such as Raschke, Taylor, Winquist, and Wyschogrod, was largely taken to be the successor to the death-of-God movement. It was Caputo who insisted on the affirmative religious passion that drives deconstruction and, in so doing, provided not only an alternative reading of Jacques Derrida but also an alternative variant to postmodern theology, one which deconstructed the verities of the death of God.[12] For Caputo, borrowing from Jean-Luc Marion, the death of God would not mean anything whatsoever from a deconstructive perspective unless it meant the death of the death of God or the end of the death-of-God movement that would speak of death as an absolute or a finality. By delinking deconstruction from the death of God, Caputo advanced a distinctively postmodern faith after the death of God. In so doing, he *read postmodernism as a postsecularism* that not only witnessed but made possible a certain return of religion. And, as I explain in the pages that follow, Caputo's critical engagement with theology is not unlike his engagement with philosophical hermeneutics: in both cases, he has deliberately radicalized the tradition.[13]

And so, the lineage of radical theology that began with the death-of-God movement has been linked to and passed through postmodern deconstruction. Likewise, its appreciation of the postsecular has provided a source of renewal for contemporary religious and theological thought. Even more, with Caputo's most recent work, this appreciation has provided a certain rehabilitation of radical theology as an identifiable lineage and a discernible tradition of thought. But, as hinted at above, the connection of radical theology to postliberal theology is more fraught. What must be said is that radical theology is not a liberal theology. Or, perhaps better, were it not for the unfortunate associations the moniker has taken on, *radical theology is a postliberal theology.*[14] It is postliberal in terms of both its lineage and sensibility.

To draw a contrast, I need to first give a brief introduction to liberal theology. For this, I turn to the work of the intellectual historian and ethicist Gary Dorrien, whose three-volume work, *The Making of American Liberal Theology,* is the authoritative and exhaustive text that makes the case for how "liberal theology has been and remains the most creative and influential tradition of theological reflection since the Reformation."[15] As Dorrien tells it, liberal theology is a three-centuries-old tradition, defined by its openness to "modern intellectual inquiry" and "the authority of individual reason and experience," its understanding of Christianity "as an ethical way of life," and its "commitment to make Christianity credible and socially relevant to modern people."[16] What has given liberal theology its critical edge as a modernizing, progressive, and democratic force has been its effort at doing theology without being based on external authority, whether that authority be tradition, the appeal to clerical or institutional authority, or the notion of the infallibility of scripture. And, finally, Dorrien makes frequent reference to the "mediationist character" of liberal theology, locating it as the "third way between conservative orthodoxy and secular disbelief."[17] In this way, liberal theology is self-consciously and consistently reformist in its intentions and sensibility and is not revolutionary.

Like the tradition of liberal theology, radical theology is also characterized by its openness to contemporary ways of knowing and critical modes of inquiry. Also like liberal theology, radical theology rejects arguments from authority. But it takes this further, which is perhaps best explained by its more recent beginnings. Whereas Dorrien dates the inception of liberal theology to 1805, radical theology traces its origin to the death-of-God theologies of the late 1950s and 1960s, in a cultural moment identified in the first book-length study of the death of God as "our post-Christian era."[18] So whereas liberal theology first arose in Germany as a creative intellectual response by the likes of Kant, Hegel, and Schleiermacher in an attempt to reconcile with—if not salvage Christianity from—the ravages of the Enlightenment rationalist critique of religion, radical theology is post-Christian insofar as it comes "after Auschwitz" in what one author describes as "the twilight of the American culture."[19] It acknowledges the loss of hegemony and moral authority suffered by Western Christian culture and thus helps to announce the end of the liberal Protestant establishment. In this way, radical theology stands to liberal theology as its historical bookend, being more liberal than its theological precursor of neo-orthodoxy and less political than its theological successor of liberation theology.

But the contrast must be drawn still deeper. If liberal theology positions itself as a third way and is deliberately reformist and not revolutionary, then radical theology rejects these options as false and arbitrary. The line from conservative orthodoxy to secular disbelief does not exhaust the full spectrum of either religious experience or theological strategy. Thus, radical theology does not aim to occupy the middle ground but rather aspires to a fundamental inquiry into the nature of theological thinking as such. In so doing, it seeks *not to conserve, but to transform.* In short, by asking the question of what it means to think theologically after the death of God, radical theology is, in the words of Mark C. Taylor, an "erring" or "mazing" discourse in search of a loss object and thus without a proper methodology to call its own.[20] Along with the search for a loss object, the very category of religion and the essentialist assumptions associated with the theoretical reflections on religious experience have come under increased scrutiny. It is for this reason that radical theology has been prone to hyperbolic proclamations, such as Thomas J. J. Altizer's early death-of-God announcement of the "gospel of Christian atheism" or Carl Raschke's argument regarding the "end of theology," which is based on his reading of the death of God through the lens of deconstructive theology.[21] As I have argued elsewhere, in this way radical theology can be seen as the radicalization of liberal theology's prerogative to demonstrate the relevance of religion to the modern world by the newfound additional need to demonstrate its *value* and *viability.*[22]

Put otherwise, radical theology does not balk at revolution. But I am referring to revolution in the most technical sense possible—revolution as distinct from reform. On this point, Paul Kahn's theopolitical reflections on the connections between sovereignty and violence are helpful. As Kahn defines it, "Revolution is change outside of law" and is therefore inseparable from violence because it "begins with the rejection of the possibility of reform through legal processes."[23] Revolution performs sacred violence not by breaking the law per se but by denying the sovereignty of the law—not violation but disavowal. More specifically, revolution operates outside the bounds of law by declaring an alternative sovereignty at work, a *domain of sovereignty beyond the law.* As Kahn puts it, "The revolutionary . . . rejects the right of the government to label his behavior criminal and, accordingly, rejects its right to enforce that law. His fundamental challenge is not to particular laws but to the government's claim of the sovereign authority to use violence. The revolutionary always claims to speak in the sovereign voice—the voice of the people."[24] The importance of this argument is that it shows the political ontology operative in the claim to revolution. I have argued elsewhere that democracy is the political instantiation of the death of God.[25] With the conception of popular sovereignty, the people perform the role once reserved for God. Thus, revolution, as the "direct action of the popular sovereign,"[26] is a constitutive act, not a reactive one. It is a new beginning, not a return—creative, not reactionary.

Further, and this point is an essential one, revolution occupies essentially an extralegal political space, which in Kahn's conception is a redundancy because the political is to be distinguished from the legal. Nevertheless, when charting the development and history of either constitutional democracy or international rights, we witness the subsumption of the political by the legal. Likewise, in the domestic sphere, the reign of law concomitant with the triumph of a free market economy is nearly complete, and both have a depoliticizing effect. This is liberalism in a nutshell, and the reason why for Kahn *there is strictly speaking no liberal concept of the political*. Revolution thereby helps to clarify the concept of the political—as distinct from the legal—and to identify a boundary, if not a transition, between the liberal and the postliberal.

Drawing on this important difference, Kahn distinguishes between the American civil rights movement and the protests by antiwar activists of the 1960s, with only the former having operated as a genuinely political movement. By the collective "demonstration of a willingness to sacrifice" and to bear the violence of the state, the civil rights movement accomplished what the American Civil War and the Voting Rights Act could not—namely, it altered "the perception of political meaning attached to the black person's body," or shifted "the image of the suffering black body from that of the lynch victim to that of the political martyr." In so doing, "[the lynching victims] are not only representations of injustice; they are a new showing forth of the sacred character of the sovereign." This functioned as something other than merely a claim for justice under the law. Kahn wrote, "It was about that intersection of being and meaning that is the politics of sovereignty."[27] While participants in the civil rights movement changed the law to be sure, as revolutionaries they stood against the law. Nonviolent resistance was an act of creative destruction constituting a new and different American identity.

We might say much the same of the so-called Protestant Reformation: *this was a revolutionary and not a reformational movement*, a contest between two sovereigns, a political operation that refused to submit to the authority of law. Too often, radical theology's revolutionary sensibility has been more stylistic than substantive and has thus failed to develop either a politics or an ecclesiology of its own. Nevertheless, I take the sensibility to be a genuine one. Whereas liberal theology has sought to preserve and extend, radical theology has sought to subvert and reinvent. In this way, radical theology stands not only outside the sovereignty of the law but also outside the spectrum between belief and unbelief by being proudly heterodoxical. That is to say, it does not just believe otherwise, it deliberately disrupts existing beliefs and creates new ones.

Finally, and to clarify my opening claim, when I say that radical theology is not a liberal theology, I certainly do not mean to disparage the tradition of liberal theology whatsoever. I accept Dorrien's claim that "the entire field of modern theology employ[s] critical tools and theories that the liberal tradition developed" and that even though liberalism has suffered a cultural crisis and decline since the 1960s, especially in the United States, liberal theology has nevertheless contributed to the development of various forms of identity-based liberation theologies and ecotheology and to the emergence of productive dialogues between religion and science and among different religions.[28] So when I distinguish between liberal and radical, it is not intended as a value judgment but instead to indicate from the outset what makes radical theology distinct. On this point I must be abundantly clear: to speak of radical theology is not to engage in self-styled posing but to align and engage with an identifiable tradition of thought.

The chapters that follow mine that tradition while also pushing its limits by making the case that a radical theology today must become political and ontological to realize whatever cultural and ecclesiastical relevancy and impact it might once have believed its birthright.

ONE

The Theological Becoming of Phenomenology

Theological inquiry today can only be a practice of phenomenology: to identify and describe the presence of the sacred, wherever it appears.

—Paul Kahn, *Political Theology*

In the introduction I defined the radical theological method I have in mind in terms of the willingness and commitment to engage in a fundamental theological inquiry that pushes against the limits of any given discourse. By returning to the difference between modern liberal theology and postliberal radical theology, we can see a dialectical reversal at work. Liberal theology began in the early nineteenth century as a creative intellectual response by the likes of Immanuel Kant, G. W. F. Hegel, and Friedrich Schleiermacher to reconcile with—if not salvage Christianity from—the ravages of the Enlightenment rationalist critique of religion. Liberal theology was forged as a result by its appropriation of modern philosophy. And even to this day, whether from neo-orthodox, radical orthodox, postliberal, or fundamentalist quarters, modern liberal theology is criticized as not having its own voice because it is too conformist, too apologetic, and too beholden to the autonomy of reason and the whims of contemporary culture. In a provocative and timely work more important for its rich intellectual history than its recommendations for political theology, Mark Lilla provides an arresting image of this idea when he identifies the concept of God operative in modern liberal thought as a "stillborn God."[1] The argument is that the modern philosophical salvaging of the concept of God comes at the expense of faith in a living God. Such an argument buttresses the claims subsequently made by Nietzsche when his proclamation of the death of God was pitched as an announcement of a long-dormant truth. One might draw the conclusion from this assertion that the death of God is the consequence of the modern philosophical becoming of liberal theology. Or perhaps more succinctly, when theology becomes philosophical, the realization that God is dead is sure to follow.

But just as theology becomes philosophical, so too might philosophy become theological. With this idea in mind, I want to make the methodological point about radical theology pushing against the limits and explore the suggestion above about the dialectical reversal at work. The question follows: at what point does philosophy become theological? The answer, of course, hinges on what is meant by the term *theology*, which, contrary to what many assume, is not as obvious or self-evident as it may seem. In fact, the traditional distinction between philosophy and theology has been increasingly blurred in contemporary thought as philosophy has appropriated many themes, categories, and concepts that once belonged almost exclusively to the realm of religious (if not theological) discourse and as theology has undergone its own process of secularization. The task of rethinking the philosophy *of* religion, therefore, requires a rethinking of the relationship *between* philosophy and theology, which necessitates as its first step an explanation of the changing nature of contemporary theological thought.

Let me begin with the irony that runs through much of contemporary philosophical and theological discourse—namely, that there is an inverse proportionality between *theology* and what might be loosely termed *God talk*. (The two are different, and this distinction which will prove absolutely central to the argument of this chapter.) In other words, if there has been, for lack of a better term, a "theological turn" in phenomenology, then there has just as assuredly been a "phenomenological turn" in theology. And thus the irony is that even as more phenomenologists are talking about God and are drawing on traditionally theological categories such as revelation and faith, self-proclaimed theologians are becoming ever more secular as the parameters of contemporary philosophical theology have seemed to be set by the early Wittgensteinian methodological rule of thumb: "The world is all that is the case."[2]

Unfortunately, however, this current within contemporary philosophical theology has been largely ignored or misunderstood by many, if not most, of the recent commentators on the theological turn of phenomenology. The result of this misunderstanding, as evidenced in Dominique Janicaud's seminal treatment of this topic, is twofold. First, it leads to a misdiagnosis of the defining issues in the contemporary relationship between phenomenology and theology. Second, it leads to an unwarranted defensive posture on the part of the phenomenologist in his effort to preserve the integrity of the phenomenological method from the encroachments of theology.[3] This chapter's argument, therefore, will be that Janicaud's notion of the theological turn of phenomenology is a misnomer and a misrepresentation of the history of the phenomenological tradition itself and, further, that this history, which tells not of a theological turn but of a theological *becoming*, parallels the recent history of contemporary philosophical theology. This theological becoming of phenomenology befits a radical theology insofar as it refuses the separation between thought and faith and contributes to the critical reflection on the proper methodology for theological thinking as such.

The Theological Turn

At what point does philosophy become theological? The first answer is that philosophy becomes theological when it speaks of God. If such were the case, then philosophy of religion would be indistinguishable from theology, as philosophers of religion have long been interested in the so-called proofs of God's existence and the problem of theodicy.

The second answer is that the philosopher stands to the theologian as the skeptic stands to the believer, so philosophy becomes theological when it begins to believe. This position not only lacks an appreciation of the hermeneutical circle of knowing but also negates the critical strand of thought that has existed throughout the history of the theological tradition, and that has become even more pronounced in the late modern and postmodern world as radical theologians have adopted the transcendental structure of critique as the crucible through which a genuinely contemporary theology must pass. These critical theologies are radically skeptical, and they have effectively transformed not only what it means to think theologically but also what it means to believe and the meaning of faith.

The third answer is that philosophy becomes theological when it takes on the category of revelation or when it assumes a confessional structure. This is the guiding assumption that Dominique Janicaud makes in his critique of the theological turn of phenomenology. At its most basic, Janicaud's concern with the theological turn is the effort to protect "the methodological from the ideological."[4] This insistence on methodological purity is, for Janicaud at least, still the great legacy of the founder of phenomenology, Edmund Husserl, and should still be phenomenology's defining feature. As Janicaud writes, "However modest it was in its intentions and in its 'fulfillments,' it [the eidetic description and the phenomenological reduction as the two sui generis methodological instruments of phenomenology] brought balance to phenomenological research in the interests of determined, stable, and universal knowledge." Moreover, even though the phenomenological tradition has since turned away from this original founding programmatic, it is nevertheless still "capable of assuming the richness of ambiguity that was already its own in Husserl."[5]

But if phenomenology is to reclaim this heritage as its own, then it must turn away from the liberties taken by the most recent generation of contemporary phenomenologists. That is why Janicaud's essay takes the form of a critical exposé on what he considers the betrayal of phenomenology. For instance, when speaking of Emmanuel Levinas, Janicaud credits him for his "talent and singular originality" but also accuses him of "strict treason" and a "biased utilization" of phenomenology, or of cloaking his theology in the guise of a phenomenology in which the "dice are loaded and choices made."[6] Why such an extreme assessment of

Levinas? First, according to Janicaud, Levinas has reduced the "two dimensions of intentionality" to one, making phenomenology strictly a matter of eidetic elucidation and forgetting or neglecting its more fundamental task of the transcendental reduction. Second, Levinas wrongly assimilates phenomenology into ontology, which is a failure on his part to recognize how the methodological discipline that phenomenology imposes provides a certain ideological independence. Third, and most seriously according to Janicaud, is the question of the very coherence of Levinas's thought. That is to say, Levinas's concept of intentionality is, in Janicaud's judgment, an "artificial operation" imposed from outside that reveals a hidden (or perhaps not so hidden)[7] theological agenda. Janicaud says, "A sham intentionality, purely representative, has been fabricated to prepare the way of the advent of the idea of the infinite."[8] Phenomenology has thus been "taken hostage by a theology that does not want to say its name." And so, Janicaud asks, "Why keep playing along at phenomenology when the game is fixed?" He means here that the game is fixed by the ideological trumping of the methodological, as phenomenology is used to hide what is actually a confessional theology. Janicaud continues by saying that "something important is at stake here: whether we can manipulate experience, or must, on the contrary, patiently describe it in order to know it."[9]

As suggested before, Levinas is not the only target of Janicaud's critique. Rather, Levinas is symptomatic of a much broader movement of supposed phenomenologists taking increasing methodological liberties. Thus, Janicaud's analysis extends beyond Levinas to the work of those such as Jean-Luc Marion, Jean-Louis Chrétien, and Michel Henry. As these figures together represent the theological turn, each in his own way also epitomizes for Janicaud a lack of phenomenological rigor and discipline. In other words, by turning to theology in their philosophical analysis, they no longer speak as true phenomenologists.

As Janicaud understands it, the theological turn of contemporary philosophy has done great damage to the integrity of the phenomenological tradition and has had an altogether negative impact on philosophical thinking by introducing an ideological bias and a confessional theology into a tradition of thought that strives for methodological purity and scientific rigor. Janicaud is therefore not the least bit interested in speculating on the nature and shape of the new philosophy of religion. On the contrary, he insists that, at least where phenomenology is concerned, philosophy and religion must be kept separate and distinct. In his words, "philosophy and theology make two."[10]

Where Janicaud's critique of the theological turn fails and where perhaps his own ideological defenses are down is in his presumption of the meaning and task of theology. For instance, like Martin Heidegger before him, he designates theology as a "positive science" and likens philosophical theology to a "square circle." But what Heidegger did not foresee (and what Janicaud fails to appreciate) is how theological thinking itself would be radically transformed by the philosophical contributions of phenomenology and hermeneutics that he helped to inspire. Much of contemporary philosophical theology operates less as a positive science and more as a method of interrogation. In other words, contemporary theology has been the subject of its own deconstruction. Indeed, this is the modus operandi of radical theology. The importance of understanding this interrogative mode of radical theology for the present discussion is that a greater appreciation of this *internal* development within theological thinking allows for a more sympathetic reading of the theological turn of phenomenology or, even better, a more sympathetic reading of the co-conspiracy between phenomenology and theology to redefine the relationship between philosophy and theology and thereby demonstrate the possibility of a new philosophy of religion.

The issue is neither, as Janicaud presents it, a matter of somehow smuggling God into a strictly phenomenological discourse nor a matter of the phenomenological appropriation of the theological category of revelation. In fact, the great irony here is that the consequence of the deconstruction of theology is that much of contemporary theological thinking is utterly devoid of God talk and has grown increasingly suspicious of the category of revelation, so much so that someone like the death-of-God theologian Thomas J. J. Altizer might argue that it is only theology proper that can truly and absolutely grasp the death of God and the absolute nihilism that lives as its consequence.[11] This kind of theological thinking, in which ideological biases have been exposed and thus deconstructed, is of a different order than the confessional or ecclesiastical theologies with which Janicaud is concerned.

One further point seems lost on Janicaud and others who would still wish for the strict separation of phenomenology and theology. A different image, besides that of Janicaud's "turning," for understanding the relationship between phenomenology and theology is that of a becoming. Phenomenology does not turn to theology as if *turning away* from itself but *becomes theological* by following its thought to its own end. It becomes theological not necessarily in the dogmatic or confessional sense but in the sense of thinking in extremis. This is a sign of its success, not of a turning away from the original founding intentions of the phenomenological tradition, for it is precisely this tradition that has taught us that *the hypothesis of God is unnecessary in order to think transcendence*. Such is the meaning of Derrida's dictum, *"Tout autre est tout autre,"*[12] by which he has radicalized Levinas's philosophy of alterity, thus collapsing the distinction between a vertical and a horizontal transcendence, refusing the logic of analogy between God and the face of the neighbor and holding nothing in reserve, not even the idea of God as the one and only infinite other.

The theological becoming of phenomenology is therefore less a turning away and more the consequence of the success of phenomenology in the reconfiguration of theology's conceptual repertoire. In many ways, it could be said that phenomenology has actually won the day in deciding what is both theologically credible and intelligible. Thus, a meaningful and relevant theology can now only be one that thinks phenomenologically.

The Secularization of Theology

Previously I stated that what Heidegger did not foresee, and what Janicaud fails to understand, was how theological thinking itself would be transformed. It is this transformation I have in mind when I claim radical theology as an identifiable lineage with a discernible tradition of thought. A number of historical factors were instrumental in this internal transformation of contemporary theological thought, a transformation that prefigured the radical theology to come. Three moments in particular help clarify what I have in mind.

First, in the wake of World War I, the Swiss Protestant theologian Karl Barth emerged onto the theological scene by announcing the moral bankruptcy of modern liberal theology and the impotency of the historical critical method of biblical scholarship. As Barth defined it, whether in the early dialectical or later neoorthodox stage of his theological development, the task of Christian theology was to recover and clarify the distinctiveness of the Christian message through a theology of revelation. This *strategy of retrenchment* coincided well with the prevailing mood throughout Western Europe during this time—namely, that World War I brought a final end to the pretense of Enlightenment optimism. Barth would remain the dominant theological voice throughout the first half of the twentieth century. His theology of revelation can be seen as the necessary counterpoint to Heidegger's revamped ontology because it embodies or fleshes out Heidegger's own cryptic remark to a group of Protestant theologians that if he were to write a theology, the word *being* would not appear.[13] This refusal of being also demonstrates a link between Barth, the neo-orthodox Protestant theologian, and Marion, the French Catholic phenomenologist-turned-theologian, in that both base their respective theologies on revelation and thus see a sharp distinction between the proper work and language of philosophy and those of theology.[14] Also, it should be noted that one of the first full-length studies of Levinas in the English-speaking world was a book by Steven Smith that compares Levinas to Barth.[15] According to Smith (and later to the radical orthodox theologian Graham Ward),[16] both Levinas and Barth share a common logic in their respective arguments to the Other. This is to suggest that when Janicaud is examining the characteristics of the theological turn and explores Levinas and Marion as two of its most important figures, he is stuck on what might very well be a time-bound moment within the recent history of the theological tradition. This moment might have led him and others to overlook the more nuanced and dynamic relationship between phenomenology and theology.

If the first moment that was important in the internal transformation of contemporary theological thought, characterized by the theology of Barth and carried forward in the thinking of Levinas and Marion, can be labeled a strategy of retrenchment and seen as the final end to the pretense of Enlightenment optimism, then the second moment, which emerges in the wake of World War II and specifically in response to the horrors of the Holocaust, can be seen as a *strategy of engagement* and as the realization of the end to the pretense of Christendom. It is at this point in twentieth-century Protestant thought that figures such as Paul Tillich and Rudolf Bultmann come to the fore. Both were one-time partners of Barth in his early efforts to rethink the task of theology after the collapse of modernity, but both would also later part with Barth for his refusal to fully engage the currents of contemporary culture. What Tillich and Bultmann helped to accomplish was the radical transformation of the *formal* nature of theological thought. For instance, Tillich's method of correlation, which came to its fruition in his theology of culture, relocates the dynamic of faith squarely within an increasingly secularized culture. It is that secularized culture that raises the questions of urgency and ultimacy to which the theologian must respond. Likewise, Bultmann's method of demythologization took on the existential and hermeneutical insights he learned from Heidegger and claimed that the biblical language of faith, to which the Christian world was still so stridently attached, was hopelessly out of date and out of touch. The time had long since passed when the modern world picture was determined by an exclusively Christian mindset, yet churches and theologians still used that religion's ancient mythological language of faith to express its truth to a world now governed by science and technology. For Bultmann, this radical disconnect called for a complete translation and remythologization of faith. What is notable about this theological innovation, and the reason why someone like Barth refused to go along, is that it conceded the diminished importance of theology by allowing the language and assumptions of contemporary culture and philosophy to establish its agenda and parameters.

Finally, if the second moment transformed the formal nature of theological thought, then the third radically transformed its very content, stripping theology of such supposed fundamentals as God, religion, revelation, and faith. It was Mark C. Taylor who saw this transition and transformation most clearly, as he shows when he writes in *Erring* that *"deconstruction is the hermeneutic of the death of God."*[17] As Taylor understood it, deconstruction, as a formal, methodological hermeneutic, is inextricably tied to the specific proclamation of the death of God, which characterizes the religiosity of late modern and postmodern Western society. This is a religiosity that stands somewhere between faith and suspicion, "between the loss of old certainties and the discovery of new beliefs." It is for those "marginal people [who] constantly live on the border that both joins and separates belief and unbelief"—an "utterly transgressive" site that makes possible a genuinely postmodern a/theology.[18] Before Taylor, the Anglican bishop John Robinson, tapping into the cultural spirit of disillusionment in the 1960s and drawing on the insights of Dietrich Bonhoeffer, Tillich, and Bultmann, argued that for Christian theology to be credible and relevant, it must be honest to God and honest with itself by admitting that the religion, supernaturalism, and mythology on which its message had long been based had outlived its usefulness.[19]

A theology after the death of God, between faith and suspicion and without religion, supernaturalism, and mythology, would be a theology unrecognizable to most. Nevertheless, this is the recent history of theology, a tradition of thought that has liberated itself from the revelatory language of God's word, a tradition that has deliberately stripped itself of its privilege and that now acknowledges itself as a strictly human enterprise. What makes this deconstructed and thus duly transformed theology still specifically theological is a question that remains unanswered. Some, such as Clayton Crockett and the late Charles Winquist, would assert that theological thinking is made theological after the dissolution of its more traditional formal and fideistic markings by isolating and dwelling within any given discourse's own formulations of extremity, by tracing the reflective folds in a discourse to their breaking point.[20] Therefore, far from the ideological trumping of Janicaud's concern, this theology is more parasitic; as Winquist writes, borrowing an image from Deleuze and Guattari, it is "a tropological strategy that makes a minor intensive use of a major discourse."[21] In other words, it is less triumphant and more subversive. As such, a whole range of contemporary critical and methodological discourses have suffered what might be considered a theological becoming, but only after theology itself accepted its secondary, marginal status.

Rethinking Philosophy of Religion

In contrast to Janicaud's rejection of the theological turn, two recent examples model an alternative, more sympathetic analysis of the philosophical turn to religion. The first example is from Hent de Vries, who argues that the recent turn to religion by philosophers and cultural theorists is structural rather than ideological. Thus, rather than interpreting the philosophical turn to religion as a betrayal of the integrity of philosophical thought in general, or of the phenomenological tradition in particular, de Vries interprets it more as a correction to the reductive and dismissive attitude toward religion that has prevailed throughout the modern age. For de Vries, in other words, it is not so much the theologians who are guilty of an ideological bias as the philosophers because they make religion into what it is not, or at least not what it is primarily or exclusively meant to be, whether treated as "'truth in the garments of a lie' (Schopenhauer), 'anthropology disguised as theology' (Feuerbach), 'ideology and false consciousness'

(Marx), 'infantile neurosis' (Freud), 'the nonsensical expression of feeling, diffused by metaphysicians without poetic or musical talent' (Carnap), a 'category mistake' (Ryle), a 'form of life' (Wittgenstein), and so on."[22] This ideological bias runs throughout the modern period because of philosophy's inordinate (and, we should add, ironic) faith in reason and its consequent inability to appreciate, let alone understand, the language of religion.

For de Vries, the brute fact of the matter is that in spite of the modern process of secularization, both religion and theology stubbornly remain, like a trauma. This is one reason why we need a new philosophy of religion that moves beyond the antagonistic relationship and mutually exclusive logic that has kept the philosopher and the theologian separate and distinct. Try as they might, philosophers "have proven unable to settle the debate [between religion and philosophy] and to silence the religious once and for all."[23]

This does not mean, as the fundamentalists might have it, that religion is now given the last word, for that would amount to no more than a reversal of privilege from the strictly theological to the philosophical and back again. Such a reversal would be the mirror image of Janicaud, who himself is caught in the modern web of exclusionary logic. No, instead, by recognizing the resemblance of religion to the experience of trauma, this new philosophy of religion proposed by de Vries begins at the point of bereavement for the sort of emptying of language and loss of old certainties in which no single word is given final say. But, at the same time, "the words *religion* and *God* remain (or have become) the most appropriate names (or simply the best we have come up with so far)"[24] for giving expression to the sense of ultimacy, ineluctable mystery, and tragic horror from which our experience knows no escape. "The task, then," de Vries tells us, "is to comprehend this intertwinement between 'faith' and 'knowledge,' but to do so 'otherwise.'"[25]

And so we come to my second and final example of this more sympathetic analysis of the philosophical turn to religion. In his recent work *After Christianity*, the Italian hermeneutic philosopher Gianni Vattimo links the Nietzschean announcement of the death of God and the Heideggerian analysis of the end of metaphysics together with Lyotard's description of the "Babel-like pluralism" of postmodern culture. This reading by Vattimo of contemporary Western culture is important for two reasons. First, it is an argument that seeks to explain the postmodern return of the religious and to counter the threat of various forms of religious fundamentalism. As Vattimo writes, "Today, it seems that the main philosophical outcome of the death of the metaphysical God and of the almost general discrediting of philosophical foundationalism is the renewed possibility of religious experience."[26] He goes on to say the following:

> The return of religion, in all its theoretical, social, and historical aspects
> . . . seems to depend on the dissolution of metaphysics, that is, on the

dismissal of all doctrines, which claimed absolute and definitive values as the true description of Being's structures. . . . In turn, though, the renewal of religion configures itself necessarily as the claim to an ultimate truth, which is indeed an object of faith rather than rational demonstration but which in the end tends to exclude the very pluralism of world pictures that has made it possible.[27]

If Vattimo's assessment is correct, then it should be no surprise that phenomenology would also be permeated by this renewed interest in matters of religion. Indeed, the fact that the phenomenological tradition demands a certain ideological independence—or, more precisely, an independence or freedom from ideological predetermination—means that it must at least entertain the *possibility* of religious belief. As both phenomenology and theology have learned from hermeneutic philosophy, what matters here is not whether beliefs will figure but what the best posture toward belief will be. This is why Janicaud does not equate his own effort at "ruling the question of God out of phenomenological legitimacy" with the restoration of "an atheist phenomenology in the manner of Sartre." For Janicaud, Sartre's rule of atheism, no less than the progenitors of the theological turn, "is of an ideological order and is the symptom of a constant contamination of the methodological by the ideological."[28]

The problem, however, is that although Janicaud allows for a distinction between on the one hand an ideologically driven phenomenology and on the other a methodologically pure one, he is not nearly as sympathetic or understanding when it comes to the theological. Indeed, the theological tradition does face the permanent threat of fundamentalism, in which beliefs grow stale and rigid, and, rather than functioning as a critical means of engagement with and understanding of the world, they become the prism through which all experience must be gathered and in which a militant ideology goes unchecked. Phenomenology also faces a permanent threat, not from fundamentalism but from a narrow scholasticism that threatens to foreclose and thus undo the possibility of discovery.

What the phenomenological tradition must understand is that there is a difference between a closed and an open theology. The closed theology is rightly designated as a positive science, and its purposes stand in contrast to the spirit of the phenomenological method. The open theology, however, not only lives in response to epistemological uncertainty but also stands as its constant reminder and is therefore a permanent argument against fundamentalism. The theology Janicaud is concerned with, it seems, is a phenomenological theology that is marked by a certain content in its elucidation of religious beliefs, a fixed point of reference within specific traditions of faith, and a center of gravity that threatens to pull and drag the phenomenologist away from his or her proper free-floating and ever-dynamic attention "to the things themselves." This concern is shared by an open theology, which is determined by neither its form nor its content but is an interrogative theology that is forever questioning the very conditions of its own possibility. In short, radical theology must remain an open theology. Like the phenomenological tradition as Janicaud defines it, this open theology is also concerned with protecting the methodological from the ideological.

This is the paradox to which Vattimo is pointing—namely, that as theology and philosophy contribute to a more pluralistic culture, there is always the chance that certain beliefs just might take hold and exact violence on the very source of their generation. This potential dilemma brings me to the second reason for the importance of this reading by Vattimo of Western culture—that there is not one but at least two internal developments that tell not of two independent truths but of just one. The philosophical dissolution of metaphysics paves the way for the methodological rigor and ideological independence of phenomenology. As with the death of God, it is both an end and a beginning for theology that by writing a void into the heart of its own discourse it becomes free to pursue a more wandering, or erring, path. It should be no surprise, therefore, that recent theologies have written of the "God without being (God)," the "being of God when God is not being God," the "God who is dead," and the "God who may be."[29] More radical still is the cultural theology of Mark C. Taylor, who speaks of religion being most interesting where it is least obvious. According to this theological rule of thumb, phenomenology has become not more but less theological as it directly assumes for itself the more obvious theological questions of God, revelation, and faith.

From this perspective, phenomenology should be warier of its unstated theological assumptions, which work on at least two different levels. First is the obvious, which Janicaud directly addresses—namely, how a given theology might inform and predetermine a phenomenology. For instance, in the case of Levinas's phenomenology of radical alterity that both supports and is supported by his idea of the infinite, we must ask whether this is an experience that is accessible and a description that is verifiable. Or, as Janicaud suspects, is this instead an experience and a description that make sense only within the particular theological tradition of Jewish propheticism?

Second is the less obvious, which concerns the politically charged question of who speaks for theology. In the strict distinction and separation that Janicaud asserts between phenomenology and theology, has he not already effectively quarantined phenomenology from theology and, further, assumed for phenomenology what it means to think theologically? Again, like Heidegger, it seems that Janicaud merely presumes that phenomenologists and theologians understand one another best when they speak in their own language. The paradoxical result of this supposition is that although Janicaud truly endeavors to preserve the freedom of both the phenomenological and theological traditions, he effectively shortcuts the theological tradition's ability to speak for itself when he establishes a single theological perspective as the norm. He thereby becomes guilty of his own ideological trumping of the methodological.

Janicaud's own ideological trump card can be seen in his conclusion, in which he cites what he considers to be the representative theological position from Martin Luther, who writes, "Faith consists in giving oneself over to the hold of things we do not see."[30] The problem with this perspective, as this chapter has tried to demonstrate, is that by allowing this single theological statement to stand for the meaning and task of theology, Janicaud has ignored and disavowed the history that has intervened. This is a history in which the fragmentation, dispersal, and pluralism of the postmodern Western culture parallel and are funded by the dissolution of theology, just as they have been by the deconstruction of philosophy.

The lineage I consider foundational for radical theology as a discernible tradition of thought starts with retrenchment and continues on to engagement and ultimately to transformation and dissolution. It operates within the province of modern liberal Protestant thought, to be sure, but by suffering a becoming of its own that parallels the more widespread secularization of the West in terms of desacralization, it still has the potential to remap the traditional boundaries of thought. Having written a void in the heart of its own discourse, radical theology wanders freely. As Taylor celebrates it, it becomes an "erring" a/theology. But the potential hubris and colonial or imperialistic overtones of this must not be missed. And so we turn from the relationship between philosophy and theology to the relationship between the ethical and the political, the passage from the one to the other, and, even more, the question of the extent to which a radical theology predicated on its own dissolution can mount a positive politics at all.

TWO

From the Ethical to the Political

This book is an effort to sketch the shifting contours of a radical theology of the future. In the previous chapter I took issue with Dominique Janicaud's critique of what has been termed the theological turn in French phenomenology. My argument was that the proper image of thought should not be that of a turn but rather that of a becoming. That is to say, phenomenology does not turn to theology as if *turning away* from its proper domain of thought as much as it *becomes* its own other as it thinks itself to the limits. The becoming other is not a consequence of an impure or faulty starting point that somehow smuggles God into an otherwise ideologically pure and methodologically rigorous discourse but is instead a consequence, an aftereffect, or a trace.

The theological becoming of phenomenology thus mirrors the radical becoming of theology, whether in Augustine's *Confessions*, in which he admits he cannot think God apart from the most intense self-scrutiny; in Ludwig Feuerbach, who argues that our talk of God is nothing but talk of humanity in a loud voice; or in Emmanuel Levinas, whose philosophy of alterity ultimately collapses the distinction between God and the neighbor, thinking (to) the (wholly) other is not just a projection but a solipsism. The question, and it is here that the work of Catherine Malabou becomes most instructive, is whether there can be an alterity without an outside—or more to the point, whether the lack of a beyond implies the lack of difference and the reduction of the other to the same. Malabou's conception, which provides me with the critical lever for the exposition and interrogation of Levinas that follows, holds that what is needed is the way to conceive of the possibility for radical transformation—true change—*without exoticism*. So whereas the previous chapter argued for a sense of theological becoming as opposed to a theological turn, this chapter will opt for change over exchange, and for transformation as opposed to transcendence.

In this way, I am pushing against the limits of radical theology as it has heretofore been employed. I do so not simply through the introduction of a new voice in that of Malabou but, more fundamentally, through the explicit inquiry into the relation between radical theology and the political. This is a separate inquiry from that of the relation between religion and politics, and it is distinct from the development of a radical political theology. What I am aiming for instead is a way of questioning the province of the lineage of radical theology as an expression and continuation of modern liberal Protestant thought. I regard this as an essential methodological point in that I strive for a decolonial effect by other means than the standard decolonial option. My choice should in no way be taken as a rejection or even a critique of the decolonial option but instead simply as a recognition of the specific tradition of thought out of which I am working. By inquiring into the relation between radical theology and the political, I want to acknowledge the potential hubris and imperialistic overtones of radical theology while holding fast to the prospect of it becoming something other. And just as a radical political theology rejects the theopolitical fatalism of a Heidegger who declares that "only a god can save us now," the methodological rule here is for the work of radical theology to be to work on itself.

This stands in marked contrast not only to Heidegger but also to Levinas, for whom change is predicated on difference. More specifically, change necessarily comes from the outside by way of the radical alterity of the other. This philosophy of alterity lays the groundwork for a messianic politics structured by transcendence, a waiting for the (wholly) other who is always to come. My argument here is that such a messianic form of politics is an insufficient conception of the political. I show how Levinas, in particular, collapses the political into the ethical, ultimately leaving politics with such a bad name that it is in need of a kind of redemption; there are ironic echoes of Heidegger in Levinas, with both sharing in a kind of theopolitical despair. So even as Levinas himself takes up political issues—most notably, Zionism and the relations between the Israelis and Palestinians—his fundamental ambivalence about the concept of the political demonstrates the inadequacy of a purely deconstructive approach to political theology, even when that deconstructive approach is informed by the most heightened ethical sensibility.

The implication, suggested but not fully developed in this chapter, is that a truly radical theological method cannot rely exclusively on a logic of transcendence and that a radical political theology would not be the messianic form of politics championed by Levinas. There must instead be some means for a more positive conception of the political, by which I intend to suggest the possibility for imagining difference and making change within this world as we know and experience it. Such a radical theology would operate not just by an immanent critique but by the recognition, harnessing, and redirection of the infinite horizon of possibilities that exist within the immanent order. A *beyond within*, by which *transformation replaces transcendence* as the operative image of thought.

Turnings

In addition to the so-called theological turn, Levinas has been credited, or at least associated, with a number of other turns in contemporary thought. The first—which remains the most common reading of Levinas and which is drawn primarily from his groundbreaking work, *Totality and Infinity*—credits him with the "ethical turn" in contemporary philosophy for the priority he gives to "ethics as first philosophy." To simplify a great deal, Derrida's work and, more broadly, poststructuralist theory and deconstructive philosophy, were seen before Levinas as largely nihilistic endeavors—that is, as simply negative thought procedures containing no fundamental commitments and contributing little to the positive efforts at determining meaning, fostering shared values, and clarifying a greater understanding of the good. Since Levinas, however, it has been precisely this nihilistic narrative of deconstruction that has itself been deconstructed.

This reversal is something that informs the reading of Derrida, deconstruction, and poststructuralism. After the Levinasian ethical turn, even ethical theory itself must answer to the radical challenge issued by that of deconstruction and must be made to account for the call of the Other. As Derrida puts it in his eulogy for Levinas, our thanks to Levinas is due at least in part for his entire recasting of the ethical, because with Levinas we are faced with an "ethics before and beyond ontology, the State, or politics, but also ethics beyond ethics."[1] Or, as Simon Critchley argues, the rupture marked by the before and after Levinas in the reading of Derrida marks "a third wave in the reception of deconstruction, beyond its literary and philosophical appropriations, one in which ethical—not to mention political—questions are uppermost."[2] We will return in due course to the question of Levinas and the political and, more specifically, the relation of the ethical to the political, but for now we must contend with Levinas's recasting of the ethical. As Critchley writes:

> The conception of ethics . . . will differ markedly from the traditional conception of ethics qua region or branch of philosophy. . . . My claim is not that an ethics can be derived from deconstruction, like an effect from a cause, a superstructure from an infrastructure, or a second critique from a first critique. . . . Rather, I hope to demonstrate that the pattern of reading produced in the deconstruction of—mostly, but by no means exclusively—philosophical texts has an ethical structure: deconstruction "is" ethical; or, to formulate the same thought less ontologically . . . deconstruction takes place (*a lieu*) ethically, or there is duty in deconstruction (*Il y a du devoir dans la deconstruction*).[3]

The ethical turn prompted by Levinas, therefore, is not away from philosophy to its prior origin in ethics but toward an "ethics beyond ethics" or, more radical still, in the words of John Caputo, an ethics "against ethics,"[4] both of which give rise to the paradoxical, if not entirely contradictory, possibility of a "postmodern ethics."[5]

Meanwhile, with the recent prominence of Italian theorists such as Antonio Negri and Giorgio Agamben, the French political philosopher Alain Badiou, and the Slovenian Slavoj Žižek—not to mention the global threat of terrorism, the hypermilitarized response from the United States and its allies in the wars in Afghanistan and Iraq, and the still-raging crisis in the Middle East—much of contemporary thought has taken a decidedly political turn as the very nature of the political and its status within contemporary thought has been a topic of much recent attention. But perhaps the most forceful theological movement during the present generation has been that of radical orthodoxy, led by the British theologian John Milbank. For many, radical orthodox theology is a welcome relief from the modern legacy of the Enlightenment and its consuming interest in matters of epistemology. Radical orthodoxy begins with the assertion of the moral bankruptcy of secular reason and seeks a more reliable foundation for values in culture through the assurances provided by a unified, comprehensive, and autonomous system of religious belief. Although beginning as a critique of liberal theology that follows the dictates of secular reason, it extends to a more generalized critique of classic modern liberalism itself. According to this critique, with the modern assertion of the autonomous self as the arbiter of all truth and reality, the liberal values of openness and tolerance are ultimately deprived of any grounding whatsoever because the very reason for the universal respect for the dignity of all— namely, the sanctity of the divine creator—is denied, if not outright in theory, then at least in practice by the secularization of our moral reasoning and public discourse. Although radical orthodoxy is a much more traditionalist movement than that cultivated by the work of the various political theorists mentioned earlier in this paragraph, what they share is an appreciation for what they identify as a crisis within modern liberal political theory. For many commentators, then, the political turn in contemporary philosophy and theology amounts to nothing less than a paradigm shift within contemporary thought, a crisis so resounding that any thinker worth considering must speak on its terms in order to garner a hearing. Each of these movements in its own way might rightly be described as post-liberal and thus align with the radical theological method I seek to articulate here.

The question this raises for us regarding Levinas is an important one and may be posed in relation to the previous chapter's concerns. Namely, as the postmodern return of religion has turned to the political, is this an extension of, or a turn away from, the ethical as conceived by Levinas? What exactly is the connection between Levinas's conception of the ethical and the political? Or, in other words, is the (ethical) promise of deconstruction also its (political) limit, and *does the political turn in contemporary thought mark the eclipse of Levinas?* After all, a Levinasian ethic is characterized first and foremost by the impossible—the unconditional demand of the Other and the infinite scope of responsibility that precedes and exceeds all intentionality. For Levinas, responsibility comes before freedom, and, as such, its obligation is absolute but also absolutely undecidable and indeterminable. The political, however, is concerned with the art of the possible and the negotiation of and for power and, at least with modern liberal thought, is predicated on the free acts of autonomous political subjects. In other words, does Levinas have a political philosophy? To the extent that he conceives of ethics as primarily philosophy, can he even have one? If so, does he belong to the tradition of modern liberalism? And, finally, what does any of this have to do with Levinas's talk of God and, more specifically, his employment of the ontological argument for God's existence?

My argument is that this political context is precisely what gives Levinas's discussion of God such urgency. Although Levinas himself steadfastly refused the designation of *theology* and most certainly would have also rejected the term *political theology*, what I propose here is to read Levinas's discussion of God for the political theology latent within it. In so doing, my effort is at least twofold. First, I attempt to place Levinas in conversation with many of the contemporary theorists who are seeking a new understanding of the political. Second, I seek to again demonstrate the enduring appeal and importance of Levinas, not only as an ethical and religious thinker of the first order but also as someone whose entire thinking, in the words of Roger Burggraeve, "can be interpreted as an immense effort to bring to light the roots of violence and racism, and as an attempt to overcome this in principle by thinking otherwise."[6]

At the same time, we must necessarily ask whether, and to what extent, his thinking is capable of meeting the challenge of this "immense effort." With this question in mind, I invoke the work of Catherine Malabou and Judith Butler for the ways that each achieves a certain critical distance from Levinas. More broadly, my concerns here are not chiefly with the legacy and limitations of Levinas per se but with the way an interrogation of Levinas provides a proxy for the interrogation of deconstructive philosophy and radical theology more generally. Insofar as this book announces the radical theology to come as postliberal, I am also concerned with the extent to which the radical theological method I am pursuing requires a postdeconstructive approach to the ethical, the political, and beyond.

Levinas's "Proof"

Truth be told, it makes no more sense to speak of Levinas's "proof" for God's existence than it does to think of Anselm's ontological argument as a proof in the modern sense of the term. As many have observed, the idea that one could somehow prove God's existence is a distinctly modern project that betrays a prior turn to the Cartesian subject as the final arbiter of truth and reality.[7] Indeed, as

John Caputo argues, the very attempt to prove God's existence is the best proof for the death of God in the modern consciousness because more than anything else it has put the conscious subject in the place of God, thus betraying the doubt that it means to erase. In other words, once the existence of God becomes a question of logic and is put to reason, the animating religious spirit of God is already dead. Caputo writes:

> So in modernity, the question of God is profoundly recast. Instead of beginning on our knees, we are all seated solemnly and with stern faces on the hard benches of the court of Reason as it is called into session. God is brought before the court, like a defendant with his hat in his hand, and required to give an account of himself, to show His ontological papers, if He expects to win the court's approval. In such a world, from Anselm's point of view, God is already dead, even if you conclude that the proof is valid, because whatever you think you have proven or disproven is not the God he experiences in prayer and liturgy but a philosophical idol.[8]

Perhaps more than anything else, it is this difference that marks the chasm between the medieval mind and the modern mind. In the first, thought proceeds almost exclusively within the realm of faith and thus God's existence is assumed, whereas, in the second, religious truth is held in suspicion and thus even the very idea of God is left wanting its own rationale and must be proven in accordance with the prevailing episteme.

From the medieval to the modern and into the postmodern, the comparison between Levinas and Anselm is not accidental, as neither falls prey to what Levinas once termed the temptation of temptation, otherwise known as the temptation of knowledge. By giving priority to knowledge, philosophy subordinates its prior commitment to wisdom. And just as this degraded, if not fallen, philosophy stands in contrast to wisdom, so too does knowledge to living. With Anselm and Levinas, though, the self does not constitute itself, and the thinking self is not its own master. On the contrary, thought is beholden to life just as the self is beholden to an-Other, and the more one thinks, the more one realizes the infinite scope of the responsibility that exceeds and precedes one's own intentionality. Levinas's treatment, then, of the ontological argument for God's existence exposes him as a quintessential postmodern thinker. In "God and Philosophy," he writes, "It is not the proofs of God's existence that matter to us here, but rather the breakup of consciousness, which is not a repression into the unconscious but a sobering or a waking up that shakes the 'dogmatic slumber' that sleeps at the bottom of all consciousness resting upon the object."[9] Perhaps more than any other postmodern thinker, it is Levinas who calls into relief both the limitations and danger of the egocentric model that predominates in modern thought from Descartes to the present.

Likewise, Levinas's philosophical turn to religion is neither coincidence nor passing fad but rather constitutive in the sense that there is a realization of how thought itself follows a certain structure of faith. Finally, then, we come to the question of the status and function of the proof for God's existence within Levinas's thinking, and, in so doing, we find at least one representative case of a postmodern thinker who employs the ontological argument but thinks it otherwise than ontotheologically. In other words, Levinas's employment of the ontological argument, rather than functioning as a founding narrative, is a *narrative of disruption* in which he leads us not to a point of realization of the necessity of God but instead to our *inescapability from God*. A founding narrative would function as a rational argument compelling cognitive assent and tempting us with a knowledge severed from life, while a narrative of disruption redoubles the ethical imperative that runs throughout Levinas's oeuvre.

Before venturing further into this line of interpretation, I must first establish the contours of Levinas's own argument as it is most clearly expressed in his essay "God and Philosophy." From the start, Levinas makes plain his argument that the traditional readings of the proofs—in his words, "the thematization of God in religious experience"—have missed their primary significance, which is, as mentioned earlier, a narrative of disruption that leads to the breakup of "the unity of the 'I think.'" Next, given Descartes's prominence in the founding of the thinking subject, we might expect that what follows in Levinas's analysis would be a critical exposé into where and how Descartes's *Meditations* goes wrong. But, on the contrary, Levinas writes, "In his meditation on the idea of God, Descartes has sketched, with unequaled rigor, the extraordinary course of a thought proceeding to the point of the breakup of the I think." And although it is true that "Descartes maintains a substantialist language here, interpreting the immeasurableness of God as a superlative way of existing," he nevertheless makes an even greater, though unwitting, contribution, in which it is not the proof that matters as it becomes the critical link for the reestablishment of an entire metaphysical edifice but instead *the inestimable excess that lies at the root of consciousness*.

After all, from whence comes the idea of the infinite? Levinas tells us that, as an idea, it exceeds the finite mind's capacity to think. Yet here it still stands before us as an idea that has already been thought and that remains a desire even within a form of contemporary thought that deliberately restrains itself to the immanent realm of ideas that can be thought in actuality. As Levinas writes, "The actuality of the cogito is thus interrupted by the unencompassable; it is not thought but undergone." He also says that "the idea of the Infinite, the Infinite in me, can only

be a passivity of consciousness . . . more passive than any passivity, like the passivity of a trauma through which the idea of God would have been placed within
us. An 'idea placed within us.'"[10]

In other words, by tracing the idea of the infinite to the thematization of God,
we learn of an unexpected reversal and overturning that lies hidden in Descartes's
own logic—namely, that before consciousness comes the idea, that it is not the
thinking self that thinks God as its highest thought, but the idea that gives birth to
thought. As Levinas puts it, "The placing in us of an unencompassable idea over-
turns this presence of self which is consciousness. . . . It is thus an idea signifying
within a significance prior to presence, to all presence, prior to every origin in consciousness, and so an-archic, accessible only in its trace."[11] As the birth of thought,
it is also an act of devastation and awakening, Levinas writes: "The Infinite affects
thought by simultaneously devastating it and calling it; through a 'putting it in its
place,' the Infinite puts thought in place. It wakes thought up."[12]

What, then, is the meaning? Although this act of devastation, disruption, and
interruption is comparable to a trauma, Levinas is careful to distinguish it from an
act of pure negativity. As he writes, "The in- of the infinite is not a non- or not of
some kind: its negation is the subjectivity of the subject, which is behind intentionality." He goes further when he says that "the not-able-to-comprehend-the-Infinite-
by-thought is, in some way, a positive relation with this thought."[13] It is positive
due to the nature of desire, which, as Levinas describes it, is the

> "more in the less" [that] awakens with its most ardent, most noble,
> and most ancient flame, a thought destined to think more than it
> thinks. . . . The negativity of the In- of the Infinite—otherwise than
> being, divine comedy—hollows out a desire that could not be filled,
> one nourished from its own increase, exalted as Desire—one that
> withdraws from its satisfaction as it draws near to the Desirable. This
> is a Desire for what is beyond satisfaction, and which does not identify,
> as need does, a term or an end. A desire without end, from Being: dis-
> interestedness, transcendence—desire for the Good.[14]

So the meaning is this: the human subject is redefined as first and foremost an
ethical subject. The idea of the infinite—the very thought that cannot be thought
by the finite mind, an idea "placed within us"—marks the human consciousness
with transcendence, which is experienced as a desire beyond satisfaction and
without end. This is a desire for the "more in the less" that makes love possible,
as the self is taken outside itself and then drawn to and beholden by the other.
It is at this point that Levinas's argument comes full circle and the religious language proves absolutely essential, for while the ethical subject is constituted by
its subjection to and responsibility for the other, there is another other that in the

words of Levinas is "otherwise and better than being; the very possibility of the beyond." This other other, which is known as God, "is not simply the 'first other,' or the 'other par excellence,' or the 'absolutely other,' but other than the other, other otherwise, and other with an alterity prior to the alterity of the other, prior to the ethical obligation to the other and different from every neighbor, transcendent to the point of absence."[15]

It should be clear from this reading that the ethical, which Levinas identifies elsewhere as "first philosophy," is here given over to a prior origin: first comes God, or, at least epistemologically speaking, the idea of the infinite now conceived of as God, to which the self responds, "Here I am." The self is thereby constituted as a distinctly ethical subject—a subject constituted by its relation with the Other, but an other who is other otherwise to the point of transcendence, *a point of beyond that draws the subject outside itself in the desire for the Good.* Or, if you prefer Levinas in the extreme, the self is a substitute for and hostage to the Other.

Levinas engages in a theologic that begins with the idea of God or the idea of the infinite, an idea that, although conceived as an idea, still cannot be thought unless it is *thought from elsewhere* than the conscious mind. Consciousness, therefore, rests on an already subjected, and thus disrupted, ground. The idea of God is an "idea put into us," an idea that is thought only as a trace that bears witness to the infinite responsibility of the self to an-Other. As such, it is true as Levinas tells it that the idea of God speaks more as ethics than as religion or theology, and ethics so conceived is an ethics that precedes and goes beyond philosophy because it remains an idea that understands more than it understands, thinks more than it is even possible to think, and carries a responsibility that is always outstanding.

It is a strange logic that begins securely with the indubitable and unified thinking self and the idea of God. As Descartes narrates it, this thinking subject was supposed to be the stable foundation from which all reality could be securely known. In Levinas's rendering, however, it leads instead to the breakup of consciousness and a transcendence to the point of absence. Perhaps it is stranger still to insist that the in- of this infinite is not entirely negative, that this devastating and overwhelming idea of the infinite that is put into us somehow has positive ethical ramifications. Add to this mix Levinas's language of the divine comedy, which he describes as "a comedy taking place in the ambiguity between temple and theater, but wherein the laughter sticks in your throat at the approach of the neighbor, that is, of his face or his forsakenness."[16] Who is it that is forsaken here, and by whom? Is it the God who is otherwise than being, who is transcendent to the point of absence? Is it the rest of us who are left behind? If this is a proof for God's existence, it is a proof that absolutely shatters the tradition. By tracing the idea of the infinite within the ontological argument for God, the one thing we can securely know is that we are on our own, face to face with our neighbor, bearing witness to the absence of God.

Beyond

From the ethicoreligious to the political and beyond, Levinas leads us on a journey of thought and human relation that follows the trace of transcendence entirely within the immanent logic of a single thought, albeit the thought of God in the idea of the infinite. But from this thought of God we are left alone, all together sharing in our forsakenness, facing our impossible obligation with no one to save us but ourselves. In so doing, Levinas stands firmly in a long line of Jewish prophets handing us over in our God-forsakenness and thus simultaneously elevating and radicalizing the ethical demand placed on us all.

This radicalization of the moral imperative is yet another example of how Levinas remains forever in close proximity to, but in fundamental disagreement with, Heidegger. For although Heidegger is led to almost the exact same point of analysis, if not despair, he finds recourse in the mystical and the poetical and asserts with resignation our now-foundering state of being:

> Philosophy will not be able to effect an immediate transformation of the present condition of the world. This is not only true of philosophy, but of all merely human thought and endeavor. Only a god can save us. The sole possibility that is left for us is to prepare a sort of readiness, through thinking and poetizing, for the appearance of the god or for the absence of the god in the time of foundering: for in the face of the god who is absent, we founder.[17]

For Levinas, however, who admits in his intellectual biography that his thinking "is dominated by the presentiment and the memory of the Nazi horror,"[18] foundering is not an option. So whereas Heidegger retreats from the political to the mystical, Levinas probes ever deeper into the critical nexus that is political theology by connecting his analysis of the idea of the infinite with his commitment to justice. This connection leads me to two observations about the nature of the political in Levinas's thought.

The first observation is that *the political is the natural progression and complexification of the ethical.* Toward the conclusion to *Otherwise Than Being*, Levinas asserts the following progression, or at least trajectory: "from responsibility to problems."[19] It would seem to most that the ethical responsibility that Levinas describes is already problem enough. But to the extent that the ethical is defined by the face-to-face relation, by the proximity to the neighbor, it remains a straightforward, if not simple, relation. Responsibility is absolute, without excess or remainder. The problems come when we introduce a third party. It is at this point that the measure of politics figures into the face-to-face relation. Levinas writes:

> If proximity ordered to me only the other alone, there would have not been any problem, in even the general sense of the term. A question would not have been born, nor consciousness, nor self-consciousness. The responsibility for the other is an immediacy antecedent to questions, it is proximity. It is troubled and becomes a problem when a third party enters. The third party is other than the neighbor but also another neighbor, and also a neighbor of the other, and not simply his fellow.[20]

He goes on to say that "the third party introduces a contradiction in the saying whose signification before the other until then went in one direction. It is of itself the limit of responsibility and the birth of the question: What do I have to do with justice? A question of consciousness. Justice is necessary."[21]

Indeed, beyond the ethical, as if counted in the natural progression from two to three, stands the necessity of the political. With the political comes a complexification of the ethical, not because the responsibility is any greater—to be sure, it could not be any greater than a responsibility that is already absolute and infinite in its scope—but because now it is bound up together with self-consciousness and in the day-to-day negotiations that mark the self's being in the world. Politics, so conceived, is being in the world and of the world. Thus the commitment to justice is as necessary as politics is inevitable.

The second observation is that *although the political stands as the natural progression beyond the ethical with the introduction of the third party, in order for the political to avoid being purely political it must continually return to its source in the ethicoreligious.* It is precisely this connection between the ethicoreligious and the political that Derrida explored in a speech titled "A Word of Welcome," which was delivered at the Sorbonne during an homage to Levinas one year after Levinas's death. As Derrida states, "The border between the ethical and the political here loses for good the indivisible simplicity of a limit. No matter what Levinas might have said, the determinability of this limit was never pure, and it never will be."[22] Having established the connection, Derrida then questions the nature of its relation, one whose limit or boundary point is admittedly "never pure" and is also not entirely clear by virtue of Levinas's own statement that suggests an ethical realm beyond the political.[23]

Does Levinas's phrasing here betray the negation of politics that is endemic to the global capital order? Does this mark a retreat from the lessons learned in his own analysis of the idea of the infinite, in which we are left alone in our shared forsakenness following the trace of transcendence to the point of absence? Not according to Derrida. Recall from Levinas's analysis of the ontological argument the meaning of the *in-* in the idea of the infinite. Levinas insists that this in- of the infinite be understood in its positive relation following the structure of desire. Likewise, Derrida insists that the "beyond the political" of which Levinas speaks be understood not as a negation but as an opening up into the transcendence that already lies within the immanent order. As Derrida puts it, "Beyond-in: transcendence in immanence, beyond the political, but in the political. Inclusion opened onto the transcendence that it bears, incorporation of a door that bears and opens onto the beyond of the walls and partitions framing it."[24] When the political is so understood, the possibility arises of an "ethical conversion" within and on behalf of our present and existing politics.[25] With this possibility, Levinas leaves us with the hope that our politics is never purely political, that by returning politics to its source in the ethicoreligious it can transcend the cynical reasoning that drives those who are interested only in power and profit and upend those who falsely equate their own thematization of God—whether in its moralizing or nationalistic guises—with the prior and more fundamental idea that stands as its source.

As Derrida notes, Levinas's politics follow the structure of the messianic as it is driven by the hope for a justice that is always to come. This fact alone is enough to affirmatively answer the earlier question of whether Levinas has a political philosophy. But, as Levinas teaches us in his discussion of the question of the third, the more difficult problem remains: to bring to light the roots of violence and exclusion, to think and act otherwise, not only with the single other to whom I might give myself in love but with each and every other from time immemorial to time everlasting and, most of all, in the here and now. This goal, of course, remains a guiding commitment of classic liberalism, and, as such, it reveals both the promise and limit of Levinas's politics. That is to say, as long as the existing present is held in relief by the messianic promise of the future, the hope for justice that Levinas so clearly expresses can never amount to more than a politics of decision. This perhaps is the ironic consequence of the deconstructive insistence on structural undecidability. As Kenneth Surin argues, the tragedy of this form of politics, whether in its Levinasian or Derridean version, "is that it has no way of inserting the subject into the domain of the actually political. We are left instead with a paralyzing Kierkegaardian pathos that provides no way of imagining resistance at the level of a politics of collective action."[26]

Although what Charles Winquist has written is true, that "epistemic undecidability does not prevent or even inhibit ethical decidability,"[27] for politics to have the positive and potent ethical force for good that Levinas desires, it must be more than the expression of individual preference or conviction, more than a politics of decision. The irony must not be missed: by Levinas's rendering, it is Carl Schmitt's concept of the political that has the most resonance.

In other words, according to Levinas's rendering, the only thing that keeps politics from being purely political, the only thing that keeps it out of the hands of those who would resort to any measure to gain power, is the goodwill and conscience of individuals. Consider, for instance, his essay, "The Rights of Man and the Rights of the Other," in which he distinguishes between what he terms a "bad peace" and a "good war." The bad peace he has in mind is the consequence of the paradox and instability of the notion of human rights—that is to say, what is freedom for one person is negation for another. Thus, the peace promised by the universal guarantee of human rights is always only a bad peace in that it remains uncertain and precarious. It is a bad peace "seeking stability in the powers of the state, in politics, which ensures obedience to the law by force. Hence recourse of justice to politics."[28]

Although Levinas admits that such a recourse might still be better than war, the insinuation is clear: *politics has a dirty name.* What's more, the concept of the political is surpassed, if not entirely trumped, by the ethical, which is why he insists that justice requires a different authority—specifically, a nonpolitical one. That different authority is goodness, and Levinas describes it by saying, "This is a goodness in peace, which is also the exercise of a freedom, and in which the *I* frees itself from its 'return to self.'"[29] Thus, beyond war and peace, beyond crime and punishment, and beyond the rights of citizenship and the laws of the nation, there is a goodness that manifests itself in the form of an inexhaustible responsibility that Levinas identifies as "the first language."[30]

Transformation

My point here is not that Levinas is some naïve optimist characterized by a political idealism. After all, as mentioned earlier in reference to his intellectual autobiography, he knew firsthand the horrors of the Holocaust, and his work was "dominated by the presentiment and the memory of the Nazi horror."[31] Likewise, in introducing Levinas's philosophy, commentators have long pointed to Heidegger's collaboration with the Nazis as the early watershed during which Levinas's thought takes shape as an ongoing effort to reverse and eventually overcome Heidegger's entire ontological enterprise.[32]

My point instead is to interrogate the consequences of this subordination of the political to the ethical. Indeed, in his radicalization of ethics through his invocation and insistence on our *infinite* responsibility, Levinas does not simply subordinate the political but disavows or erases it. The political gets entirely subsumed within the ethical. The mistake that Levinas makes, then, is to insist on a prior and transcending goodness. As Malabou puts it, Levinas has his own conception of the fantastic in that his philosophy is ultimately immaterial and utterly incapable of explaining the passage from that which is otherwise to being to either being itself or the world of beings.

It is on this point that Malabou and Derrida starkly disagree, both in their ultimate assessment of Levinas and correlatively in their position on the viability of
the messianic form of politics he espouses. Recall from earlier Derrida's careful
wording: "No matter what Levinas might have said . . . " He goes on to explain that
although Levinas spoke in terms of a "beyond the political," what he meant, or
how he ought to be understood, is that the "beyond the political" is a beyond-that-
remains-within the political—not a negation but an opening. This presents the permanent possibility of an "ethical conversion," or a kind of redemption of politics.

Even still, we must ask: whence comes the conversion? For Levinas, goodness
has a preoriginal quality that precedes and exceeds the subject. One need look no
further than well-known titles from Levinas's oeuvre to see that the ethical conversion necessary for the redemption of politics comes from "outside the subject";
it is "otherwise than being" and "beyond essence." Malabou responds by saying,
"I have serious reservations about such a 'beyond.'" She goes on to specify that
the problem with the "alterity of pure dissymmetry" lies in its modality: "What
changes from 'being' to 'otherwise than being'?"[33] Put differently, the question is
not just about where alterity comes from but about how exactly it gets expressed,
experienced, or imposed. In a stark reversal from Levinas and from Derrida, who
comes to Levinas's defense, Malabou insists that change comes before difference,
that difference is the product of change, and that *difference only happens* and thus
can never be conceived as some preoriginal state or quality. "Alterity can only
impose itself fundamentally through its *power of transformation* and as this same
power," Malabou says. She also writes that "transformation is the origin of alterity."[34]

To make the point clear, the significance for radical theology of this internal
debate among three French thinkers turns on the respective views of transcendence and immanence. Levinas's critique of ontology is well known; he claims
that ontology operates on an immanent economy by which its comprehensive
gaze reduces all differences to the same. It is thus totalizing, and its supposed neutrality masks the risks of total annihilation. This totality must be broken up from
the outside, whence comes the prior and transcending goodness that gives philosophy its proper grounding. Such is the meaning of Levinas's claim that "ethics is first philosophy." But here is the crucial point: the prior and transcending
goodness not only gives philosophy its proper grounding but also is the necessary
source of redemption. Just as ethics saves politics from itself, the hope for justice
depends on a messianic logic.

Malabou's position is not nearly as well known. She is a nonreductive, materialist thinker whose thought is built on the concept of plasticity. As such, although
she, like Levinas, acknowledges that ontology operates by an immanent economy,
for her this is not a problem to be overcome; rather, it is the condition of possibility

for thinking and being otherwise. While, in her words, "we cannot leave Being" and "Being is impossible to escape," this does not destine us to a circle of the same. On the contrary, being itself is destined to metamorphosis. We do not need to get beyond essence to make way for or to appreciate difference, because, as Malabou demonstrates, "the essence of a thing . . . is its alterity."[35] That is because "nothing exists that is not already changed, transformed, metamorphosized."[36]

The meaning for radical theology should be clear: our hope does not rest in the world beyond or in the world to come but in the *world here and now. Our hope is in change, not in an exchange,* whether that be an exchange of one world for another or one self for another. *Transformation is the means, not transcendence.*

Cohabitation

Finally, no discussion of Levinas's politics can be complete without taking up the concerns from the recent book by Judith Butler, *Parting Ways: Jewishness and the Critique of Zionism.* Butler, of course, is a profoundly Levinasian thinker who conceives of ethics as a relational practice that originates outside the subject. But, unlike Levinas, she has taken greater care in conceptualizing the political and in schematizing the relationship between ethics and politics. Specifically, Butler takes issue with Levinas's suggestion of the preoriginary or preontological ethical demand of goodness. She makes clear that "the demand from elsewhere is part of the very structure of address by which language operates to bind people," and that it is "always known and experienced through 'some' language, idiom, media, or another, or some site of convergence between them."[37] In addition, the ethical address is never simple or straightforward but always already multiple, containing within itself the possibility of being misaddressed, contradictory, and inconsistent. In contrast to Levinas, for Butler there is no "noninterpretive moment." And because "receptivity is always a matter of translation," the ethical demand must always be thought together "in a critical relation to power."[38]

This difference becomes especially apparent when Butler addresses Levinas's apparent disregard for the suffering imposed on Palestinians by the state of Israel. Butler cites an interview given by Levinas in which he claimed that "the Palestinian had no face," and that the absolute ethical obligations he had done so much to articulate and even radicalize extended only to those of Judeo-Christian and classical Greek origins.[39] For Butler, this moral insensitivity, callousness, or blindness on Levinas's part should not be used as an indictment against Levinas's ethics-cum-politics altogether. On the contrary, Butler insists that "in some ways, he [Levinas] gave us the very principle that he betrayed"—namely, that "we are bound to those we do not know, and did not choose, and that these obligations are, strictly speaking, precontractual."[40] At the same time, however, she identifies the fatal flaw in Levinas's particular political calculation in an insight that has its source in affect theory but that helps illuminate the much-needed passage from the ethical to the political:

> But if only certain populations are deemed grievable and others are not, then open grieving for one set of losses becomes the instrument through which another set of losses are denied. If Jews only mourn the loss of Jews in the conflicts of the Middle East, then they affirm that only those who belong to one's own religion or nation are worthy of grief. This way of differentiating between valuable and nonvaluable populations emerges not simply in the aftermath of violent conflicts, but provides the epistemological condition of the conflict itself.[41]

Consider by comparison black liberationist theologian James Cone's treatment of Reinhold Niebuhr in his book *The Cross and the Lynching Tree*. Cone acknowledged the debt he owed to Niebuhr, especially for Niebuhr's clarification of the social dimension of sin that took into account the factors of power and self-interest. Nevertheless, he rebuked Niebuhr in the strongest possible terms for his moral blindness regarding the question of race and the legacy of racism in the United States. Although Niebuhr did more than any other modern Protestant theologian to point out the tragic dimension of sin in human history, for Cone, Niebuhr himself was guilty of "theology's great sin"—that is, the evil of white supremacy by which Niebuhr could rest comfortably, ignoring the structural sin of racism reflecting his privilege as a white theologian. The case against Niebuhr, which I explore in more detail in the following chapters, is that he lacked empathy and moral imagination. The result is that he never mustered up the prophetic outrage that the systemic violence against African Americans demanded. In Cone's words, there was no "madness in his soul."[42] For Cone, this theological silence reveals a moral bankruptcy that suggests a fatal flaw in the white liberal Protestant consciousness he represented.

Butler may ultimately be gentler in her treatment of Levinas as she reads Levinas against himself and thereby seeks to salvage his ethics from his faulty politics. To do so, she established a point of contact between Levinas and Hannah Arendt through the idea of cohabitation. Just as Levinas "gave us a conception of ethical relations that make us ethically responsive to those who exceed our immediate sphere of bellowing and to whom we nevertheless belong, regardless of any choice or contract," Arendt condemned Adolf Eichmann for thinking he could choose "with whom to cohabit the earth." As Butler writes of Arendt, "Cohabitation is not a choice, but a condition of our political life. We are bound to one another prior to contract and prior to any volitional act."[43]

But note here that in establishing this point of contact Butler is assuming there is a parallel or equivalence in his ethics and that politics is ethical. Yet the passage

from the ethical to the political is the very passage that has proven to be so problematic for Levinas. Although no doubt translatable, the ethical nevertheless must
not be treated as equivalent to the political, as Butler herself acknowledges when
she writes, "If the process of translation comes to define retroactively religious resources for ethical thinking, then to derive an alternative political imaginary from
such resources is to make them anew or, indeed, to scatter and transmute them."[44]

Return again to the first observation made about Levinas's politics—that the
political is the natural progression and complexification of the ethical. The point
of this observation is that ethics stands to politics as the number two stands to the
number three. If, for Levinas, ethics presents the self as a hostage to the other, a relational self given over entirely to the other without reserve, then politics requires
a standing reserve, a more complex calculation by which determinations must be
made regarding to whom one owes one's loyalty, obligation, and belonging and
regarding whose losses are worthy of grief and whose are denied. The nation is a
religiocultural product. So conceived, whereas ethics is preoriginary and precontractual, politics operates by essentially by a liberal, social contract theory. The
point of the idea of cohabitation for both Arendt and Butler, by contrast, is that we
do not get to choose who is worthy of our grief and who is not, and we do not get
to choose with whom we share the earth. The point is also that we are precontrac-
tually bound together in modes of sociality that require an alternative politics, one
that is beyond the modern, liberal notion of the sovereignty of the nation-state.

To the extent that this is a fair reading of Levinas's concept of the political,
my concerns go deeper. It is not simply that his notion of the ethical redemption
of politics is nothing more than a pious wish but, more cynically, that the hyper-
ethical sensitivity hides a political calculation and callousness that is ultimately in-
humane. Put succinctly, *a political theology based on the beyond provides no basis for
the realization of justice.* With this tentative conclusion in place, we might cite the
important work done by Charles W. Mills in what he calls "the racial contract."
For Mills, social contract theory in particular and Western philosophy in general,
when read through the lens of critical race theory, are histories of an obfuscation
that hides the fact that white supremacy is "the unnamed political system that has
made the modern world what it is today."[45] As Mills makes clear in his study, the
pernicious legacy of racism is not a deviation or exception within our history but
is the norm, the very basis of our political order. And the evasion of our ethical
and political responsibility operates by a profound self-deception that is not accidental but prescribed by what he terms "an epistemology of ignorance" or a
"structured blindness."[46] In light of the political norm of conquest, colonization,
and enslavement, Mills calls for a heightened moral naturalism that begins from
actual moral consciousness and actual political realities that would better explain

the basic tragedy begging an explanation: "How were people able consistently to do the wrong thing while thinking they were doing the right thing?"[47]

By posing this question in the conclusion to this reading of Levinas, I mean it as a challenge—and certainly not just for Levinas but also for the self-styled radical theology that I explore throughout this book. There is no doubt that the lineage of radical theology is a real one that can be traced back at least as far as the death-of-God theologians of the late 1950s and 1960s. There is also no doubt that, with very few exceptions, the lineage of radical theology has been largely an internal conversation comprised almost entirely of Euro-American male voices and concerns. Ever since deconstruction was linked with the death of God as its proper hermeneutic, the circle has closed even tighter, making Continental philosophy the de facto methodological norm.

Perhaps it is time for radical theology to radically delink itself from its chosen hermeneutic. If so, the cohabitation invoked by Arendt and Butler yields not just the modes of sociality and politics promised but also new theological methods for truly subverting the norm.

THREE

The Political Becoming of Hermeneutics

The last chapter mentioned Martin Heidegger's collaboration with the Nazis as the time at which Emmanuel Levinas began a sustained effort to reverse and eventually overcome Heidegger's entire ontological enterprise. Along the way, Levinas radically recast moral philosophy by showing how Heidegger's fundamental insight into the nature of *dasein* as a being-with-others carries with it a prior ethical demand by which the self is constituted not first and foremost as an intersubjective being but as a moral being.

Nevertheless, the passage from the ethical to the political proved to be a difficult one for Levinas. His difficulty suggests at least two lessons for the present exploration of a radical theological method. First, as I discussed in the previous chapter, my tentative conclusion in reference to Catherine Malabou is that any political theology based on the beyond provides no opportunity for the realization of justice, and that a radical theology should therefore stake its hope in transformation, not transcendence. Second, the moral naturalism that is the product of critical race theory's interrogation of modern, liberal social contract theory provides one methodological resource by which radical theology might delink itself from deconstructive, Continental philosophy as its de facto methodological norm.

Although in this chapter I shift focus from the case study of Levinas to that of Heidegger, I continue this line of inquiry. As in the previous chapter, I invoke Malabou as interlocutor and intermediary. Also as in the previous chapter, I seek to accomplish a methodological delinkage of sorts, here by way of the decolonial theory of Walter Mignolo. And finally, I explore here as in the previous chapter the passage to the political—more specifically, I inquire whether a postmetaphysical philosophy and theology can produce a positive politics at all or whether postmetaphysics always and necessarily must remain only in a deconstructive mode.

A Reckless Mind

In his book *The Reckless Mind: Intellectuals in Politics*, Mark Lilla rehearses the familiar condemnation of Heidegger for his association with the Nazi Party. For Lilla, Heidegger was just one of many contemporary intellectuals who had no business commenting on or involving oneself in politics. Lilla believes it is better to avoid the political sphere altogether than run the risk of the philosophical love of wisdom degenerating into what he calls a philotyranny. For Lilla, modern European history is replete with examples of other philosophers that betrayed, in league with totalitarian regimes, the ideals of freedom and intellectual inquiry and were so utterly deluded that they failed philosophy's first and most enduring test—to tame the passions. The primary lesson of the twentieth century is how the temptation of the philotyrannical mind operates by an internal force that, in the words of Lilla, blinds by "the allure of an idea."[1] This sordid recent history is juxtaposed with the philosophical ideal as held by Socrates and Plato in which it is doubtful that the demands of politics and philosophy can ever be made to coincide.

In contrast to Lilla, Gianni Vattimo and Santiago Zabala accomplish the nearly unthinkable task. They not only take on the mantle of Heidegger for their entirely original and sorely needed articulation of the meaning of the politics of hermeneutics but convincingly demonstrate that a truly Heideggerian politics would be communist, not fascist. In so doing, Vattimo and Zabala reinvigorate the politics of the left and, what's more, redefine and redirect philosophical hermeneutics. As such, their book, *Hermeneutic Communism,* is the first salvo in the political becoming of hermeneutics.[2] Interpretation is a political act. By philosophically reflecting on the nature of interpretation, a particular, if not certain, politics is bequeathed—a reinvigorated communism severed from its metaphysical foundations, an antifoundationalist and postmetaphysical politics that eschews violence, and a weak Marxism that by its "South American alternative" aims to dissolve the Euro-American death grip on geopolitics.

My interest in this bold project is threefold. First, along with other recent scholars in critical philosophy, Vattimo and Zabala have paved the way for a renewed appreciation for Heidegger. They have accomplished what Malabou has termed a Heidegger change, even going so far as to suggest a new perspective on the prevailing view of Heidegger's cruel, opportunistic, and inept politics. Theirs is not as much a demythologization of Heidegger that reads Heidegger against himself to salvage what is good and enduring from the shame of his Nazi involvement as an actual invocation of Heidegger's hermeneutical philosophy as a potential political model or an actual claim—however counterintuitive it might seem—that a properly Heideggerian politics would be a communistic one. For this first point, I read Vattimo and Zabala's invocation of Heidegger in conjunction with Malabou's equally ambitious study in which she reappropriates Heidegger as a thinker of ontological mutation and thus as a viable ethical guide. In both cases, whether with Vattimo and Zabala or with Malabou, there is a fresh new critical engagement with the work of Heidegger that does not dismiss or shy away from his political past. Theirs is admittedly a dangerous undertaking. It is much easier and safer to stand with the likes of Lilla and issue a blanket condemnation of Heidegger. But in so doing, the connection between thinking and politics would still be left severed—our thinking bereft of any ethical or political direction and our politics left to its own devices as nothing more or less than the game of power we already know it to be.

Second, because they make their contemporary political reference point what they term the South American alternative, it is worth exploring the degree to which this endeavor toward a hermeneutic communism can be seen as a decolonial project. For this, I will take Walter Mignolo as my guide. He has been at the forefront in taking pains to define and distinguish decoloniality from both postcolonial theory and Marxist-oriented leftist politics. Although there is considerable overlap and compatibility between these three movements, they are nevertheless irreducible to one another. In the words of Mignolo, they "walk in the same direction, following different paths."[3] The chief difference is that they have different points of origination. Postcolonial theory and the politics of the Left are and remain essentially Western projects, with Western intellectuals grappling with their own troubling legacies, cultural biases, and complicity in networks of power and control. Decoloniality, however, is more than, and different from, "third world thoughts . . . processed in European intellectual factories."[4] It is a radical shift in the point of origin and reference. Or, better, it is the radical subversion of the very idea of the point of origin and reference. That is to say, decoloniality is defined by its embrace of a genuinely polycentric world, a dispelling of the myth of universality. So if postcolonial theory and the politics of the Left confront capitalism and colonialism from within the West itself, decoloniality stages a similar confrontation but from the perspective of the ex-colonies and the once colonized. In so doing, at least Mignolo's variant of the decolonial option distances itself from communism. For Mignolo, both communism and capitalism belong within the horizon of modern Western civilization and are thus unfit for a proper decolonial form of thinking and politics. This point will be important to consider when evaluating the viability of Vattimo and Zabala's reenvisioned hermeneutic communism. What's more, the question of what can or cannot authentically claim to call itself decolonial has already been posed regarding the possible decolonial effect of relating radical theology to the political. The question is not just whether but the extent to which the traditions of radical theology and radical hermeneutics can do the necessary deprovincializing work on themselves.

Third, I pursue the connection between hermeneutics and politics—or, better, the politics of hermeneutics as envisioned by Vattimo and Zabala—because although it seems clear that their project is intended as an effort to revitalize the radical politics of the Left for the expressed purpose of changing the world, it is simultaneously a work in critical philosophy. In making the case for the political becoming of hermeneutics, it is important not just to stake its claim within the history of hermeneutical philosophy but also to provide its very own critique and corrective to that history. Their claim is much stronger than simply that hermeneutics might be applied to politics. It is that *hermeneutics properly understood eventuates in a particular form of politics, specifically a communism of and for the twenty-first century*. This assertion is a departure from the way their postmetaphysical hermeneutics of weak thought has typically been portrayed, and I regard it to be the single most significant aspect of their project. But they must clear a high bar in proving there can be a postmetaphysical politics at all. And to the degree that they are successful, they provide important methodological insight for radical theology.

Changing Heidegger

The case against Heidegger is well established. The agenda was set by the argument from Karl Löwith that Heidegger's Nazism "was not born of a regrettable miscue" but is consistent with—indeed, is a necessary outgrowth of—his existentialism. It was in a 1936 conversation with Löwith, after all, that Heidegger agreed "without reservation" that "his partisanship for National Socialism lay in the essence of his philosophy."[5] So, in the words of Richard Wolin, "We know that Heidegger's alliance with Nazism, far from being a temporary marriage of convenience, was grandiose and profound: at least for a short period of time, Heidegger labored under the delusion that he could play the role of 'philosopher-king' to Hitler's *Führersstaat* . . . so that the 'National Revolution' might fulfill its appointed metaphysical destiny."[6]

Nevertheless, this justifiable condemnation of Heidegger still speaks only to his person, of how he fell into the grip of his own self-importance and of how his political decision was a legitimate interpretation at least in his own mind, if not in the minds of many of those (including Löwith and Karl Jaspers) who knew him and his work the best. What this condemnation does not determine or settle, however, is whether and to what extent alternative interpretations and applications of Heidegger might be made. For instance, John Caputo has effectively demythologized Heidegger, reading Heidegger *against* Heidegger through the lens of what is essentially a Levinasian ethic. For Caputo, Heidegger's philosophy poses the reader with a choice "between dangerous myths and salutary myths; between privileging, elitist, and hierarchizing myths and myths that promote justice and multiplicity; between exclusionary and oppressive myths and liberating, empowering myths."[7] It is clear that Heidegger made the wrong choice, that he failed to heed the dangers of the path of thinking and action that he was on, but if indeed his philosophy presents us with a genuine choice then his failure need not translate into a wholesale repudiation of his thought. Perhaps, regardless of how he saw it, his politics were *extrinsic* to his thought, so therefore Heidegger should be the least qualified of all to operate as authoritative guide for how his thinking ought to be interpreted and applied. Because of his delusions of grandeur, his political opportunism, and his callousness and cruelty to those he once regarded as friends, teachers, and mentors (think Husserl), Heidegger has forfeited the right to be his own privileged interpreter. It is at this point that the recent commentaries by Malabou and by Vattimo and Zabala fit in regarding the invocation of Heidegger as a potential political model. Theirs is more an actual reclamation of Heidegger than a demythologization. This reclamation, moreover, is not of a Heidegger purged of his politics but is more ambitiously a critical argument about what a properly Heideggerian politics would actually be.

First, we hear from Malabou. In her book *The Heidegger Change* she continues in the same vein as her earlier work, *The Future of Hegel*. In both she employs her signature concept of plasticity to demonstrate how these philosophical castoffs might be reappropriated—or, better, she warns against dismissing Hegel and Heidegger too quickly by reading them in light of plasticity, a concept whose time has only now come to fruition and that we are only now in a position to appreciate. What this means is that the caricatures that have been made of Hegel and Heidegger by their critics say less about Hegel and Heidegger than they do about the outdated nature of the critiques. Malabou's reappropriation of Hegel turns on the question of the future—whether there is a future *for* Hegel when it seems that the scholarship on him has retread such familiar ground for so long that it has exhausted all possibilities for new and different interpretations. The more significant question, though, is whether there is a future *in* Hegel's own dialectic or, as originally charged by Heidegger, Hegel is unwilling to think the future and is incapable of doing so.

Her analysis of Heidegger also turns on a question, but the question here regards the concept of change. Her pattern of questioning, however, is the same: whether there is the possibility for a change in how Heidegger can be interpreted and whether and to what extent the concept of change is operative within Heidegger's own philosophy. But to inquire about change *in* Heidegger, one must talk not just about change but also about what Malabou terms the "triad of change," which is comprised of the notions of *Wandel* (change), *Wandlung* (transformation), and *Verwandlung* (metamorphosis), or simply W, W, & V for short. Malabou argues that by reading this triad of change within Heidegger, it not only "confers on Heidegger's thought its power and vigor" but also is "a device whereby Heidegger is changed."[8] That is to say, the triad is about Heidegger's understanding of change and about how an appreciation of that distinct and overlooked understanding might effect a change in how Heidegger is understood.

In other words, Malabou is able to put to rest entirely the debate over the so-called Heideggerian turn, which refers to how he changed after his Nazi involvement, by showing a consistency within Heidegger's thinking from beginning to end that conceives as being *qua* change. It is for this reason that Malabou calls this triad of change the "secret agent" of Heidegger's philosophy.[9] By attending to

W, W, & V within Heidegger's corpus, Malabou makes manifest the ontological difference, not in terms of the history of the forgetfulness of being but in terms of the "originary mutability of being" and of being as "nothing but its mutability."[10] As Malabou puts it, the better understanding of the ontological difference is an exchange of difference for change, a shift from the epoch of writing and its consequent philosophies of language to plasticity. By letting ourselves be "put under the spell of the leitmotif of W, W, & V," we are on the way to reaching "another Heidegger." This is not so much an ontological revolution as a moral-political one in which—irony of ironies—Heidegger is deployed as the engine of resistance against capitalism.

In Malabou's telling, Heidegger is the defender of the precariousness of life. He is not a messianic thinker in the tradition of Derrida. His promise of change does not rest on transcendence, as in the case of Levinas. He does accomplish a disarming of the metaphysics of presence, but not by contrasting presence with absence or identity with difference. Instead, it is the originary nature of exchangeability that allows him to affirm a metamorphosis *without rest*, a change without beginning or end, a change that is imminent to time—indeed, constitutive of it. In this portrait, the caricature of Heidegger standing passively by, letting being be, or waiting for a god to save us, is replaced by a nonrevolutionary concept of change. Change has always already happened. We are changed in advance, and the world never stops the change. The world never stops being changed. "The genius of Heidegger," Malabou writes, consists "in having inscribed the possibility of revolution not in a future event to come but in fact (so modest, slight, and tiny) of *being-there, of still being there after the accomplishment that was never accomplished.*"[11]

There is enormous political power and vigor in this thought because it schematizes human freedom and establishes the ontological conditions for political resistance. But resistance to what? Malabou gives a name to the site and target of resistance—capitalism. The culture of late capitalism establishes the biopolitical norm of flexibility wherein the human is merely acted upon, wherein the worker is made to change at the whims of market forces but cannot—is utterly unable to— make change. When being is conceived of as change, however, *dasein* is known as a change agent. Malabou is careful and consistent in distinguishing the flexibility demanded and valorized by free market capitalism from the adaptability associated with plasticity. Change, exchange, and metamorphosis happen, but those need not translate into pure malleability. The human is not a passive subject who is merely acted upon. No matter how much management might wish it otherwise and no matter how much working conditions mitigate against it, our time, our bodies, and our intellectual property are ours alone. This permanent potential for resistance manifests our freedom. It is this plastic form that remains, no matter how often it is transformed, or even deformed. In Malabou's words, it is "up to us to contend."[12] Our fates are in our hands—not written in stone as if being had some eternal essence or left entirely blank as if the future was merely a play of differences. The plasticity of being teaches us that being qua change has the potential both to *receive* form and to *give* form. That knowledge is the way we know that if it is always up to us to contend, then real change is possible. There is nothing that cannot change. Moreover, there is nothing that is not change, that is not always already changed and changing. This idea is the strongest repudiation of the very ideology of capitalism that renders capitalism as completely natural and inevitable and thus irresistible. Our fates are never written in stone but in plastic.

Like Malabou, Vattimo and Zabala invoke Heidegger as a source for political resistance against the machinery of capitalism and the way that capitalism divvies up the winners and losers in the global economy. The logic of capitalism sets the powerful against the weak, whether on the scale of individuals or on the scale of the neoliberal geopolitical order in terms of nation-states. Whether we recognize it or not, this is a state of emergency, but it is left to the weak and dispossessed to sound the alarm because entrenched power is invested in preserving the status quo. Thus, the weak, postmetaphysical thought of hermeneutics "becomes the thought of the weak in search of alternatives." It is a weak form of thought that does not claim universality and "does not believe that politics can be founded on scientific and rational grounds, but only on interpretation, history, and event."[13]

When compared with Malabou, this invocation of Heidegger by Vattimo and Zabala is a more traditional one that stresses Heidegger's project at overcoming metaphysics but with a twist. By *reading Heidegger into Marx* and thereby suggesting the possibility of a hermeneutic communism, they correct Marxist philosophies of their own excesses—or more precisely, purge Marxism of its metaphysical bearings. The fault with Marxism is not its revolutionary charge to change the world but its framing of this demand for change "within the metaphysical tradition."[14] Vattimo and Zabala set aside the general call for revolution in lieu of a more basic defense of the weak. They admit that this strategy of reading backwards, "from Heidegger to Marx," goes "further than Marx or Heidegger intended."[15] Nevertheless, by so doing, they articulate a conception of a "communism of the twenty-first century," or a "weakened communism." This would be a humbled communism that keeps its distance from both the historical Soviet and contemporary Chinese models. It is humbled by the hermeneutical attitude that must always contend with the conflict of interpretations and thus places a premium on respect for differences. And, as a hermeneutic communism, it is also necessarily a democratic communism but is not the reigning democracy that has made the fateful mistake of conflating freedom with free markets and that has felt justified in spreading democracy through the barrel of a gun. Although humbled, this hermeneutic communism still presents itself as the best, if not the last, hope for those they identify as the "discharge of capitalism."[16]

The audacity in this work is how it cites Heidegger as an ally. After all, how Heidegger repudiated communism is well known. But Vattimo and Zabala argue that this repudiation was not an outgrowth of his early Nazi sympathies "but rather because of his need to overcome metaphysics."[17] As evidence of this, they cite his simultaneous repudiation of Western-style democracy and free-market capitalism. In their reading, Heidegger was trying to think politics otherwise. The problem with the existing forms of communism, capitalism, and democracy is that they all strived to complete a "metaphysical organization of beings" and, in so doing, failed the thought of Being and failed to acknowledge "philosophy's groundless realm."[18] Heidegger was a postmetaphysical thinker of Being, one whose philosophical project was defined by the quest to overcome metaphysics, and this is the key to thinking his politics otherwise; this is the "other" Heidegger who can be claimed as a political ally in the articulation of a hermeneutic communism despite his protestations to the contrary.

Vattimo and Zabala have conceived of Heidegger's postmetaphysical politics in complete sympathy with those of his contemporary Carl Schmitt. Given philosophy's groundless realm or when dwelling within the remains of Being, the concept of the political becomes nothing else besides the prerogative to decide. This political decisionism fills in for the abyss left by Being's departure. Both Heidegger and Schmitt saw in modern liberalism an onslaught of a technocratic order, a tragically ironic process in which the human subject was eclipsed and modern politics was rendered apolitical. When politics is essentially managed as a bureaucratic state—or as the science of a technocratic bureaucracy—it is desperately in need of either a political ontology or a renewed political theology, which might very well amount to the same thing. But in both cases the actual political projects are set up in opposition to democracy. As I have argued extensively elsewhere, Schmitt saw political theology and democracy as mutually exclusive and defined the essence of the political in terms of the friend-enemy distinction that directly goes against the democratic ideal of inclusion.[19]

The case was not so simple for Heidegger, and it is at this point that the differences between Malabou on the one hand and Vattimo and Zabala on the other are most significant. It is simply not the case that Heidegger never developed the political dimensions of his thought, as Vattimo and Zabala assert.[20] Even if it was only for a brief time, there is no question that Heidegger's Nazi period involved his own political translation and application of his thought. He decisively and unapologetically involved himself in an explicitly political project—and an explicitly fascist one at that. The argument, then, is not whether Heidegger was a political thinker and certainly not whether he deserves the prerogative to be his own privileged interpreter. Instead, it is whether and how his thinking can be a resource for rethinking and reorienting our politics today.

We see precisely this being done by Malabou and by Vattimo and Zabala. In Lilla's words, Heidegger was no doubt a "reckless mind." We can add that he was also egotistical, opportunistic, and cruel. But someone no less than Emmanuel Levinas still acknowledges that all thinkers in his wake owe him a debt of gratitude—albeit a regrettable one. Just as Levinas turned Heidegger's anthropology of *dasein* as a being-with-others into the moral imperative that was the basis of his revisioning of metaphysics as ethics, others are reclaiming Heidegger for today's political challenges. He was reckless but not irredeemable, and the redemption in mind here has nothing to do with spirituality, with Heidegger's soul or his person. It is instead a more ancient or archaic understanding of redemption by which we regain possession of something we have lost. A debt is cleared, specifically the debt we owe not to Heidegger the man but to the thought—the thought that was hijacked and distorted by Heidegger himself, the thought that we ourselves have been scared away from by the cautionary tale that is Heidegger.

By reading change in Heidegger, we release the "secret agent" of Heidegger's thought for today. *Dasein* is exemplary by its plasticity. It is *subject to* change by being impressed upon by all sides in an immanent order of interpersonal relations structured by care, and it is a *maker of* change and thus always already a revolutionary. And with the hermeneutical strategy of reading backwards—from Heidegger to Marx—we see the emergence of not only a new politics but also a potentially new concept of the political. The politics is new communism for the twenty-first century, a politics that is weakened, if not cured, of its metaphysical foundations so that communism might once again—even if for the very first time—defend the interests of and stand in solidarity with the weakest citizens.

The Decolonial Option

The question must nevertheless be asked: why Heidegger at all? And not only why Heidegger but why communism? Are they so necessary to the political project that they are worth the baggage they carry? Is there not some other way to imagine a global future that escapes the Euro-American stranglehold on geopolitics, an option that does not depend so much on the internal confrontation of the West with itself as on exploring alternative genealogies of thought and practice? This would be not so much a Eurocentric critique of modernity that still traffics in systems of knowledge and institutional practices that Walter Mignolo refers to as the "Western code" as a horizon of thinking outside the West that nevertheless—or perhaps precisely thereby—recognizes the "darker side of Western modernity."

This alternative has been called the decolonial option. Like Vattimo and Zabala, Mignolo, in his articulation of this decolonial option, also stages a confrontation among the winners and losers of the current global order. But in Mignolo's estimation it is not simply a competition of the strong against the weak but a competition among an entire colonial matrix of power that includes the obvious markers of racism, patriarchy, environmental degradation, and resource depletion as well as the not-so-obvious characteristics within epistemology and ontology. After all, what counts as knowledge, Mignolo contends, is still based in modern scientific rationality. And personhood is still framed by the supposedly universal code of human rights. "Decoloniality shall dispel the myth of universality grounded in theo- and ego-politics of knowledge," Mignolo writes, leaving open these questions: "what kind of knowledge, by whom, what for?"[21]

It is a struggle to find the right words to describe the significance of this decolonial option. Perhaps this is why Mignolo so often resorts to sloganeering. No doubt there are times when his arguments and analyses amount to little besides pronouncements, albeit richly evocative ones. But there are other times when the slogans give us an urgently needed visualization—a visualization of not so much a different world as an obscured and neglected one in which the blindness and hubris of the West rehearsing its own past sins and promises might be shattered once and for all. This visualization is of a genuine *penetration* of the elaborately constructed defenses of the current global order, defenses that have been nearly impenetrable precisely because they are virtually invisible. That is to say, the colonial matrix of power has been so strong and has endured for so long because it has managed to contain within itself not only its staunchest defenders but also its critics. It has been able to absorb or eliminate any and all resistance unto itself as a functioning totality.

The point is not original to decolonial thinking but certainly takes on a different salience thanks to its emphasis on the idea that colonialism was constitutive of modernity. It is that globalization functions as a kind of hypermodernism and thus as an extension of colonialism. The world is interconnected by a single, interconnected global economy. The colonial matrix of power is nearly complete. Yet although the world is economically interconnected, there remains a diversity of political theories, practices, and institutions. Capital functions as a trans- or supranational sovereign power, with almost no one or nothing capable of keeping it in check. So although various individuals and movements rise to voice their dissent, which might be the noblest and most serious and scrutinizing form of self-critique, this dissent can and has been used to shield the West from the rest of the world. This ongoing dialectic has at times been vicious, with the very world hanging in the balance. At the same time, whereas this dissent or self-critique has essentially been a protracted civil war—a war of the West with itself, a contest for supremacy that designates entire swaths of the world to third-world status—its collateral damage has been largely externalized. And just as the Western world's damage has been largely externalized, its most penetrating critique might also come from outside. This possibility is why Mignolo begins his book *The Darker Side of Western Modernity* by distinguishing decoloniality, precisely by virtue of its externality, from other types of critiques of modernity—whether those critiques come from psychoanalysis, Marxism, poststructuralism, or even postcolonialism.

Thus, to penetrate the global defenses requires changing both *who* partakes in the conversation and the very *terms* of the conversation. The decolonial option provides an epistemological and ontological alternative for making this change. And *alternative* is the operative word here, more so than *revolution*, because it is extrinsic to the normative code. "I am where I think" is the slogan Mignolo gives to this alternative epistemology and ontology, a repudiation of the presumed universality of the modern Cartesian subject.[22] This is an epistemology of dwelling that makes reference to local habitats and cultures but is also fully immersed. The accompanying political ontology acknowledges and provides for overlapping and conflicting spheres of sovereignty and different possibilities for conceiving of what counts as a person and what or whom is deserving of rights as determined by bonds of mutual obligation and care. To make place central to epistemology and ontology is to put the lie to the universal code proffered by the West. Place matters. And when we say place matters, we mean not just one single place but different places and different peoples—*from the universal to the pluriversal.*

In this context, Mignolo takes distance from communism in an important disclaimer, in which he says, "In a nutshell, the difference is this: the Marxist Left confronts capitalism first within Europe itself. . . . The decolonial confronts all of Western civilization, which includes liberal capitalism and Marxism. And it does it from the perspective of the colonies and the ex-colonies rather than from the perspective internal to Western civilization itself."[23] This disclaimer must be kept in mind when considering what Vattimo and Zabala identify as the South American alternative, by which they mean specifically Hugo Chavez's "Bolivarian Revolution." As Vattimo and Zabala tell it, the South American alternative "differs substantially" from previously existing forms of communism because it follows "democratic electoral procedures and also manage[s] to decentralize the state bureaucratic system."[24] The initiatives that were put into place by Chavez in Venezuela and Evo Morales in Bolivia have effectively spurred economic growth, contributed to the alleviation of extreme poverty, and greatly increased literacy and access to health care. This success is proof of the viability of weak communism for the twenty-first century, and the evidence is the way these two leftist governments have, in the words of Mark Weisbrot, "delivered on their promises to share the income . . . with the people."[25]

Another distinguishing characteristic of the South American alternative for Vattimo and Zabala is how the governments in the countries of that continent feature a militant, but not armed, form of communism. International partnerships must necessarily be forged to withstand the mounting and unrelenting pressure from American interests and the neoliberal economic policies they prescribe and impose. Vattimo and Zabala are right to expose the concerted, if not coordinated, effort to delegitimize Chavez and, to a lesser extent, Morales. In the opinion of Vattimo and Zabala, intellectuals and media figures in the West are "obsessed" with South America "because its governments represent a political alternative to the global capitalism of framed democracies."[26] That any alternative exists at all makes questionable the entire presumed *raison d'être* of globalization. That is, we have no further need for globalization if we have reached the end of the history of ideological conflict in that global capital has finally achieved its inner purpose of expanding its reach to the entire globe. As we saw in Mignolo's work, South America's ideological opposition to the rules of global capitalism puts the lie to the fatal logic that there is no outside to capitalism. Just as these South American regimes are being singled out for their responsiveness to and solidarity with the poorest and neediest—those who are the "discharge of capitalism"—the regimes themselves, to the extent that they are deliberately established as external to and independent from the neoliberal global order, are also capitalism's discharges and, as such, are the world's, or at least the region's, best hope.

And finally, consider what Vattimo and Zabala say about the conditions of possibility for hermeneutics: that hermeneutics is a distinctively postmetaphysical philosophy. As we examined earlier, it is what corrects Marxism of its excesses by purging it of its metaphysical bearings. But what is so interesting and important about the particular genealogy of hermeneutics that Vattimo and Zabala provide in this work is that it is more than a development within the history of (Western) philosophy. Indeed, "hermeneutics would not have been possible," Vattimo and Zabala tell us, "without the end of Eurocentrism." In other words, the conditions of possibility for hermeneutics require an externality, one that "confirm[s] the disarray of the Eurocentric convictions" and the "dissolution of metaphysics." By penetrating the defenses of the West's own self-obsession, the very possibility of hermeneutics is revealed as a political becoming announcing the end to the "pretense to universal 'Western' rationality."[27] The importance of this revelation for the similar province of radical theology must not be missed.

Further, as Vattimo and Zabala see it, this recognition of the conditions of possibility for hermeneutics that lays the groundwork for the political becoming of hermeneutics provides "a chance for the return of communism."[28] But on this point we should already hear Mignolo asking why there is the need for a return at all. Why a return and not an alternative? Why remain within the province of the

West and its internal alternatives rather than seek out a genuine externality? As Mignolo narrates the origins of decolonial thinking, he points to the Non-Aligned Movement (NAM) during the Cold War as the beginning of the political project of decolonization. From its inception, decolonization has pinned its hopes on neither communism nor capitalism. On the contrary, decolonization opened up "a new horizon . . . beyond capitalism and communism."[29] Over time that essentially political project mutated from decolonization to decoloniality, the comprehensive theory that lays out the systematic critique of how the colonial matrix of power is constitutive of modernity and charts not only an alternative political alignment but also an alternative epistemology and ontology. It is not a question of a return, a reproduction, or even a renewal. Instead, for once over the long history of Western modernity, there is the possibility of an embrace of a genuinely polycentric world.

Vattimo and Zabala's articulation of the South American alternative is an important gesture toward that end, and, thus, their hermeneutic communism should be seen as having a "complementary trajectory" to that of decolonial thinking. At the same time, we must be cautious that hermeneutic communism is not simply another instance of "third world thoughts . . . processed in European intellectual factories." Vattimo and Zabala have successfully linked the end of Eurocentrism with the dissolution of metaphysics and thus the political becoming of hermeneutics. But is their weak communism weak enough, sufficiently dissolved of all remnants of its modern Eurocentric convictions? If so, it might be worth asking whether we are then better off calling communism by some other name entirely.[30]

The Passage to the Political

Regardless of its name, I remain deeply interested in and committed to what I consider to be the even more fundamental and enduring aspect of Vattimo and Zabala's project in *Hermeneutic Communism*. In broad terms, this aspect has to do with the connection they have established between hermeneutics and politics. More specifically, it addresses the question of whether a postmetaphysical philosophy can produce a positive politics at all or whether postmetaphysics always and necessarily must remain only in a deconstructive mode. It is by addressing this question that the resonances between hermeneutics and radical theology indicate a possible methodological guide for the thinking to come.

Perhaps the most comprehensive and damning critique of postmodernism comes from the famed British left-wing literary critic Terry Eagleton in his book from 1996, *The Illusions of Postmodernism*. Like Žižek after him (with whom he has been frequently compared),[31] Eagleton has criticized postmodernism from a political perspective, noting how its presumed radical ideas of negativity and undecidability are actually an announcement of political defeat by the left, a form of micropolitics and political subjectivity perfectly in concert with, and thus completely unable to resist, the cultural logic of late capitalism. After all, as Eagleton points out, "Capitalism is the most pluralistic order history has ever known." Therefore, by relativizing capitalism as just one form of totality among others and by refusing to organize itself in an explicitly anticapitalist fashion, postmodernism has effectively pulled out the rug from beneath itself. For instance, in a characteristic passage, Eagleton writes:

> For in a period when no far-reaching political action seems really feasible, when so-called micropolitics seems the order of the day, it is relieving to convert this necessity into a virtue—to persuade oneself that one's political limits have, as it were, a solid ontological grounding, in the fact that social totality is in any case a chimera. It doesn't matter if there is no political agent on hand to transform the whole, since there is in fact no whole to be transformed. It is as though, having mislaid the breadknife, one declares the loaf to be already sliced.[32]

More bluntly, and more directly to the point of Vattimo and Zabala's hermeneutic theory, Eagleton questions the political value and viability of an epistemology in which everything is subject to interpretation. "Everything would become an interpretation," Eagleton writes as he narrates the philosophical genealogy of postmodernism, "including that claim itself, in which case the idea of interpretation would cancel all the way through and leave everything exactly as it was. A radical epistemology would issue, conveniently enough, in a conservative politics."[33] It is with this idea in mind that Eagleton announces his overall assessment of postmodernism. He writes variously that "it is the upshot of a political failure" or "the backwash of a political debacle," that it has allowed the so-called left to remain in a state of "political illiteracy and historical oblivion," and that the power of capital has never been "so sublimely omnipotent and omnipresent."[34]

Put schematically, the problem with postmodernism, especially the postmetaphysical postmodernism to which Vattimo and Zabala subscribe, is a political one. It is a political problem because its actual politics are in fact a form of postpolitics, a politics of evasion that has sidestepped the most vital and intractable political problem of our time—namely, the presumed naturalism of capitalism and, concomitantly, its near-total, and totally unresisted, spread. Although much of postmodern discourse has effectively historicized normative values and operative ideologies, Eagleton is correct to point out that historicizing in and of itself is not necessarily a radical act and most definitely does not belong to the left alone. Postmodernism might very well be oppositional, but it is a *framed opposition* allowing for a nearly infinite multiplicity. This multiplicity, however, has no sustained and targeted critique of the lone governing logic that keeps those multiplicities in a perpetual and almost purposeful state of play. They are "politically oppositional but economically complicit" is how Eagleton concludes his critique.[35]

Eagleton's critique is a potent but generalized one. Kenneth Surin provides a much more fine-grained analysis of what we might term postmodern politics in his article "The Ontological Script of Liberation."[36] He begins with an acknowledgement of how the transnational flow of capital operates as a sovereign power and how the modern model of the secular nation-state is powerless to control or hold accountable the new regimes of capitalist accumulation. In the era of globalization, our economy has become global but our political institutions have not. This has weakened or neutralized state power and contributed to a postpolitical citizenry. Citing his colleague Fredric Jameson, Surin argues that this apparent triumph of global capital is so dire, or so complete, that "it's easier for us nowadays to contemplate the total destruction of the earth through some ecological catastrophe than it is to believe that capitalism will come to an end."[37]

In the wake of this reality, Surin outlines four contemporary political options for the left. The first option is the politics of identity, which Surin promptly dismisses for how smoothly it dovetails into actually existing capitalism. The second, which he associates with the ethicopolitical deconstructive work of Derrida and Levinas, is the politics of subjectivity. For Surin, the politics of subjectivity becomes an unwitting politics of decision. Further, he says, "it has no way of inserting the subject into the domain of the actually political" and, as a consequence, "provides no way of imagining resistance at the level of a politics of collective action."[38] The third option, associated with Alain Badiou and Žižek, is labeled as the politics of the Event. This option is the most fervently anticapitalist contemporary mode of political resistance, but it might also be guilty of a kind of political romanticism. Moreover, because it is predicated on the notion of a truth-event as a radical rupture, it is incapable of providing any norms whatsoever. The state of exception that Badiou and Žižek might seize upon to mobilize anticapitalist resistance could just as easily and more frequently be mobilized by the right as a justification for a seizure of state power that violates constitutional norms and limitations, as was seen in the aftermath of 9/11. This leaves the fourth and final option for Surin, which is the politics of the multitude, identified with Deleuze and Guattari as well as with Michael Hardt and Antonio Negri. The virtue of multitude theory, as described by Surin, is how it conceives of political power as autogenerating. In Surin's words, "the multitude directs itself according to its own powers and its own history."[39] The politics of the multitude is a decentralized form of political power befitting a polycentric world. At the same time, it recognizes the logic of the global flow of capital as a transnational sovereignty.

By now, it should be abundantly clear that on nearly every count Vattimo and Zabala have risen to this sweeping challenge issued by Eagleton and, in so doing, have provided a fifth option to the four outlined by Surin for organizing the contemporary politics of the left. Vattimo and Zabala have taken the hermeneutical theory of interpretation and given it a fully fleshed political body. Theirs is no politics of evasion. It is oppositional without being economically complicit. On the contrary, its chief theoretical opposition comes by virtue of its concept of a "framed democracy." This term describes a democracy in name only, a democracy held hostage by a neoliberal economic policy that continues to divide the world between haves and have-nots and to divvy up the winners and losers of globalization. As Derrida has told us, there are no actually existing democracies. Democracy instead is a promise, one that will keep its stranglehold on power and its death grip on geopolitics as long as it is framed by economic interests as opposed to people's power.

Eagleton has accused postmodernism of only a framed opposition, by which he means that the single most vital political question is left entirely out of the equation. This would be not only a politics of evasion but also rightly a politics of defeat. Vattimo and Zabala have put the picture back in the frame; they have accomplished a political becoming of hermeneutics and, in so doing, have provided the single most important innovation in hermeneutics since the time of Heidegger's grandiose partisanship for Nazism as the political actualization of the essence of his philosophy. But what we now can see, maybe for the very first time, is that the reckless mistake on the part of Heidegger was not that he injected politics into his hermeneutics but that he had the wrong politics. If Vattimo and Zabala are correct, what our politics need is not less hermeneutics but more—and the more hermeneutical our politics, the more that even communism itself can deliver on its own democratic and decolonial promises.

FOUR

Changing Ontotheology

Tillich is not a postmodern theologian. He clearly works within the ontotheological tradition.

-Charles Winquist, *Desiring Theology*

Thus far we have seen how the work of Catherine Malabou might be employed
as a critical reversal of Emmanuel Levinas and a critical rehabilitation of Martin
Heidegger. In both cases, her fundamental ontological insight regarding the essence of being as change is central. Malabou again proves decisive in this chapter
as I shift attention away from the methodological issues raised by relating the concept of the political to radical theology and toward the question of the proper relationship between philosophy and theology. In particular, I want to explore how
Malabou's ontology of change might help us change our understanding of the
so-called problem of ontotheology.

Judging by his identification of God with being-itself, Paul Tillich is an ontotheologian par excellence. Indeed, Tillich may be seen as the last unabashed ontotheologian. Although this relatively straightforward claim has been contested by
many leading scholars of Tillich,[1] my argument is that the radical Tillich is the ontotheological Tillich. Moreover, as is spelled out in greater detail in the conclusion,
by virtue of Malabou's alternative conception of being, radical theology may completely adjust its approach to ontotheology, seeing it not as a problem to be overcome but as the condition of possibility for thinking anew.

Thus, whereas much of contemporary philosophical theology has been preoccupied—nay, even consumed—with the task of overcoming ontotheology, a task
largely set by Tillich's contemporary Heidegger, I do not intend my argument regarding the radical Tillich as the ontotheological Tillich as a critique. On the contrary, by taking with the utmost seriousness Tillich's identification of God with
being-itself, we have the potential for a radical reconceptualization of the so-called
problem of ontotheology. In other words, by embracing rather than resisting the
ontotheological dimension of Tillich's thought, not just his radicality but his originality and contemporaneousness are brought into critical relief. The radical (that
is, ontotheological) Tillich is our contemporary because he forces us to come to
terms with the ontotheological condition of thought and thereby helps us to move

not only *beyond* theism (and atheism) but also *after* the death of God. In short, by virtue of the concept of plasticity, we might say that God is not dead; rather, God has changed. God *is* change.

The Problem of Ontotheology

At least since Heidegger the problem of ontotheology has been (taken as) well established. John Thatanamil is certainly correct when he asserts that the problem of ontotheology is the rubric by which "the postmodern critique of reason's pretentions, especially with respect to thinking about God" has been understood.[2]

Consider Jacques Derrida here. In his first direct and extended foray into religion with his essay "How to Avoid Speaking: Denials,"[3] he famously distinguished deconstruction from negative theology and *différance* from God. Derrida accepts Heidegger's claim that metaphysics is inevitably and necessarily ontotheological. As such, the problem of ontotheology must be seen as a variation on the problem of the metaphysics of presence. Whereas some considered negative theology as a way to bypass, if not overcome, the problem of ontotheology, for Derrida, this does not avoid the problem. Instead, negative theology only extends the metaphysics of presence by presuming a hyper- or superpresence to the divine. This is why negative theology's mystical God beyond being is not to be confused with *différance*. On the contrary, negative theology is ontotheological in that it "saves" the name of God by locating the presence of God beyond being. As John Caputo puts it, negative theology operates by a "double bind" that endeavors toward a "double save":

> When negative theology says that God is beyond every name we give to Him, that is a way of saying and saving "God such as he is," beyond all idols and images, a way of "respond[ing] to the true name of God, to the name to which God responds and corresponds." Every time negative theology engages in negation, "it does so in the name of a way of truth," of a goddess whose name is *aletheia,* under the protective auspices of a truthful and authoritative name.[4]

From this deconstructive perspective, therefore, Tillich's God beyond God is to be seen as a quintessential ontotheological gesture. Far from overcoming ontotheology, such a gesture only reifies the problem.

But Derrida and Heidegger go even further. They assert not just that metaphysics is inevitably and necessarily ontotheological and thus caught up on the metaphysics of presence but that theology too is necessarily ontotheological. This latter point is not so much argued as it is suggested by a consistent linkage of theology with the problem of ontotheology. Therefore, the religion without religion

that Caputo has insisted is the affirmative, animating passion of Derrida's deconstruction is necessarily a private one. Religion cannot be thought or spoken. Theology corrupts, or at least alters, pure faith, turning a living wellspring of passion
into a rigid dogma, an idol of thought.

Or, to borrow Heidegger's formulation, which we saw at work earlier in the
critique of the theological turn of phenomenology by Dominique Janicaud, theology, unlike philosophy, *does not think*. Theology not only corrupts faith but also
contaminates pure thought. Theology and philosophy are "absolutely different."[5]
The difference between the two is the same as the difference between thinking
and science. Philosophy asks the question of being. It is a thinking of an indeter-
minate origin and end. Theology, though, is the science of faith. It proceeds by
way of certainty as a self-explication of faith. It knows its end thought before it
ever begins the task of thinking. It answers to a God who is the name of a limit, a
limit that encloses theology in a circle of the same.

Given this truth, and given how the problem of ontotheology is typically construed, religious faith must be distinguished and protected from theological thinking, just as philosophy must be kept separate from theology, for each speaks its
own language.[6] This is why Heidegger likens the notion of Christian philosophy to
a "square circle,"[7] an oxymoron that betrays a fundamental lack of understanding
of both the nature of faith and the nature of thought. Once again, therefore, Tillich's philosophical theology is a violation of the strict separation between philosophy and theology insisted upon by Heidegger—a separation that has been
largely accepted without question by nearly all those who have followed in Heidegger's wake.[8]

Finally, in case one were to incorrectly conclude that this quest for a purity
of thought as dictated by Heidegger comes only from the side of philosophy, we
may look to the example of the Swiss Protestant theologian Karl Barth, often regarded as the most significant theological voice of the twentieth century. Barth
shared with Heidegger the basic concern of the dangers of the contamination of
thought. For Barth, this concern resulted in a self-critical theology that attempted
to preserve for the Church the autonomy and integrity of the Word of God. By
reading Barth in conjunction with Heidegger's unfolding critique of ontotheology,
we can discern a surprising similitude—surprising because Barth famously showed
a "benign neglect" of currents in contemporary philosophy, often expressing frustration and distress over what he considered to be the spectacle of his theological
contemporaries pandering to philosophy.[9] As he once explained to Rudolf Bultmann, "I will not defend in principle what you call my ignoring of philosophical
work. . . . It is also a fact that I have come to abhor profoundly the spectacle of theology constantly trying above all to adjust to the philosophy of its age, and thereby

neglecting its own theme."[10] For Barth, as is well known, the proper theme—or, better, the proper subject—of theology must remain the God of revelation. Barth replaces modern philosophy's grounding in human consciousness with his own theological grounding in the subject of God. For him, the proper question for thought is not epistemological: "How do we know what we know?" Rather, it is exegetical: "How does God make Godself known to us?"

This brings us to the most profound irony of contemporary philosophical theology. Namely, that it is Barth, more than any of the theological students or followers of Heidegger (consider Bultmann and Tillich and also Gerhard Eberling, Ernst Fuchs, and Friedrich Gogarten), who realizes most fully Heidegger's vision for theology in the wake of the critique of ontotheology. Specifically—wittingly or unwittingly, independently or derivatively—Barth is the one who follows the prescriptive Heidegger offered to a group of German Protestant theologians that if a "proper theology" were to be written, the word "being" would not appear.[11] Although Barth himself never develops a critique of ontotheology per se, the mixing together of, or the collapsing of the difference between, philosophy and theology remains a problem for him. Extending Barth's distress over the theological pandering to philosophy, we might say that the problem of ontotheology from a strictly theological perspective is that it does not know which way to turn, whether to God or to creation as the source of truth. For him, philosophy works best when it limits itself as an endeavor to test the boundaries of human understanding. Theology, however, speaks from a different source, derived not from the horizon set by knowledge but from the Word of God spoken by faith. Ontotheology is undesirable because it puts humans in the place of God by forgetting the infinite qualitative difference. Barth resists ontotheology, even without naming it as such, because it constrains the absolute freedom and transcendence of God.

Tillich follows a different path. Whereas Barth's preservation (or is it a recovery?) of the purity of theology is achieved by a recovery (or is it a preservation?) of the personal God of biblical revelation—God as subject, the transcendent being of God for Tillich is expressed in nontheistic terms—God beyond God. Once again, then, Tillich stands guilty as charged of the sin of ontotheology. In this case, the charge comes from the side of theology. Tillich has conflated, and thereby confused, what ought to be regarded as two distinct discourses. His is an ontological philosophy masquerading as a theology. And, irony of ironies, although it is Tillich who imbibes from the Heideggerian well more than any of his other theological contemporaries, it is he who is most in violation of the direct prescription that Heidegger gives to the theologian. So we must ask: if the way for the theologian to avoid the problem of ontotheology is to write a theology without the word "being," then what, if any, possible defense of Tillich can be offered?

Race and Ontotheology

Before turning to Tillich's defense, there is still one additional concern that must be lodged. Specifically, it is the concern over the connection between liberation theology and Tillich's ontotheology—or, in other words, over theology's contribution to the struggle for justice. Mary Ann Stenger and Ronald H. Stone have done a great service for scholars of Tillich in their book, *Dialogues of Tillich*, which stages encounters between Tillich and other streams in contemporary Christian thought as well as in Buddhism, feminism, Marxism, liberation theology, and fundamentalism. It is Stone's chapter on "Religious Socialism and Liberation Theology" that best sets the stage for the concerns I wish to raise here. The chapter begins with this statement: "The religious socialism of Paul Tillich preceded liberation theology and consequently never entered into dialogue with it. Liberation theologians of Latin America do not know much about Tillich's religious socialism and have not engaged it in dialogue. This chapter is an attempt to bring into dialogue two traditions which themselves have not engaged in conversation."[12]

As I discussed in chapter 2, James Cone's *The Cross and the Lynching Tree* stages a similar but much more critical encounter between Reinhold Niebuhr and liberation theology. Recall from Cone how Niebuhr, specifically his appreciation of the social nature of sin and the tragic dimension in human history, had always figured prominently in his work. This is why Cone argues that Niebuhr should have been more sensitive to the sin of racism and the tragic dimension of American race relations. Instead, Niebuhr was largely silent throughout the worst ravages of the lynching era, and Cone declares this silence to be "profoundly revealing."[13] The more Cone has reflected on his one-time theological mentor the more he has come to the conclusion that Niebuhr's silence amounted to a certain theological apathy born of privilege and reflecting "a defect in the conscience of white Christians."[14] And so, Cone concludes, "Thus, I have never questioned Niebuhr's greatness as a theologian, but instead admired his intellectual brilliance and social commitment. What I questioned was his limited perspective, as a white man, on the race crisis in America."[15]

Theologian J. Kameron Carter has shown how over the course of Cone's life, he has increasingly drawn on Tillich as a way to counter the excesses of his earlier reliance on and employment of Barth. Although Barth's radically transcendent God initially provided Cone with the firm theological footing for his social protest against racial injustice, that footing has eventually come to be regarded as a "false start."[16] Tillich's dialectical theology of culture has been instrumental in an explicit shift in Cone's thought from what he has termed an abstract revelation to a more contextual theology that arises out of and directly addresses a concrete social situation. In addition, just as Tillich interprets Heidegger's project of overcoming metaphysics as an existentialist task in the "courage to be," Cone interprets Tillich's notion of courage or struggle as black power. Although Cone remains sympathetic and indebted to Barth, he ultimately comes to the conclusion that "although God is the intended subject of theology, God does not do theology. *Human beings do theology.*"[17] For Cone, this means that there should be no pretensions to objectivity or universality when doing theology. On the contrary, theology is always already an interest-laden procedure. In this way, Tillich's theology of culture provides a guide.

Carter accepts this methodological theological insight of Tillich's insofar as it goes but, largely due to Tillich's ontotheology, stops short of fully embracing him. The ontological question of being underlies Tillich's theology and helps to reveal its dialectical structure. That is because, as Tillich puts it, "In our search for the 'really real,' the search for being-itself," or the search "for the power of being in everything that is," the theologian is on a "search for ultimate reality beyond everything that seems to be real." As Carter puts it, "The human pursuit of ultimate concern is a search to transcend *the* Finite. . . . It is eternity conquering temporality."[18] Specifically, it is Tillich's "beyond" that raises Carter's ire, not only because it is a gesture of ultimate transcendence that would seem to contradict what Carter terms the "anti-Barthian nature of Tillich's thought" that expresses itself in terms of a dialectical philosophy of life (a la Nietzsche) but more fundamentally because it follows a well-established Christian theological pattern of antimaterialism, antihistorical spiritualism, otherworldliness, and abstraction.

In fairness to Tillich, he goes to great lengths to expose the false dichotomies of religion/culture, transcendence/immanence, autonomy/heteronomy, and so on. Likewise, by Tillich's rendering, a theological ontology provides the fertile ground on which human relationality—not only among humans but also between subjects and objects and between humans and the divine—is best established. Nevertheless, to the extent that Tillich insists on the God *beyond* God— the theology that always already contains the answer to the questions posed in different ways by different cultures at different times and places and the sense of ultimacy that lies hidden in the passing phenomena of concrete human existence—Carter says that "it follows that cultures, history, and people groups have no lasting value in and of themselves." Carter continues by linking this Tillichian gesture toward the beyond to the age-old, essentially Gnostic tendency within the history of Christian thought. As he says, "Like the historical Jesus who is overcome by the universal Christ and in this way realizes infinite unity, so, too, is it the case that cultures, histories, and people groups must be overcome." And just in case the racial significance of this is lost, Carter makes the point clear with his question, "Is this not an anti-Jewish philosophy of culture?"[19]

What we see here, therefore, is a different concern with the problem of Tillich's ontotheology. It is not simply that Tillich's identification of God with being classifies him as an ontotheologian par excellence, that his theological ontology does precisely what Heidegger explicitly forbids, or that by his outsourcing of his theology to the currents of contemporary philosophy he has somehow sacrificed the autonomy and much-needed clarity of his theological voice in a time of crisis. Tillich's ontotheology is a problem precisely because it participates in and reifies the very processes by which Christian thought has racially constituted the world. In other words, Tillich's ontotheology is exemplary of what Carter terms "the theological problem of whiteness."[20]

A Defense of Tillich

Comparative theologian John Thatanamil offers the most thorough defense of Tillich against both of these charges—the charge of ontotheology and, by extension, the charge of ethnocentrism. He begins with the statement, contra Barth, that not every theological appeal to ontology is necessarily ontotheological, especially not if the theologian's ontotheological claims are "hypothetical and so vulnerable to correction." With this important caveat, he then turns directly to the question of whether Tillich is guilty of ontotheology. He admits "at first glance" that Tillich seems "to be the very embodiment of what is now widely regarded as an obsolete and unsustainable kind of metaphysical theology."[21] He also concedes that, in light of Derrida's differentiation of deconstruction from negative theology, Tillich's apophaticism is not enough for him to escape the charge of ontotheology.

So given, Thatanamil nevertheless provides a five-pronged defense. First, he points out that Tillich's reference to God as being-itself does not yield, or even promise, conceptual knowledge of God. In Thatanamil's language, the "term's meaning remains shrouded in mystery."[22] The point here is a profoundly Heideggerian one—namely, being is presumed but can never itself be thought as such. This is why Tillich supplements his identification of God as being-itself with the claim that the identification is a "nonsymbolic statement." That is to say, as a term shrouded in mystery that does not generate determinate knowledge of God, this identification necessitates religious symbolism. But the symbol of God must never be confused with the being of God. Second, Tillich speaks of God both as the ground of being and as an abyss. Tillich's theology is thus a nonfoundational and therefore postontotheological theology. Third, Tillich's God is neither a determinate being among beings nor an infinite or Supreme Being. Instead, what must be said is that God does not exist, at least not as existence is traditionally conceived according to the metaphysics of presence. Fourth, for Tillich, the categories of neither causality nor substance can be ascribed to God. Although God is nontheistic, it would be incorrect to speak of God in Aristotelian terms as an unmoved mover.

Likewise, the substance of God must not be thought of in terms of a fullness of being—or, more accurately, in terms of pure actuality. On the contrary, being includes nonbeing, and thus the negative element within the divine—or, more accurately, the divine potentiality—must be preserved. Fifth, Tillich is a "wholly impure thinker—a thinker of boundaries and margins," whether those margins are between theology and culture, theology and philosophy, or Christianity and other world religions.[23] Based on these five points, Thatanamil concludes that "Tillich's God can in no way be reduced to an ontotheological foundation" and "is simply not the ontotheological God that Heidegger rejects."[24]

Thatanamil must be commended for this defense. His knowledge of the Tillich corpus is masterful, and the way he extends—we might even say, radicalizes—Tillich's late concern with comparative religion continues to breathe new life into the study and employment of Tillich. But it is at this point that we might twist Thatanamil's opening declaration slightly to say that *while it is true that not every theological appeal to ontology is ontotheological, it might also be said that not every form of ontotheology is necessarily a problem.* Thatanamil has gone to great lengths to insist that Tillich is not an ontotheologian, but perhaps this cedes too much authority to Heidegger's original analysis of the ontotheological problem. The result is a reactive, rearguard defense, which may succeed in clearing Tillich's name but only by demonstrating his palpability. Echoes can be heard here of Barth's consternation over the spectacle of theology's losing its distinctiveness, conforming to certain philosophical norms, and chasing after the latest wave in contemporary philosophy.

What if, instead, we came clean to the obvious—that Tillich is an ontotheologian, at least of a certain sort. After all, Tillich's theological ontology is one of several aspects of his thought that sets him apart from his contemporaries. Consider that Tillich's formulation of the "God beyond God" has been read as preparing the ground for, or as a forerunner to, the radical death-of-God theologies of the 1960s.[25] Tillich's remark that "God does not exist" has been employed to cut through the debates over the so-called New Atheists.[26] Tillich's theology of culture continues to serve as a model for the nonsectarian academic study of religion and has developed into what is sometimes referred to by the oxymoron "secular theology."[27] And Tillich's forays into the theological engagement with other world religions and the history of religion have been cited as a contemporary model for the burgeoning field of comparative theology.[28] Yet his theological ontology, which is at the very heart of his systematic theological doctrine of God, is somehow sidestepped or explained away.[29]

If the above account is accurate, and Tillich's contributions in each of these arenas of contemporary religious thought have been cited, recognized, employed, and to a certain extent absorbed, then it seems all the more reason to assert that

there is one remaining arena in which the truly radical Tillich might be discerned—
to wit, in the concept that the radical Tillich is the ontotheological Tillich.

We are in a position, therefore, to ask a different question. Instead of asking whether Tillich is an ontotheologian, we must ask the degree to which Tillich's particular ontotheology is amendable to change. With this question in mind,
we return briefly to Carter's theological account of race and the way that Christian identity formation has been racialized and is thus a prime contributor to the
problem of racism in the modern world. Recall the argument that it is to the extent that Tillich's theology is predicated on a "beyond" that his theology of culture actually amounts to an anti-Jewish, antimaterial, and antihistorical theology
of culture. Although there is a certain relationality at work in Tillich's ontology,
by Carter's assessment it is only a relative relationality, a mere passing moment to
a higher unity. Therefore, the God *beyond* God not only claims a false universal but
contributes to the Christian supersessionist problem by which religious identity
formation operates according to a racial—if not yet racist—logic.

Carter's project asks "how the discourse of theology aided and abetted the
processes by which 'man' came to be viewed as a modern, racial being."[30] His
answer is that "modernity's racial imagination has its genesis in the theological
problem of Christianity's quest to sever itself from its Jewish roots." This severing
is accomplished by the Christian spiritualization of the fleshly, material existence
of Jesus's Jewish body. In Carter's words, "Christ did not assume a 'psychic body'
but a material one." And not to put too fine a point on it, Jesus's God was not a
God *beyond* God, but the God of creation, of history, and of Israel. Jesus's Jewish,
covenantal flesh is the key to redemption for both Jews and Gentiles alike. "Given
this," Carter adds, "we must say that Christ's flesh in its Jewish constitution is 'mulatto' flesh. That is to say, in being Jewish flesh it is always already *inter*sected by
the covenant with YHWH and in being *inter*sected it is always already *intra*racial
(and not merely multiracial). Its purity is its 'impurity.'"[31] In place of the false universal of the beyond—which is a unity predicated on purity—Carter is suggesting
a "unity-in-distinction" or a "discontinuity-in-continuity," by which the material
existence of Christ's covenantal flesh reveals God's saving grace. The covenant lib-
erates identity from the fiction of (racial) purity, which is why Carter proclaims
Christ to be a "linguistic liberation."[32]

What must be observed here is that just as Thatanamil claims Tillich to be a
"wholly impure thinker," so too is Carter. But Carter's is a different sort of impurity. Whereas Tillich is a genuine thinker of boundaries and margins, he still presumes discrete identities and discernible parameters. Carter, by contrast, invokes
miscegenation, with all the sociopolitical implications this term carries. Theology
might be radically reformulated based on changing cultural norms, but the question is whether this reformulation also includes a change in the very essence or

being of theology. Is what it means to think theologically fundamentally altered, or merely repackaged? How one answers this question determines the degree to which Tillich is rightly or wrongly regarded as a radical theologian. It also just might address the issue of whether ontotheology is a genuine problem or a false one, and thereby suggest an alternative future for a truly radical theology.

(Re-)Introducing Malabou

To address this issue, an intervention is in order. Although Malabou has worked with much of the same philosophical archive as Tillich, her contributions to contemporary Continental philosophy have yet to be applied to him or to the problem of ontotheology more generally. In chapters 2 and 3, I employed Malabou first as an alternative to Levinas and second for her critical reinterpretation of Heidegger. In both cases Malabou uses the concept of plasticity to articulate a philosophical ontology of radical immanence. It is her realization of ontological mutability that prevents her ontology of radical immanence from closing in on itself as a totality. That is to say, as long as we understand being as change, the prospect for transformation need not be predicated on transcendence or radical alterity. Instead, the capacity, reality, or even inevitability of change is the being of beings—being's ownmost possibility. This is what Malabou means when she invokes the possibility for radical transformation without exoticism.

Evidence for Malabou's creativity and significance can be seen not just in the fecundity of her signature concept of plasticity but also in how her readings of the modern Western philosophical canon are entirely original, bucking academic trends and fashions. For instance, the contemporary philosophical dismissal of Hegel is well established. For Malabou, the various iterations of this dismissal are all variations on the question of the future, both in terms of how Hegel's dialectic conceives of the future and whether there is a future for critical engagement with Hegel. If we put it in schematic form, we can look at three versions of this dismissal. First, Hegel's philosophy aspires to a total comprehension of history in which all of human culture—for example, art, religion, politics, and so on—is subject to the *aufhebung*, the process of sublation that both suppresses and preserves everything that came before it in a final synthesis that is the realization and culmination of the absolute spirit. For Hegel's contemporary critics, however, the problem is that once history has been fully comprehended, it has ended. Or, more precisely, the problem is that history can be fully comprehended only when it has come to an end. Therefore, to the extent that Hegel is a thinker of the end of history, there is no future in Hegel. Second, Hegel is merely of historical interest. To the extent that Hegel is merely of historical interest, there is no future for Hegel. Third, for many critics, there is no real contingency within the Hegelian dialectic, only a contained contingency. In the end, for Hegel, there

is no doubt of what the end will be. Although the Spirit may achieve its final destination in many different ways, it will always—necessarily and inevitably—achieve
its final destination. The Hegelian dialectic does not permit a different or alternative destination, only infinitely different means of getting there. As John Caputo
has written, "Hegel's future means that what is going to happen next is an open
question, but in the end, no matter what happens, there will have been an explanation and a necessity. . . . In that sense, there is no chance and no event."[33] The
concept of plasticity employed by Malabou, then, can stretch only so far. Malabou
cannot stretch plasticity far enough as long as she is contained within the Hegelian dialectic. If the end or the outcome is never called into question, then there
is no future. This would be a plasticity without any explosive potential, and thus
the future would merely be a repetition and a perpetuation of the same. Therefore, to the extent that the Hegelian dialectic is merely a perpetuation of the
same, there is no future in Hegel.

Malabou counters the argument that Hegel is a relic of the past by showing
how he conceived of humanity, divinity, and philosophy as inherently amenable
to future transformations. Regarding humanity, consider the material practice of
habit. Through habitual behavior, human beings fashion a second nature for themselves. Routines become internalized, and rituals and customs become automatic.
Taboos become written into the very fabric of the ego's identity formation. In Malabou's rendering, this process is the accidental becoming essential and revealing
the plasticity of human subjectivity. Given this understanding, then, the constitutive role of habits breaks down the dichotomy between nature and culture—not
simply because nature is always already inculturated but because nature can be
changed or altered by the taking on of a second nature. Conversely, in the Hegelian dialectic, the divine must be thought of as a "plastic God," the becoming accidental of the essential. It is the same with philosophy—Hegel's dialectic is itself
plastic, and so according to Malabou it is "capable of being transformed by those
who read it, and capable of transforming those same readers." In other words,
Absolute Knowledge rightly conceived is characterized by "metamorphosis," not
"stasis,"[34] the dialectic process does not stop but changes and transforms,[35] and
the *aufhebung* undergoes its own *aufhebung*.[36] It is in this sense that, for Malabou,
Hegel is both open to and productive of change.

This rehabilitation of Hegel for contemporary Continental philosophy also
provides the template for how Malabou reads Martin Heidegger and Sigmund
Freud. For my purposes here, I return to what she terms the Heidegger change,
in which she develops her fundamental ontological insight—namely, how an ontology of change lies beneath and goes beyond Heidegger's famed identification
of the ontological difference. To repeat, by attending to the concept of change
in Heidegger's oeuvre, Malabou is able to show that this is a consistent insight

that runs throughout Heidegger's career, from beginning to end, irrespective of the so-called Heideggerian turn. That is to say, both before and after his Nazi associations—whether in the development of his existential analytic and fundamental ontology during the period of *Being and Time* or in his later, more contemplative, poetic works (and perhaps even unbeknownst to him all along)— Heidegger's interests were driven by a sense that being as such is being *qua* change, that the very condition of possibility for the ontological difference is the self-differing made possible by an ontological mutability. Nothing is without change. Or, in other words, nothing is prior or more fundamental to being than change. Change makes what is to be.

Before considering how this alternative understanding of ontology might be applied to Tillich, we must first revisit the so-called problem of ontotheology. Heidegger's clearest and most fully developed analysis of the problem comes from his work *Identity and Difference*. There the problem of ontotheology was located within his larger project of overcoming metaphysics. Indeed, in arguing for the ontotheological constitution of metaphysics, he identified metaphysics as an ontotheological problem in that it operates by both a theologic and an ontologic. The concern with metaphysics is how it conceives of being in terms of identity and is therefore forgetful of the ontological difference. Metaphysics has the character of ontotheology by its conflation of theology and ontology and thus renders what is different as the same. Using this analysis, the problem with ontotheology is that it is at once the highest and most fundamental expression of identity. Being is hardened as the self-same. Moreover, being is held up or set aside as an object of thought. Such is the comprehensive, totalizing gaze of Hegel's dialectic. Such is the idolatry of those who dare speak of or for God. In Thatanamil's words, "The argument . . . claims that any thinking of God that identifies God with being will constrain and even determine the conditions under which God is permitted to appear."[37]

It is at this point that we must attempt the intervention by Malabou. If earlier I insisted that the radical Tillich is the ontotheological Tillich, here I must defend the claim that the problem of ontotheology is perhaps least understood by Heidegger himself. This claim is the key to Malabou's radical reinterpretation of the significance of Heidegger's work—namely, that by attending to the notion of change in Heidegger's work, Heidegger himself is changed. This idea is more than a demythologization or deconstruction of Heidegger, a salvaging of the good from the bad or the subjecting of his fundamental ontology to an ethics as first philosophy. Instead, Malabou's provocative suggestion is that there is a "secret agent" at work in Heidegger's philosophy, so clandestine that it remains radically unknown even— or especially—to him. *If change comes before, and is more fundamental than, difference, then Heidegger's project of overcoming metaphysics*—which for him is the context in which the problem of ontotheology is rightly understood—*is misguided at best*. It operates by a logic of identity (and difference), effecting a reversal of, but not a way out of, the binary.

In short, *Heidegger misdiagnosed the problem of ontotheology*. He misdiagnosed the problem because he misunderstood—or simply missed—his most important insight into ontology. It is not, as he supposed, that he clarified the ontological difference and recovered the ontological question but that beneath both something more fundamental was at work. The word *being* was consistently evoked in connection with terms such as *change, metamorphosis,* and *transformation.* The ontological difference was derivative of this ontology of change because it is change that makes differences happen.

Put in different terms more resonant with Carter's concerns about the theological problem of whiteness, the trouble with Heidegger's analysis of the problem of ontotheology is that it belies a quest for purity. This is the critical argument I pursued in my book *Between Faith and Thought*.[38] In this respect, I see Heidegger and Barth as flip sides of the same coin, each recognizing the limits of language and thought but nevertheless taken by the desire for purity. In *Between Faith and Thought* I appealed to Levinas's notion of the trace as a way to make clear that there are no pure actions or intentions and that the ontotheological condition of thought renders any prospect of either a pure identification or pure differentiation an impossibility. In the place of Heidegger's project of overcoming (metaphysics), I suggested a thinking that is "otherwise than overcoming," an ethical interrogation of the misguided quest for purity, a recognition that it is perhaps the desire for overcoming itself that is the problem.

Caputo is helpful here as well. Where I talk of Heidegger's quest for purity, Caputo speaks of Heidegger's mythological gesture that "takes the form of a myth of origins, of a Great Beginning, of a great founding act back at the beginning of the tradition, which gives flesh and blood—mythic form—to a philosophical insight."[39] Heidegger constructs a grand narrative of monogenesis, to which Caputo asks, "Why must there be *the* history of Being *and not rather* many such histories, a whole host of them, a proliferation of histories, which tell us many stories, so many that they are impossible to monitor and to organize into a grand narrative of Being's singular upsurge and decline?"[40] And lest one suppose this effort at thinking otherwise is merely semantic, Caputo gives a name to Heidegger's fatal flaw. He says that "the fateful, fatal flaw in Heidegger's thought is his sustained, systematic exclusion of this jewgreek economy in order to construct a native land and a mother tongue for Being and thought."[41]

Returning to Malabou once again, we may pose the possibility of a series of changes. She herself admits that even with the completion of her book on Hegel she had still not recognized the decisive shift from plasticity to metamorphosis that it effected.[42] It was only by virtue of her book on Heidegger, which came after her book on Hegel, that she was able to go back and recognize that her probing of the future of and for Hegel was really a question about the possibility for making change, for a way of affirming the dialectic without being trapped in a merely retrospective gaze or without reifying the perpetuation of the same, and for a radically immanent form of thought that still holds out the possibility for difference. It is this nascent thought that leads her to the interrogation of the Heideggerian concept of change itself, which even further clarified her real question: *if her interest in plasticity was really a way at getting at metamorphosis, then what Heidegger's metabolic ontology helps to clarify is that the fundamental question of philosophy is about transformation and whether transformation is achieved through immanence or transcendence,* or, in Malabou's terms, through ontogenesis or as a pure rupture. Malabou's views should be clear—she believed that the notion of the pure rupture is a dangerous fantasy that plagues any and all quests for purity. "There is no outside," she writes, and then adds the important caveat, "nor is there any immobility."[43]

By changing Heidegger, Malabou gives us a way to think otherwise, an "alterity without an outside," a "lack of beyond" that does not imply a lack of difference or the reduction of the other to the same. In other words, we come to realize that *transformation—and not transcendence—is the origin of alterity.* There is neither messianism here nor a need for this pure figure of the wholly other or of the absolute future. There is *no messianism, only metamorphosis.* That is because not only do we have the capacity to change but our very being is change. Once again, this is "a radical transformation without exoticism."[44]

The Radical Tillich

In the preceding, we were presented with at least two ways to rethink the problem of ontotheology and, by extension, two ways to remember and reclaim the radical Tillich. There is miscegenation, and there is metamorphosis. Both are figures of the reject. Think of the mulatto lieutenant governor Silas Finch from D. W. Griffith's cinematic masterpiece *Birth of a Nation*. Finch was a power-hungry, wanton sex fiend whose every look exposed even more his deviance and danger. And think of Kafka's Gregor Samsa, the character who awoke to find himself metamorphosed into a "monstrous verminous bug," a figure so absurd and so grotesque that he lay beyond the scope of human care.

Despite his suggestion that Tillich's theology of culture is in effect an anti-Jewish theology of culture, Carter nevertheless appreciates the appeal of Tillich's reconfiguration of transcendence for the development of black liberation theology. Tillich redefines transcendence as a self-transcendence in the existentialist guise of the quest for authenticity and the "courage to be." This existentialist moral fortitude provides a schema for articulating black power and resistance. But, as Carter sees it, this language of courage comes at a cost—namely, that Tillich's reconstrual of transcendence is an immanent transcendence predicated on the immanence of being. Further, this immanence is total. Even God is housed in being, albeit as its ground. So conceived, the threat of nonbeing is an existential threat, and the quest for authenticity requires not just the overcoming of one's anxiety by way of courage but the overcoming of finitude itself. The irony Carter seems to be suggesting is that by Tillich locking himself into immanence of being he is that much more beholden to a beyond.

By this reading, Tillich is no radical theologian at all. On the contrary, he is a theologian of culture who in actuality sees no lasting value in cultures. He is an existentialist thinker of finitude whose work is animated by a quest for transcendence. Recall Carter's words when he said, "It is the case that cultures, histories, and people groups must be overcome: that is, they must exhibit courage in order to be liberated into the infinitude of their existence."[45] This infinitude operates as a universal norm and thus not only is anti-Jewish but also eviscerates black liberation theology's claim on the revelatory significance of black culture and experience. Therefore, because Tillich is an ontotheologian par excellence, his identification of God with being contributes to the total erasure of difference. It matters little that Tillich carefully avoids calling God either the first cause or the highest being. His ontotheology is problematic in traditional Heideggerian terms because he privileges identity over difference and the one over the many.

But *with a changed Heidegger we might also hold out hope for a changed Tillich.* Or better, by unleashing the secret agent of change onto Heidegger's conception of being and the problem of ontotheology, we might be in a better position to appreciate how Tillich's ontotheology is both radical and contemporary. Carter makes the mistake of reading Tillich more in Hegelian than Heideggerian terms. But, as Malabou has shown, regardless of whether Tillich is rightly or wrongly characterized as Hegelian or Heideggerian, the two together may be read as a "transformational mask," with the face of the one rendering the other more or less visible. Like Hegel's notion of transcendence, Tillich's can be characterized as either a self-transcendence or an immanent transcendence. In both cases, there is a radical immanence at work. The question is whether this radical immanence constrains God and. correlatively, places a limit on, or immobilizes, being.

Given Tillich's identification of God with being, we may now say that God is change. The God beyond God is a plastic God. As Malabou has written of plasticity more generally, the characteristics of plasticity include the capability of receiving form (of being changed), of giving form (of making change), and of explosion (of transformation and metamorphosis). In this respect, Tillich's ontotheology is not a problem, and neither is his radical immanence. On the contrary, these are productive, if not necessary, conditions for conceiving of miscegenation and metamorphosis. Ontotheology is a mixed discourse. The ontotheological condition of thought recognizes the ethicopolitical significance of thinking on the border. Thinking ontotheologically is a rejected way of thinking that nevertheless gives birth not so much to something new as to something old, something impure. A miscegenated form of thought does not reject the reject but instead rejects the misguided quest for purity in the task of overcoming.

As it is with metamorphosis, the traditional reading of the problem of ontotheology is concerned with how it establishes an artificial limit with a determinant floor (being as ground) and ceiling (God as the highest being). So conceived, ontotheology sets us in a trap of radical immanence in which there is nothing beyond and thus no hope for change. The longing for transcendence typical of the theological gesture is nothing more than the effort to escape the trap of the ontotheologian's own making. As such, it is the ultimate alienation; liberation is predicated on an impossible infinitude. And it is a fundamental self-contradiction—radical immanence betrays a secret desire for transcendence.

But what if, as Malabou insists, there can be "radical transformation without exoticism"? What if just because there is no outside does not mean there is immobility? Instead, difference is made by way of a self-differing, by the strangeness and otherness that lie within. It's not just that we are capable of change but that we necessarily and inevitably change because being is change, because to be is to change. This profound insight into the ontology of change goes all the way down and all the way up, from being as ground to God as the highest and most complete expression of plasticity.

Combining Malabou's ontology with Tillich's ontotheology, then, we may say that the identification of God with being means that God is seen as the very being and source of change. This claim does not rest on the hope for the impossible but is instead grounded in the very nature of our being. Once we regard ontotheology not as a problem to be overcome but as the necessary condition of thought, radical theology may put aside once and for all the misguided quest for purity and affirm the divine in the impure, the polluted, the reject, and the flux. In so doing, we may announce the death of the moral-metaphysical God defined as being otherworldly and unchanging and proclaim a new faith in a plastic God forever bearing the marks of the wounds of history while still retaining the possibility for change.

FIVE

The Hermeneutics of the Kingdom of God

The last three chapters have invoked Catherine Malabou as an agent of change for a more radical theological thinking. When I traced the path of transcendence for Emmanuel Levinas, Malabou provided the alternative possibility of an "alterity without an outside" and thus a way to conceive of the possibility for radical transformation without exoticism, which means a nonmessianic politics of radical rupture predicated on an ontology of change, mutability, and transformation. When I considered the potential viability and liabilities of a weakened communism, Malabou's bold reinterpretation of Heidegger as a thinker of ontological mutation was enlisted in common cause with Gianni Vattimo and Santiago Zabala's political reclamation of Heidegger. And when I searched for a more radical Paul Tillich by way of a reexamination of the so-called problem of ontotheology, Malabou's concept of plasticity was employed to redirect the preoccupation of much of contemporary philosophical theology. In other words, the problem with ontotheology is not the identification of God with being (à la Tillich) but the fixed understanding of being as immobile and immobilizing. By virtue of Malabou, we may affirm our God as a plastic God—that is, as the being and source of change.

In the next few chapters, John Caputo will stand in the place of Malabou as intermediary and interlocutor. This will simultaneously be a reading *of* and reading *with* Caputo, allowing me to better position the postliberal radical theology I have in mind. Caputo figures in these pages as foil to some and mediator to others. He is deserving of this place of priority not simply for the contributions he has long since made in establishing the field of Continental philosophy of religion as we know it but also, more recently, for articulating and defending his own particular variant of radical theology. As I have sought to show elsewhere, his is not a radical theology of the death of God but is instead a radical theology *after* the death of God.[1] This important distinction places Caputo in interesting positions with regard to his various contemporaries—as the pious one to Mark C. Taylor's erring a/theology, as the postmodern antimetaphysician to William Desmond's theistic metaphysics, and as the voice of moderation to both John Milbank and Slavoj Žižek's extremism.

After the Death of God

Recent years have witnessed a change in tone in the still-developing field of the Continental philosophy of religion. The tone of the first theological encounters with postmodern theory and deconstructive philosophies was primarily critical toward traditional forms of religiosity. Representative of this primarily critical tone was Taylor's assertion in *Erring* that *"deconstruction is the 'hermeneutic' of the death of God."*[2] By identifying deconstruction so closely with the radical death-of-God theologies from the 1960s, Taylor both established a distinctively postmodern theology and marked postmodern theological thinking as necessarily a/theological and, for many, as intrinsically antagonistic toward traditional religion. Such a postmodern a/theology sought a new theological paradigm for what was thought to be a rapidly secularizing culture, a form of theological thought for those uncertain in, if not outrightly suspicious of, their faith.

Also representative of this still-early encounter with and engagement of Continental philosophy and religion was Paul Ricoeur's now-famous identification of Karl Marx, Friedrich Nietzsche, and Sigmund Freud as "masters of suspicion."[3] Ricoeur's notion of a hermeneutics of suspicion provides a slightly different genealogy of contemporary Continental philosophy of religion from that of Taylor but still shares with Taylor the assumption of a primarily critical tone toward religion (Ricoeur's own personal religious convictions notwithstanding). Thus, whether by way of Taylor's postmodern a/theology or by way of Ricoeur's hermeneutics of suspicion, the first wave of the Continental philosophy of religion assumes a certain self-distancing from religion and, as such, is symptomatic of the spirit of secularism that pervades the thought and culture of late modernism.

There are a number of contemporary indications that this secularist mindset has undergone a decided shift. Indeed, one of the most surprising aspects of our postmodern culture is the global resurgence of religion; although, as noted by Gianni Vattimo in the introduction to the book that first brought this resurgence to the attention of philosophers, this return of religion is taking place "more in parliaments, terrorism and the media than in the churches, which continue to empty."[4] It is the public visibility of religion that has caused widespread discussion of the proper role of religion in public life, a reconsideration of church/state matters, and the degree to which religious considerations impact the relations between different nations and cultures.

Religion's public visibility has caused a reconsideration not only of the contemporary cultural situation but also of the lineage of modern philosophy and theology. For instance, a number of important recent works have reexamined Ricoeur's so-called masters of suspicion in such a fashion that the *affirmative* quality of their religious thought has been emphasized.[5] The best known of these recent works is perhaps Van Harvey's *Feuerbach and the Interpretation of Religion*.[6] Although Feuerbach himself was not included in Ricoeur's official pantheon, Feuerbach's work has been considered by many, because of his reading of theology as anthropology, to be a forerunner of the insights from the critical attitudes of Marx, Nietzsche, and Freud toward religion. For Harvey, however, just as important as Feuerbach's hermeneutic of suspicion is Feuerbach's *constructive* and evolving theory of religion, which has much significance beyond his well-known Hegelian critique of religion as alienation. It is likewise with Tyler Roberts's book on Nietzsche, *Contesting Spirit: Nietzsche, Affirmation, Religion*,[7] and James DiCenso's book on Freud, *The Other Freud: Religion, Culture and Psychoanalysis*.[8] Each book challenges the scholarly consensus that Nietzsche and Freud, respectively, are somehow enemies of religion. Roberts argues in his book that Nietzsche's critique of religion is in fact an affirmative religious practice that eventuates not in the rejection or overcoming of religion but in its transformation and renewal. Although DiCenso admits that Freud's orientation toward religion is atheistic and generally critical, Freud's critique of religion nevertheless yields constructive insights into the meaning of religion in culture. And even beyond DiCenso, Mark Edmundson—who draws his argument largely from Freud's last work, *Moses and Monotheism*—has gone so far as to describe Freud as a "defender of the faith." As Edmundson writes in *The New York Times Magazine*, Freud argued that religion, or, more precisely, Judaism, "helped free humanity from bondage to the immediate empirical world, opening up fresh possibilities for human thought and action. He also suggests that faith in God facilitated a turn toward the life within, helping to make a rich life of introspection possible."

Although this scholarly reconstructive effort is ongoing, leading to fresh insights and a renewed appreciation of the nuances within these respective theories of religion, it has been Caputo's reading of the affirmative religious passion that drives Derridian deconstruction that has been most responsible for providing an understanding of our contemporary postmodern situation with regard to religion that is different from that of Taylor's postmodern a/theology and the tradition of radical theology that he inherited. One way to put this is to say that, beginning with *The Prayers and Tears of Jacques Derrida*, Caputo has been engaged in a sustained effort to deconstruct deconstructive a/theology. As Caputo first wrote in *Prayers and Tears*, "The problem with *Erring* is that it is insufficiently aporetic, that it allows itself to be led straight down the path (*poreia*) inerrantly I would say, of the death of God. . . . That version of deconstruction is undone by deconstruction itself, which refuses such closure, such exclusions and clean sweeps."[9] That same critique—not only of Taylor but of the entire way in which deconstructive analysis had been received within religious studies and theology—has been carried forward and expanded in his more recent works in which he explains how the death of God immediately implies the "death of the death of God" and how the modern secular world has undergone its own process of "desecularization."[10]

This point of distinction that Caputo has drawn between himself and Taylor is a technical one, but it is not merely semantic. Caputo emphasizes the affirmative religious passion that drives deconstruction and he claims that this emphasis better accounts for our lived cultural reality in which the religious remains stubbornly like a trauma long after its predicted demise. In the words of Hent de Vries:

> Religion, in this light, resembles the experience of trauma: its modality is the impossible mourning of an immemorial loss. . . . It consists, first, in the affirmation of the mere fact of this original bereavement or emptying of language and experience, for which the words *religion* and *God* remain (or have become) the most appropriate names (or simply the best we have come up with so far). Second, this response manifests itself in the affirmative of the impossible yet necessary rearticulation of this troubling fact . . . in ever-changing idiomatic and institutional contexts.[11]

Or, as Caputo has expressed it, what the persistence of the religious or the postmodern return of religion reveal is that beyond or after the death of God there remains the *desire for God*. In other words, the death of God is not the final word, and religion is more fundamentally about desire—even, or especially, when our old beliefs have been worn away or stripped apart, whether by the brutalities of modern life to which we have all become spectators or, more complex still, by the pretense of self-sufficiency. God is the name (or at least one of the names) that we give to this desire, and religion is the means (or at least one of the means) by which it takes its institutional form. But even when the name rings hollow and the form grows stale, it is the desire that stirs beneath that we still strive to articulate, that we still mean to affirm.

In addition to the advantage this alternative sensibility gives us in describing our contemporary cultural situation, it also has more immediate applicability. This applicability has been amply demonstrated in Caputo's first admitted foray into theology in *The Weakness of God*, in which he begins by confessing his "weakness for theology." This confession came after years of accepting the rather rigid boundaries that academics draw between philosophy and theology, so that even though theology might be the secret desire or aspiration of the philosopher of religion, it is where he dare not tread. The reasons for this reticence are clear and well founded, for, as Caputo tells us, "theology signifies a passion in which everything is at stake."[12] By giving a name (God) to desire, the theologian, unlike the philosopher, is fully exposed. By giving a name (God) to desire, the theologian has also set for herself an impossible task. In Caputo's idiom, theology is precisely this prayer for the impossible, a prayer not unlike the caution that Karl Barth once gave to a group of aspiring ministers when he said, "*As ministers we ought to speak of God. We are human, however, and so cannot speak of God. We ought therefore to recognize both our obligation and our inability and by that very recognition give God the glory.*"[13] More provocatively still, think here of Martin Luther's advice "to sin boldly, yet more boldly still believe." Caputo has said on many occasions that Derrida "loosened [his] tongue," that it was Derrida who freed him to speak in his own voice.[14] The absolute conceit of a philosopher parading as a theologian is where the rubber of Caputo's reading of deconstruction as a form of liberation meets the road. By trying his hand at theology, Caputo might have transgressed the self-imposed limitations of philosophy, but these more theological works are characterized by a rare and refreshing boldness.

WWJD?

Throughout this section, I want to focus on Caputo's *What Would Jesus Deconstruct: The Good News of Postmodernism for the Church* as an instantiation of a radical theological method that ups the ante even more.[15] Here, Caputo not only parades as a theologian but actually dispenses theological, moral, and political advice to a deliberately targeted evangelical audience. The book is published in The Church and Postmodern Culture series edited by James K. A. Smith for Baker Academic. As explained by Smith in the preface, the series is intended to allow "contemporary philosophy and critical theory to 'hit the ground,' so to speak, by allowing high-level work in postmodern theory to serve the church's practice." The goal of the series is to have "high-profile theorists [like Caputo] in continental philosophy and contemporary theology . . . write for a broad, nonspecialist audience interested in the impact of postmodern theory on the faith and practice of the church."[16] Of course, one might ask, what does a deconstructive philosopher of religion born and bred in the Roman Catholic Church have to do with evangelical Protestantism? Or, conversely, what reason would those from the Bible Belt have for reading a book by, let alone taking the counsel of, an East Coast intellectual?

This incongruity is precisely what gives the book its charm. Indeed, one could even say that it is the very point Caputo is trying to convey. It is true, and readily acknowledged by Caputo himself, that he is speaking as an outsider—that while he might play the part of the theologian, dispense pastoral counsel, and repeatedly (even gleefully) call the religious Right to task, he does not count himself among their fold. Nevertheless, what he and they have in common is a shared fidelity to Jesus. Although Caputo might relish the role of the outsider looking in, what we know from Jesus's life and witness is that wherever he was and whenever he might arrive, he was the consummate outsider. Thus, the question—which began with Charles Sheldon's bestseller *In His Steps,* first published in 1896, and has recently become a veritable industry—is "What would Jesus do?" This question is the thread that runs throughout Caputo's book and, perhaps surprisingly, is also the tool that he wields in his running critique of the religious Right. As he writes in the opening paragraph, "My hypothesis is if our friends on the Right really mean to *ask* that question instead of using it as a stick to beat their enemies, they are in for a shock."[17] That is because the question, when genuinely asked, is inevitably shocking. After all, in what is perhaps a surprise to many of those wearing the WWJD merchandise, the narrative in which Sheldon first set that question treats it as a call for radical social justice. It is a call to Jesus, but then, if the New Testament is any guide, one can never know or safely predict precisely what Jesus might do next. In other words, the very posing of the question of what Jesus would do "requires an immense amount of interpretation, interpolation, and self-questioning." In short, not only does posing this question deconstruct the pretense of those who claim to speak for God or to know God's will with absolute certainty, but the posing itself is a "scene of *deconstruction*."[18]

Careful readers will note that this might not be the way that the term *deconstruction* is typically utilized. Again, this is the very point that Caputo is trying to convey. As he defines the *work* of deconstruction: "It simply tells the truth, meticulously, uncompromisingly, without disguise, amelioration, or artificial sweeteners. . . . Deconstruction is organized around the idea that things contain a kind of uncontainable truth, that they contain what they cannot contain. Nobody has to come along and 'deconstruct' things. Things are auto-deconstructed by the tendencies of their own inner truth."[19] More directly still, deconstruction is defined by Caputo as "a way of making, or letting, the truth happen":

> Up to now, deconstruction has gotten a lot of mileage out of taking sides with the "*un*-truth." That is a methodological irony, a strategy of "reversal," meant to expose the contingency of what we like to call the "Truth," with a capital *T*. . . . While deconstructors have made important gains exposing the hypocrisy of temporal and contingent claims that portray themselves in the long robes of Eternal Verity, it is also necessary to point out that deconstruction is at the same time a hermeneutics of truth, of the truth of the event, which is not deconstructible.[20]

Throughout the book, Caputo makes reference to many other scenes of deconstruction—besides the posing of the question "What would Jesus do?"—that are drawn from literature, film, and popular culture. One of the scenes he describes is the much-acclaimed HBO crime series *The Wire*. This show is a scene of deconstruction because it provides us with an unflinching look at the crime, poverty, drugs, and despair of inner-city life in Baltimore. Its characters—whether drug lords or cops, teachers or students, city hall officials or the forgotten masses who bleed out into the streets—are all three-dimensional and self-conflicted. There is no knight in shining armor, although good intentions, as well as shady political and business dealings, abound. It is deconstructive because it exposes the myth of the American dream to its all-too-realistic underbelly. It ties together with the question "What would Jesus do?" because to the extent that Jesus cared about the poor and the outcast, helping them is where the good news of the church meets its contemporary challenge.

Other scenes of deconstruction that Caputo mentions include Khaled Hosseini's *The Kite Runner*, Dostoevsky's "The Grand Inquisitor," Dan Brown's *The Da Vinci Code*, the *Mission Impossible* films, the music of Frank Sinatra, and so on. Although these references help to illustrate his argument and establish reference points for his audience, who might otherwise be intimidated by the high theory and litany of philosophers embedded in the analysis, they are not central to his discussion. Instead, the whole of the text can be organized into four main themes: the critique of the religious Right, the application of the gospel to concrete social and political issues, the status of Jesus and the authority of scripture in light of a deconstructive analysis, and, finally, the rewriting of deconstruction as the hermeneutics of the kingdom of God. I now briefly take each one of these themes up in turn.

(1) *The critique of the religious Right.* The indictment of the religious Right has already been mentioned several times in this chapter. Although the criticism is never laid out in a systematic fashion and is oftentimes mentioned by Caputo simply as an aside to his primary concern, it does cohere as a twofold charge. First, Caputo takes issue with the self-assured posturing of the religious Right as represented by its well-known, outspoken leaders. The problem here is not simply the personal style of these leaders but a deeper philosophical matter. By presenting their faith as a series of moral absolutes, they are making a fundamental epistemological mistake in confusing faith with knowledge.

For Caputo, who draws on the lesson hammered home by his years of study of Kierkegaard, faith goes hand in hand with doubt. Indeed, as Caputo writes in his discussion of John McNamee's *Diary of a City Priest*, doubt is not the opposite of faith but its very condition of possibility. As a priest in North Philadelphia, McNamee has to face crime, drugs, poverty, and despair on a daily basis. In a situation like this, especially, "One is called on to have faith in a world in which it is impossible to believe anything," and in which "doubt is more humane than faith." So for those on the religious Right whose faith leaves no room for doubt, Caputo adds his deconstructive analysis—which is, namely, that their lack of doubt is the "fuel for fanaticism."[21]

Second, in addition to the religious Right being philosophically or epistemologically challenged, they come across, at least to self-confessed outsiders like

Caputo, as angry and domineering. As Caputo writes in his characteristic style, "Now ask yourself, what does the Religious Right look like? . . . Are they mad with their love of the poor and oppressed, or are they just plain mad because somebody is asking them to reach into their pockets?"[22] And not only are they mad, but, even more troubling, they are in cahoots with the American military and its tendency toward aggression and the patently unjust defense of preemptive war, as Caputo laments:

> Strategically, diplomatically, socially, morally, economically, evangelically, in every possible way, we are witness today to a low point in American leadership, an ethical, social, political, and biblical catastrophe. Jesus would hardly recognize himself . . . . Instead of denouncing such policies in no uncertain terms, . . . the Christian Right cheers them on. Instead of serving as the prophetic voice of Amos giving President Jeroboam holy hell, instead of being the voice of Jesus and of the gospel in an act of unilateral American military aggression, the Christian Right dreams of a Christian Empire.[23]

I have two brief comments about Caputo's respective charges against the religious Right. First, the reader will be pleased to note that even while Caputo's critique sometimes reads like a blanket condemnation of both political conservatism and evangelical Protestantism, he does at least mention and commend the growing list of progressive evangelical thinkers such as Jim Wallis, Brian McClaren (who contributed the foreword to the book), Jimmy Carter, and others. Thus, his critique is not nearly as categorical as it might at first sound, especially when one takes into consideration the target audience for his book. After all, the book was deliberately written for an evangelical audience and published in a book series edited by a prominent evangelical theologian. The critique, therefore, is fundamentally theological in calling into question who rightly speaks for Christianity. Second, recalling Caputo's long tutelage under the writings of Kierkegaard, the reader might wish for a more careful treatment of the religious Right, one that does not turn it into the proverbial straw man, but one must also appreciate that Caputo's rhetoric functions as the act of a provocateur. Any attention to his tone and style throughout should guide the reader to understand that Caputo's critique is deliberately hyperbolic and intended for effect. Satire, wit, and even sarcasm are the hallmarks of his style.

(2) *The application of the gospel to concrete social and political issues.* As the subtitle of his book suggests, although Caputo does try to demonstrate "the good news of postmodernism for the church"—and in that sense the book is a case of *applied* theory—he is not writing a "politics of Jesus" per se. He makes that clear by saying, "I have avoided speaking of the 'politics of Jesus,' an expression that I

think is inherently ambiguous and too easy to abuse."[24] As a case in point, Caputo asks (and answers) the rhetorical question, "What would it look like if there were a politics of loving one's enemies, not of war, let alone, God forbid, preemptive war? Would it not be in almost every respect the opposite of the politics that presently passes itself off under the name of Jesus?"[25]

That being said, Caputo is not at all reticent when it comes to applying the message of Jesus to the social and political realm. Indeed, in what is perhaps the most courageous and refreshing part of the book, Caputo *directly* takes up the questions of economic justice, militarism, patriarchy, abortion, and homosexuality. In his examination of these cultural hot-button issues, Caputo falls on the liberal-progressive end of the political spectrum. Although Caputo is reliably or predictably (depending on one's own political persuasion) progressive in his social and political convictions, it cannot be said that he is ideologically rigid in his analyses. The difference is that a politics of Jesus would imply that the New Testament is straightforward, direct, and transparent when it comes to contemporary social and political issues, whereas an effort to apply the message of Jesus to the social and political realm acknowledges the need for interpretation. Put simply, a politics of Jesus would be too literalistic, whereas Caputo's approach is hermeneutical. As he explains, "It is *our responsibility* to breathe with the spirit of Jesus, to implement, to invent, to convert this poetics into praxis, which means to make the political order resonate with the radicality of someone whose vision was not precisely political."[26]

(3) *The status of Jesus and the authority of scripture in light of a deconstructive analysis.* Returning to the question of "What would Jesus do?," we might ask ourselves the actual difference that Jesus makes as the specific reference point in question. It is perhaps on this point that Caputo's analysis is most insightful, even revolutionary. After all, when the question of "What would Jesus do?" is typically posed, it is as if we, armored with the best of intentions, are calling on our better angels, summoning up the moral fortitude to do the right, good, and decent thing that we *know* we *ought* to do. But as long as that is the role the question plays, what real need is there for Jesus at all, except to stand in as a moral exemplar? Would Jesus not be interchangeable with other moral exemplars? What would the Buddha do? Or George Washington, for that matter? What practical difference does it make as long as we already know the answer in advance? As Caputo puts it, "What is the uniquely Jesus-inspired thing to do? I do not mean some universal-rational thing (as if there were one!) that we might get from Socrates or Kant, but the specific genius, the divine madness that characterizes Jesus in particular."[27]

Critical race theorist George Yancy has posed a similar question in order to expose the normative structure of whiteness operative in traditional Christology. Yancy sees whiteness as a form of structural sin and a "site of idolatry, fanaticism, obsession, and narcissism."[28] This link between whiteness and Christology has infected Christian theology and practice despite the clear incompatibility of the two. As Yancy explains, "I argue that through a certain hermeneutic lens Christian theology and whiteness—that is, whiteness as a historical process that continues to express its hegemony and privilege through various cultural, political, interpersonal, and institutional practices, and that forces bodies of color to the margins and politically and ontologically positions them as sub-persons—are incompatible."[29] To counter this incompatibility, Yancy calls for a "race realism" that recognizes race as a social construct that nevertheless has "real and profound *socio*-ontological, existential, political and psychological implications for those who are categorized as white and nonwhite."[30] Through the lens of this race realism, we should come to a better "conception of Jesus whose life and message were implicative of overcoming domination and oppression."[31]

The point of this discussion when it comes to our reading of Caputo is that Yancy then subsequently shows how even asking the question of "What would Jesus do?" can, in the words of Karen Teel, be "dangerously misleading":

> *In His Steps* suggests that asking "What would Jesus do?" can inspire Christians to read the gospels carefully and cultivate intimate relationships with God. Yet this seemingly innocuous question displays an insidious ability to distract white Christians from broader issues. Insofar as it fails to prompt us to critique our own social positions, it can allow us to skim right over the problem of whiteness, to think and act as if it is not there, to remain oblivious to—or at least helpless in the face of—unjust social structures. In other words, it can enable the continuation of the white unreflectiveness about whiteness. . . . As a method for white Christians to discover how to address whiteness, asking "What would Jesus do?" lends itself to answers that address symptoms, not the disease itself.[32]

Both Yancy and Caputo reject the idea that we already know what we ought to do because Jesus activates our preexisting moral consciousness and fortitude, and they agree with Teel that what is really needed is a *"discomfiting* Jesus."[33]

Only once we achieve some clarity about the actual specificity of the question, are we in a position to appreciate its radical nature. It is at this point that Caputo's "weak theology" comes into play. Consider the following:

> While other cases of "divine men" are to be found in ancient literature, Jesus is unique precisely because Jesus is not a typical superhero or mythological power who slays things and crushes his enemies with his might. What is most riveting about Jesus is that he is defeated,

executed, and abandoned, and that he is a man whose symbol is an
instrument of public execution, like a gallows, and whose message is
radical peace and nonviolence.

If we . . . think of a Jesus who really is crucified and who really
feels abandoned, then the icon of God we find in Jesus on the cross
is not an icon of power but of powerlessness, or at most of a power
of powerlessness.

What rises up in majesty from the cross is not a show of might
but rather forgiveness, not power but a protest against the unjust execution of a just man, a great prophetic "no" to injustice and persecu-
tion, a prophetic death rather than a sacrificial exchange that buys a
celestial reward.[34]

There are echoes of Rene Girard, to be sure, but in keeping with the book's main
concerns and key question, we are back to the previous point about the absolutely unpredictable nature of Jesus. What Jesus adds to our moral reasoning is
not simply the reduplication of our rational ethical theories. More precisely, what
Jesus adds to our moral reasoning is the *confounding of* our rational ethical theories.
For instance, it is said that we should love and care for our own, that any father
or mother who does not show special regard for his or her child has neglected the
responsibilities of parenthood, and that children should show their parents the
proper honor and respect. But Jesus says that anyone who does not "hate" his or
her father and mother cannot be his disciple. Jesus calls for unconditional love,
thereby negating the special concern and attachment that is our birthright and by
all accounts the natural and necessary basis for society. Jesus commands us to love
our enemies, but any study of our psychosocial development would tell us that it
is imperative to our survival that we learn to distinguish friend from enemy, those
we can trust from those we cannot.

In other words, only once we consider the "uniquely Jesus-inspired thing to
do" can we begin to understand the extent to which Jesus is a stumbling block
and a scandal. Recall Yancy's project of troubling the comfortable world of white
Christians by deconstructing white Christian identity formation. When we consider Yancy's view, it must be said that a proper Christology would not see Jesus as
the paragon of bourgeois virtue but would instead recognize Jesus in the hooded
African American teen, an outsider figure who inspires an unspoken fear, one who
troubles our own liberal fantasies about equality and fairness. In light of that,
there is nothing so secure or stable on which we can fasten our beliefs—this applies even to the very authority of scripture itself. Although the Bible is oftentimes
cited to settle political scores or to decide moral convictions, for Caputo it too is

always in need of being hermeneutically interpreted. When this question of authority is raised, Caputo answers directly: "My answer is that I am not an idolater. In deconstruction, the Scriptures are an archive, not the arche (which means they are not God). I take the second commandment very seriously and I do not put false gods—like books (biblical inerrantism) or the Vatican (papal infallibility)—before God, who is the 'wholly other.'"[35] This allows Caputo the freedom to argue that on certain subjects—most notably, homosexuality and abortion—the Bible might be either wrong or at least ambiguous by its silence. He quotes from Elizabeth Schussler Fiorenza to say that no text "that perpetuates violence against women, children, or slaves should be accorded the status of divine revelation if we do not want to turn the God of the Bible into a God of violence."[36] Likewise, there is no shame in admitting that the Bible's views of sexuality are outdated and reflective of a patriarchal culture. By Caputo's hermeneutical interpretation, there is no requirement to deny science in order to remain faithful.

(4) *The rewriting of deconstruction as the hermeneutics of the kingdom of God.* Now I return to where I began regarding the changing tone within the Continental philosophy of religion and Caputo's sustained effort at deconstructing deconstructive a/theology. Like the French philosopher Jean-Luc Nancy's project of deconstructing Christianity[37] and, before him, the German biblical scholar Rudolf Bultmann's project of demythologizing scripture,[38] there is something of a rehabilitation that is accomplished by Caputo's reading of deconstruction as the hermeneutics of the kingdom of God. That is to say, rather than being characterized by its antagonism toward traditional religion, Caputo's deconstructive analysis is fundamentally affirmative. So whereas Mark C. Taylor once spoke of deconstruction as the hermeneutics of the death of God, Caputo speaks of the kingdom, because, in his words, it helps us "get at the prophetic spirit of Jesus. . . . In my view, deconstruction is good news, because it delivers the shock of the other to the forces of the same."[39] And elsewhere, Caputo explains, "The deconstruction of Christianity is not an attack on the church but a critique of the idols to which it is vulnerable—the literalism and authoritarianism, the sexism and racism, the militarism and imperialism, and the love of unrestrained capitalism with which the church in its various forms has today and for too long been entangled, any one of which is toxic to the kingdom of God."[40]

Although Caputo adds that there is nothing new in this claim, that "it is the ageless task imposed on the church and its way to the future,"[41] I would counter that, in shaping the burgeoning field of the Continental philosophy of religion, it in fact continues and expands on the something new that he has contributed and promises something new and different for the evangelical audience he is targeting.

The Political Becoming of the Kingdom of God

It is worth inquiring, as I conclude this chapter, whether and the extent to which Caputo's hermeneutics of the kingdom of God is subject to the political becoming detailed in Vattimo and Zabala's weakened communism. As I already noted, in *What Would Jesus Deconstruct?*, Caputo offers a disclaimer: because of how prone the term is to abuse, he avoids speaking of the "politics of Jesus." In lieu of using this phrase, Caputo is content to apply the message of Jesus to the social and political realm by directly taking up the questions of economic justice, militarism, patriarchy, abortion, and homosexuality. As an application, it is a hermeneutical, and thus nondogmatic, practice.

Beyond that, however, I want to argue that there is the concept of the political operative in Caputo's hermeneutic theology. Specifically, this concept goes by the name of "sacred anarchy." To be sure, this is not politics as normally conceived. It is not hierarchical, producing instead a kind of "hieranarchy."[42] It does not authorize power with the prerogative to rule but initiates a "disturbance or a holy disarray."[43] As Caputo explains, "My idea is to stop thinking about God as a massive ontological power line that provides power to the world, instead thinking of something that short-circuits such power and provides a provocation to the world that is otherwise than power."[44] It is in the world but not of the world, just as the name of God "*harbors* an event" that is "uncontainable,. . . endlessly translatable," and excessive.[45] And as a political theology, this sacred anarchy is a direct repudiation of Schmitt, whose political theology is predicated on the concept of sovereignty. Caputo, by contrast, suggests the idea of a God—*after the death of God*—without sovereignty.[46] So although he stops short of identifying this concept of the political with the politics of Jesus, Caputo nevertheless does claim biblical warrant. Sacred anarchy is the politics called for in the New Testament.

At this point, a comparison in order. That is, to the extent that Caputo remains a messianic thinker whose ethics is deeply informed by Levinas,[47] does his deconstructive approach to politics get us any further than the difficult passage from the ethical to the political discerned in Levinas? As we have already discussed, Levinas's politics follows the structure of the messianic, as it is driven by the hope for a justice that is always to come. Likewise, Caputo runs Levinas together with Derrida, Vattimo, Walter Benjamin, and St. Paul to develop his weak messianic theology. The figure of thought he invokes for this messianic view of history is Benjamin's "angel of history," whose very being is sustained as a recollection of the dead. Caputo cites the angel of history as a weak messianic power because it has no ability to raise the dead back to life—there is only remembrance, not resurrection. Each moment in time is what Benjamin calls the "now-time" through which the messianic figure may pass to remember the ruin of history such that the dead will not

have died in vain. Nevertheless, the dead are left behind. Time marches on ineluc-
tably toward its future.

This is a messianic force so weak as to be unnoticed, a Messiah who might just
as well have come and gone without so much as a second glance or a moment's
thought. The one who would redeem history, the one who would proclaim that
nothing is lost, nothing forgotten, is the one who slips through the straight gate of
time only to be plotted in the ever-expanding sequence of events that is the single
and continuous catastrophe of history. There is no new, exalted life born from
the ash heap of history, no recovering what has been destroyed. For Caputo, such
a despairing view does not leave enough room for hope. Here is where he turns
from Benjamin's "backward-directed messianism" to Derrida's "call for a justice
to come." Caputo comments that "unlike Benjamin's, Derrida's is not a 'tragic'
view." He goes on to explain by saying, "The messianic is concerned not only with
redeeming the dead, the *revenants*, but with redeeming the future, the children, the
arrivants; the ones to come, which is the more usual meaning of hope."[48] Caputo
puts it another way when he says that "Benjamin should remember not only the
history of ruin but the original *yes* that Elohim inscribes on history."[49]

Caputo finds an example of this paradoxical divine affirmation in the New
Testament story of the crucifixion of Jesus. Here Caputo updates Martin Luther's
theology of the cross. That is to say, God's yes to the world is paradoxically found
in the world's most profound and absolute rejection of God—God's love abounds
in the death of God. God's will stirs even as it is usurped, thwarted, mocked, and
ridiculed. God's power is revealed in God's weakness. But—and this is the point at
which Caputo's hermeneutical theology suffers its own political becoming and at
which he ultimately parts company with Luther—this weak power of God is *not
soteriological*, as if Jesus's brutal death were all part of a clever ruse by which God
could declare God's ultimate victory over Satan. It *does not operate by an exchange
economy*. The sovereignty of God *does not remain intact after the death of God*; on
the contrary, *by Jesus's death, God's will was undone*. Jesus's death was not willed by
God but does reveal how far and how often humanity has departed from God's
intended purpose for humankind. It is neither an atoning sacrifice required by a
bloodthirsty God nor a ransom to pay the price of sin for the purchase of salvation for those who believe. Instead, *the weak power of God is a subversive, insurrectionary power*.

Jesus dies a torturous death as the mocked "King of the Jews." For Caputo,
Jesus's announcement of the Kingdom of God was neither premature nor quix-
otic; rather, it was ironic. It subjected the brutality of Roman imperial power to bit-
ter ridicule, and it posed a *counterpower*, an alternative logic of the world through
the rule of weak, vulnerable forces. And as the Jesus of History scholarship has
taught us, *if we cannot understand why Jesus was regarded as an enemy of the state, then*

we do not yet understand the mission that animated his life. Caputo is correct that Nietzsche understood better than most the subversiveness that Jesus's radical vision represented. In Caputo's words, the kingdom of God operates by a "divine madness" in which the lost one is preferred to the ninety-nine, in which we are told to forgive the unforgivable wrongdoing deserving of our condemnation and punishment, and in which we are told to defy the truth we know from evolutionary psychology and to disavow the fundamental concept of the political as Schmitt tells it in order to love our enemies and to hate our own father and mother.

So given, we can see how Caputo's weak theology is political in the same sense as the historical Jesus as portrayed by John Dominic Crossan, who has drawn his analysis from perspectives in social and cultural anthropology to reconstruct a revolutionary biography of Jesus.[50] In Crossan's view, for instance, Jesus's practice of eating with outcasts was an expression of his commitment to God's radical justice. Crossan calls this practice "open commensality," which was an enactment of Jesus's vision of "shared egalitarianism." By eating with outcasts, Jesus flaunted the boundaries between rich and poor, male and female, pure and impure, and patron and client, thereby challenging normative social relations and customs and attacking the social system built on patronage. As Crossan has developed this insight in books such as *God and Empire*, he has shown how Jesus's anti-imperialistic message of nonviolence and egalitarianism remains as scandalous and as often met with religiopolitical resistance now and throughout the history of Christianity as it was in Jesus's own time. Crossan has revealed that even the pages of scripture contain an unresolved tension between the violent normalcy of civilization and God's radical vision of nonviolent justice.[51] And as Crossan reads the Lord's Prayer, it is a call for redistributive economic justice more than an expression of religious piety and devotion.[52]

My argument here is that although Caputo still proclaims the messianic politics of the to come, in his ironic reading of the Kingdom of God as a counterpower that is rightly perceived as a threat to normative sociopolitical relations and customs, Caputo is attentive to the concrete political demands for justice. It is a weak messianic power that does not violently impose its will but rather quietly *insists.*[53] As such, it might be either ignored or rejected, but it nevertheless persists, just as the desire for God persists after the death of God. It is that original yes inscribed in history that provides Caputo with a more full-fledged concept of the political than that of Levinas. It is a politics of love rather than of enmity, based in a reading of the crucifixion of Christ that sees beyond the narrow preoccupation with individual salvation to the becoming of an alternative community that threatens the powers that be. It is a subversive and insurrectionary force that stands strongest in its most absolute vulnerability. It is anarchic in that it upends and disrupts but also in that it offers no guaranteed outcome or happy ending.

This is a theopolitics about more than using Jesus to sacralize or authorize one's politics. It is about the nature of subjectivity, community, cooperation, and justice that gets at the root of the political—a radical political theology. Caputo's rendering of the politics of the kingdom of God as a sacred anarchy, then, is a theorization of democracy as a primal, positive, generative power. More than a discontinuity, rupture, or break with sovereignty, it is a sovereignty undone or interrupted by its own overflow, its own excess—an uncontained and uncontainable energy that reverberates out of itself, beyond itself.

This divine yes is a moment or force or energy of decision that is *prior to* the founding of sovereignty—and, as such, more fundamental. This is not a sovereign power that has already been constituted, designated, or authorized. On the contrary, it is constitutive. Therefore, it provides a rich *concept of the political that is prepolitical inasmuch as it is radically theological*—a persistence of the divine yes by virtue of the weak power of God after the death of the sovereign, omnipotent, moral-metaphysical God.

SIX

The Radical Becoming of Theology

Lord, my God, who am I that You should forsake me? The Child of your
Love—and now become the most hated one—the one—You have thrown
away as unwanted—unloved. I call, I cling, I want—and there is no One to
answer—no One on Whom I can cling—no, No One.—Alone. . . . Where is
my Faith—even deep down right in there is nothing, but emptiness &
darkness—My God—how painful is this unknown pain—I have no Faith—
I dare not utter the words & thoughts that crowd in my heart—& make me
suffer untold agony.

—Mother Teresa

This chapter will be a brief one. It is structured around a question asked half in
jest: What does John Caputo have in common with Mother Teresa? Or, more
seriously, what does radical theology have in common with a living religious
faith? My suggestion is that radical theology not only gives voice to a kind of
religious faith for the disenchanted but also is an authentic expression of biblical propheticism. In this sense, the radical becoming of Caputo's weak theology
is not an external, ideological critique of religion that requires a self-distancing
from faith but is instead an inner outworking of a distinctly biblical faith. In other
words, *it becomes radical insofar as it remains biblical* and *it affirms faith insofar as it
suffers doubt.*

Such a reading of Caputo is prompted by a critical study written by
Christopher Ben Simpson that compares Caputo unfavorably with William Desmond.[1] Its inclusion in the pages of this book is not for the purpose of defending
Caputo against scurrilous charges. For one, Caputo has proven himself perfectly
willing and able to handle such defenses on his own.[2] More significantly, I want to
affirm the real value in Simpson's study. It is true, as Simpson presents it, that Desmond and Caputo represent two possible tracts for a contemporary philosophical
theology engaged with Continental thought. But Simpson's work helps to put into
critical relief many of the changes that have taken place in Caputo's developing
work in the philosophy of religion and theology. Further, whereas Simpson contrasts Caputo with Desmond to show two different ways of doing contemporary

philosophical theology, Caputo develops his own contrast in which he identifies two kinds of Continental philosophy of religion, one he calls a "postmodernism light" version and the other he calls a radical theological version. And whereas Simpson claims Desmond as the antidote to the antimetaphysical, deconstructive bent of Caputo's Derridean-inspired religion without religion, Caputo becomes increasingly insistent about the radical implications of the event of truth harbored within the name of God, within the practices and beliefs of religion, and within confessional theologies as traditionally conceived. For a theology to attend to the insistence of the event, it has to *become radical* insofar as it must succumb to the pent-up pressure of an uncertain faith seeking an understanding that knows no bounds. In this case, Caputo's self-identified radical theology is a theology that gets at the root so as *to uproot, to disrupt, and to open up a tradition of thought and practice from within.* So given, Simpson provides me with the opportunity to reprise some of the early, formative influences that shaped Caputo's thought and thus helps to round out the portrait of Caputo in service of the present effort to develop a radical theological method.

Between Metaphysics and Antimetaphysics

In his book from 2001, *The Predicament of Postmodern Theology: Radical Orthodoxy or Nihilist Textualism,* British theologian Gavin Hyman opens with the observation of the "strange condition" we faced at the beginning of the new millennium wherein we seemed to have arrived at the end of time or, more accurately, at an entire constellation of endings: the end of history, ideology, and dogma; the end of art; the end of the planned system; the end of Marxism, socialism, and the welfare state; the closure of the book; the disappearance of the self; and the death of God. "Nowhere is this strange condition more evident than in religion," Hyman tells us. He goes on to say, "For if religion was thought to have ended, there is a sense in which it has also returned. And yet it is evident that if religion is returning, it is returning *differently.*"[3] And from there, he lists the two viable postmodern alternatives for thinking theologically, albeit differently. The first, which he associated primarily with the work of Don Cupitt in Great Britain and Mark C. Taylor in the United States, "claims that the 'end' of foundationalism brings with it also the 'end' of theology" as we know it. The second, which he associated primarily with the work of John Milbank, "claims that the 'end' of foundationalism actually opens the way for the 'return' of theology" of a radically orthodox sort. "It may be said," Hyman continues, "that radical orthodoxy and nihilist textualism provide two radically antithetical theological responses to our postmodern predicament. What is particularly striking, however, is that these two responses have largely failed to confront and engage each other."[4] And thus we might say that the predicament of postmodern theology is that the field of philosophical theology finds itself divided and primed for a robust debate, which heretofore has effectively been a *nondebate*.

Jump forward over a decade, and it is worth asking whether Hyman's observation remains: is it the case that radical orthodoxy and postmodern deconstructive theology are like ships passing in the night, each going their separate directions, with neither even remotely disturbed by the other? Has the field of philosophical theology been caught in a protracted period of nondebate? Beyond Hyman's book, in which his allegiance ultimately comes down more on the side of what he describes as the nihilist textualism of Cupitt and Taylor, there has been no shortage of books and book series brandishing respective movements in contemporary philosophical theology and no shortage of interesting collaborations that combine those of the more traditionalist or orthodox bent and those who count themselves as postmodernists or deconstructivist. Consider on one side the dialogues between Slavoj Žižek and John Milbank in *The Monstrosity of Christ* and *Paul's New Moment* and on the other side the dialogues between Kearney and Caputo, Caputo and Vattimo, and Vattimo and Girard.[5]

Likewise, a recent work by Christopher Ben Simpson, *Religion, Metaphysics and the Postmodern: William Desmond and John D. Caputo*, doesn't so much straddle the divide as identify the appeal, animating concerns, and key ideas of both sides in this heretofore nondebate. But whereas Hyman's allegiance ultimately comes down more on the side of the nihilist textualist, Simpson makes clear the superiority of Desmond's philosophical system to alternative visions, here represented by the work of Caputo. Simpson does this both in his expressed gratitude to Milbank for his guidance and in the stated aims of the book's main argument and purpose, which is to demonstrate this superiority along with the viability of Desmond's system. Simpson describes himself as a "young would-be Derridean" but for his encounter with Desmond. In reference to his early attraction to the postmetaphysical vision of those such as Heidegger, Levinas, and Derrida, Simpson states, "Desmond's writing struck me as a loosening of the fetters and blinders—the assumed answers and latent liturgies—of these supposed liberations, and thus it presented me with an engaging and surprising (curious, perplexing, astonishing) vision . . . opening another way to see."[6] The thesis of Simpson's work, then, "is that William Desmond's approach to thinking about religion and God in relation to the domains of metaphysics and ethics provides a viable and preferable alternative to the like position represented in the work of John D. Caputo." And further, "Beyond this main thesis—of the superiority of a theistic metaphysical frame . . . over the kind of late-twentieth-century postmodern anti-metaphysical frame represented by Caputo—I suggest that Desmond's work can be seen as part of a larger emerging scholarly movement advocating such a theistic metaphysical frame."[7]

Finally, to put some flesh on this thesis, Simpson explains precisely why he finds Desmond's vision both viable and superior to Caputo's:

> Desmond's vision is viable in that it answers Caputo's critiques—showing that they need not be the case. Here Desmond shows how metaphysics (and ethics and religion informed by metaphysics) escapes Caputo's narration/location. Desmond defeats Caputo's defeaters, as it were—negates Caputo's negations in order to make Desmond's vision a possible position. On a deeper level, Desmond's vision is arguably preferable inasmuch as it can be used to critique Caputo's vision—largely in that it (Desmond's vision) can be seen to fulfill Caputo's motivating concerns in a more satisfying manner than Caputo's own LeviNietzschean vision. It does this in two ways. First, from Desmond's vision one can see how the LeviNietzschean vision tends to, in fact, betray its motivating concerns. Second, Desmond's position shows how a metaphysical vision/stance/picture (like Desmond's) is, in fact, necessary for one to fulfill these concerns—or simply necessary, as such. In this manner, Desmond out-narrates the "postmodern" LeviNietzschean position, showing Desmond's as a preferable position—as possessing a broader explanatory reach.[8]

Simpson is to be commended on several points, not only for this honest and clearly stated perspective in defense of Desmond but also for the clarity and fairness with which he approaches the subject of his critique of Caputo's work. Simpson is correct when he identifies Caputo's radical hermeneutics as a seeking out of a "minimalist metaphysics" and a postmetaphysical ethics (against ethics). Likewise, Caputo's postmetaphysical religion, at least in its earliest stages of development, is a religion without religion, pitting faith against knowledge or, perhaps better, in the words of Simpson, forcing a "choice between a 'faithless' metaphysics and a genuine religious faith, true to religion."[9] In sum, Simpson is correct to follow Caputo's "logic of the sans" in the making of a metaphysics without metaphysics, an ethics without (or against) ethics, and a religion without religion.

Further, and more technically, by showing how Caputo's concern with metaphysics as a will-to-knowledge or a will-to-mastery is present within Desmond's own discussion of the instrumental mind, Simpson successfully completes the first part of his dual task—namely, he shows how Desmond's metaphysics escapes Caputo's critique, or at least how Desmond's more nuanced position more than accounts for the sweeping, generalized, antimetaphysical bent of Caputo's. As Simpson puts it, "Desmond's position is able to answer Caputo's critique of metaphysics by showing that the understanding of metaphysics represented in his work is not guilty of the errors that Caputo levels against metaphysics as such."[10] Given this reasoning, even those like myself who are steeped in the postmetaphysical lineage of Heidegger, Levinas, Derrida, Vattimo, Caputo, and so on must concede that Desmond's metaphysical position is indeed a "possible position," which leaves the question not only of whether it is a viable one but of whether it is a preferable one. That is, how convincing is Simpson's case that "Desmond's position is able to genuinely address the motivating concerns that can be seen to be inspiring Caputo's treatment of metaphysics"? And, further, how convincing is Simpson's argument that "Desmond's position can be seen as preferable inasmuch as it presents a broader perspective from which the LeviNietzschean position can be seen to betray its motivating concerns and from which these concerns can be better addressed"?[11]

Caputo without Caputo

I would like to give a two-part response to these questions posed by Simpson's reading. First, although Simpson's treatment of Caputo is fair, clear, and fully documented throughout, that is not to say it is entirely complete. By consistently reducing Caputo's vision to a LeviNietzschean understanding, Simpson treats Caputo's religion as if it is nothing more than an exalted way of speaking about ethics. In other words, if we had only Simpson's reading, we would be left with a Caputo *without passion and without faith*—in short, a Caputo without Søren Kierkegaard. I would argue that a reading of Caputo's religion that fails to account for the deep and abiding impact of Kierkegaard is incomplete at best. And if we put that incomplete Caputo into a debate with Desmond, Caputo is left entering the fray with at least one hand tied behind his back. Second, although there is no denying that Desmond's metaphysical position on religion and ethics provides a viable alternative to Caputo and therefore proves that Caputo's critique of religion need not be the case, this by no means exhausts the full range of appeal for Caputo's work. Caputo might still speak for the disenchanted. And, to give credit where credit is due, in his most recent work Caputo has effectively rehabilitated a distinctly biblical theology of the weakness of God.

First, Simpson's reading of Caputo that collapses his religioethical vision to that of a LeviNietzschean understanding is true insofar as it goes—which is basically to the point of the Caputo of *Radical Hermeneutics*. But its incompleteness effectively ignores the actual—clearly and consistently articulated—religio-passionate faith of Caputo. Although Caputo credits Derrida for "loosening his tongue," the distinctive philosophical style of Caputo's rhetoric was an emulation not of Derrida but of Kierkegaard, for whom Caputo admits he long nurtured a closet love. While Caputo sees Derrida as the more "subtle, elusive, playful and avant-garde writer," he praises Kierkegaard not only as a brilliant humorist but as the "more accessible stylist." Caputo makes it clear that Kierkegaard, rather than Derrida, has had the more consistent influence on him. As Caputo said in an interview from 2002, it was Kierkegaard whom he would read "secretly at night, after the lights went out." It was Kierkegaard who "was [his] secret hero—passionate, Protestant, and provocatively funny." It was Kierkegaard's comic genius that was the antidote to the solemn humorlessness of Heidegger.[12] And it was this humor, as Caputo learned from Johannes Climacus, that served as "the incognito of the religious."

Thus, Caputo's affection for and emulation of Kierkegaard is not merely a matter of literary styling. Kierkegaard not only provides Caputo with the enduring image of the Knight of Faith but also provides him with a comic, irreverent, and provocative style that is the bearer of the religious dimension within Caputo's own work. It is in Kierkegaard's works of love that Caputo finds the fine line between, or aspires beyond, either irony or cynicism. And by recognizing Kierkegaard in Derrida—for example, in the fear and trembling that is so clear and apparent in Derrida's gift of death—Caputo came to his own original insight with regard to postmodern deconstruction. By sometimes calling deconstruction "Danish deconstruction," Caputo is identifying the necessary element of faith that drives the affirmative religious passion in Derrida's own work. In so doing, Caputo was able to recognize "what a bad take it was on deconstruction to view it as aestheticism, as antireligious or irresponsible."[13] And, as we have already seen, it is from this recognition that Caputo effectively redefined postmodern deconstruction from the hermeneutics of the death of God (à la Mark C. Taylor) to a hermeneutics of the kingdom of God.

The Profundity of Faith

Second, there is Simpson's suggestion that the viability of Desmond's metaphysical vision is preferable because Desmond better achieves Caputo's own animating concerns. Again, if we return to Kierkegaard, we can see that Caputo is appealing to those who feel left out or left behind by the conventional treatment of religion. Whereas Kierkegaard's attack on Christendom takes place in a society in which everyone thinks they are Christian, rendering the prospect of living in the likeness of Christ all but an impossibility, Caputo's critique of the historic faiths takes place in a society haunted by the specter of religious fanaticism and the threat of religious violence. Unlike those guilty of confusing their faith with knowledge, Caputo dwells on not only those such as Kierkegaard, who only dares to *aspire* to Christian faith and never claims it as a birthright, but also those such as Dietrich Bonhoeffer and Mother Teresa—those who *know* enough about religious faith to live it out in the midst of their doubt and uncertainty.

As revealed by the publication of Mother Teresa's more-than-sixty-six-year correspondence with her superiors, her saintly life and steadfast allegiance to the

Church, both in terms of the Church's spiritual authority and the rightness of its teachings, continued in the midst of a prolonged dark night of the soul that proved to be no passing phase.[14] On the contrary, it was the private wound that consumed her thoughts throughout her adult life, even in the midst of her increasingly public ministry to the poor and the sick and the outcast. For some, this was a shocking story. For others, such as Christopher Hitchens, it was further confirmation of Teresa's duplicity and further proof that religion is nothing but a human fabrication. Like the rest of Hitchens's writings on religion, this explanation is far too easy because it fails to acknowledge the true complexity of the human psyche. What Teresa's religious torment shows, is that religion can never be reduced to simply a matter of belief or unbelief, which is a truth illustrated in its most focused manner in the vast existentialist literature on the subject. Indeed, as Kierkegaard taught us nearly two hundred years ago, doubt is the necessary companion to faith.

It is precisely this doubt and anxiety that has drawn generation of readers to the spiritual writings of one of Teresa's own Catholic contemporaries, Thomas Merton. Merton's classic modern spiritual autobiography, *The Seven Storey Mountain,* tells the tale of his conversion, and his subsequent writings as a contemplative Trappist monk demonstrate how an authentic faith is no panacea. From the vantage point of the Trappist monastery in rural Kentucky, Merton remained deeply engaged in the modern world as his commitment to a life of contemplation forced him to speak out on various issues ranging from the civil rights movement to nuclear armament and eventually even the need for greater interreligious cooperation and dialogue.

Whereas Merton was held up as a model of the modern man who came to religion only after years of spiritual wandering and futility, Teresa's more straightforward good works and obedience have been seen as a sort of counterpoint. Many assumed that her work with the poor left her little or no time for the self-obsessed quest for authenticity that was the hallmark of Merton and the bulk of his contemporaries. Now we discover that just as Merton's solitude was the means by which he became the critical voice of cultural engagement, so too was Teresa's public life of good works the inevitable and necessary flip side to a penetrating, scathingly honest, and deeply personal internal spiritual quest.

For perhaps what is the closest analogy to this newfound window into Teresa's soul, we should recall the classic story from the Spanish existentialist Miguel de Unamuno, "Saint Manuel Bueno, Martyr." This story, which is set in a small provincial Spanish town in the early twentieth century, is about a simple but saintly parish priest who devotedly carries out his duties by visiting the sick and instructing the faithful. He is beloved and revered by his parishioners. But through it all, he harbors his own secret burden—namely, he cannot bring himself to believe the very truths he proclaims to others. As Unamuno writes of Don Manuel, he "feigned belief, even if he did not feel any." Don Manuel's faith was a *willed unbelief* and a *deliberate hypocrisy*, but the paradox was that it was precisely by this ruse that he lived such a life of integrity and was such a source of blessing and inspiration to others. By asserting a truth that he could not bring himself to believe, others stood as witnesses to his goodness and were saved from his own private despair. Thus, his lie established a truth in a reality that even he himself could not see.

This is the profundity of faith. With these existentialist forbears in mind, what we might say about Teresa's private spiritual agony is that, far from suggesting a "startling portrait in self-contradiction," as the *Time* journalist David van Biema writes, it is only now that we may know Teresa as our fellow sojourner on the path of life. It is by her doubt that her true faith is confirmed, and it is by that fuller and more honest account of her faith that her true vocation as a saintly witness is confirmed. If only we had more faith in doubt, we might move beyond the dogmatic certainties of the believers and unbelievers alike.

Becoming Radical

By my reading, *both* Caputo and Desmond are to be commended for making this very point and appeal. As Simpson eloquently puts it, "Far from providing the assurances of such a pure access to reality, metaphysics as Desmond conceives it disquiets our thinking and strains our language—metaphysics is an insomniac, migraine-courting encounter and struggle with the excess of being that gives rise to the astonishment and perplexity that constitute the abiding engine of metaphysical thought."[15] But again, that one might be disquieted in one's thinking by a metaphysics properly understood does not exhaust the full realm of religious possibility. Of course, Kierkegaard's rejoinder to Hegel is well known. But I should add that *Teresa's spiritual agony was not a metaphysical problem.* When—in the midst of genocide and the general silence, if not complicity, of the Church—Bonhoeffer wrote, "Yet our business now is to replace our rusty swords with sharp ones," he was decidedly not calling for greater metaphysical precision.

That is a long way to go to make a relatively simple observation—one that Caputo no doubt would have made with much greater wit—namely, that there is a difference between the prophet and the philosopher. By invoking the voice of the prophet, Caputo's philosophy of religion performs a timeless and necessary task, a task that must be renewed with every generation.

And this is to say nothing of what I think it is probably most important to say: not only might Caputo's philosophy of religion speak for and to the disenchanted, and not only does his philosophy of religion perform the prophetic task, but, ever since his recent "coming out" as a theologian, he has effectively rehabilitated a distinctly biblical theology of the weakness of God. There are no doubt those who still prefer the magisterium of the Christian tradition along with the metaphysical accoutrements it has accumulated through the centuries. But there are others whose experience and testimony center on the crucified Christ, whose death on a cross was and remains a scandal and a stumbling block. It is for these, whose primary fidelity remains with the living messiah who was left for dead, that a theology of the weakness of a God without sovereignty is a welcome relief.

By using the word *relief*, I do not mean to imply that Caputo's weak theology is a safe and reassuring one. On the contrary, a biblical theology of the weakness of God is a faith that testifies to doubt, that understands doubt as the necessary accompaniment to faith. It is a theology that troubles all certainties, and therefore it is a radical theology. Or, in Caputo's words, it is "the becoming-radical of confessional theology," a nonfoundational way of thinking that begins wherever we are, or wherever we might find ourselves, and follows thought to the edge and beyond. It is radical in the sense that it is "radically exposed," not knowing the full risks of faith, where the thought will lead, or what the future holds. *Radical* here means risky, without guarantees. Following the original semantic meaning of the word, we see that the term *radical* seeks to get at the root, but as Caputo insists, "goes to the roots of classical theology and uproots them, pulling up by the root the *logos* of the old theology and replacing it with a poetics."[16]

This uprooting does not just trouble certainties but also troubles authorities. It is on this point that the distinction Caputo makes between two types of Continental philosophy of religion is instructive. First, there is the Kantian type, which he describes as an "abridged edition of postmodernism," or as "postmodernism light," in the sense that it ultimately serves the apologetic aims of a confessional theology.[17] This kind of Continental philosophy of religion resembles radical theology in that it subjects faith to the most radical critique, purging religion of its excesses, its dogmatism, and its superstitions. It reads, understands, and has absorbed the modern and postmodern critiques of religion, whether those critiques come from the Enlightenment philosophes, those proclaiming the death of God, or, more recently, those who invoke the specter of religious violence and terrorism to link religion with a fundamentally antimodern, antiscientific, and irrational fanaticism. But it accomplishes this by accepting a basic Kantian Enlightenment epistemology that separates faith from knowledge. So while it subjects faith to the most radical critique, the faith itself is not so much purged as safely quarantined.

The problem with this thinking is that it simultaneously goes too far and not far enough. It goes too far in the sense that faith is not only epistemologically distinguished from knowledge, but also purified from it. Faith is sacralized and is therefore made untouchable. By delimiting knowledge to make room for faith, the impulse to disassociate faith from knowledge and power is taken to the extreme such that faith is disassociated from history and culture as well. Religion is reduced to a kind of fideism, a will-to-faith that operates by the neoliberal cultural logic of identity.[18] This first type of Continental philosophy of religion does not go far enough—or, as Caputo puts it, "fails to get as far as radical theology"—because it fails to truly uproot the logos at work. The classical binary distinction between two worlds and two orders of knowledge remains intact, but now it is merely assumed rather than defended, merely asserted rather than argued.[19]

In the second type of Continental philosophy of religion—by contrast more Hegelian than Kantian—faith is not separated from knowledge as much as it becomes the stuff of thought. Just as Caputo's earlier "coming out" as a theologian was a great turning point in his work, so too is this identification with Hegel. By testifying as a "born-again Hegelian" (albeit, in Caputo's words, a "heretical version of Hegel" or a "headless [Hegelian] without the Concept"), Caputo has departed from his earlier dismissive attitude toward Hegel for Hegel's totalitarian tendencies.[20] In so doing, he has breathed new life into the lineage of radical theology. Religious faith cannot so easily be separated from theological thought, even the religiosity of the private prayers and tears of a deconstructed religion without religion. Likewise, theological thinking cannot so automatically be associated with ontotheology. Or, better, drawing on the argument from chapter 4 and perhaps radicalizing Caputo beyond where he himself is willing to go, ontotheology cannot so automatically be identified as a problem to be overcome. Thinking theologically about God as first cause or highest being no more locks us into a self-same world without change than does saying revelation is *tout autre* imply a supernatural message from beyond. "A revelation does indeed break in upon us as a *tout autre* interrupting our lives," Caputo insists, "unsettling beliefs and practices, not because it comes from outside space and time but because it interrupts the spacing and timing of the given world with a new form of spacing and timing, a new and unforeseen way to be. A revelation is not a message from another world, but a new and unforeseeable messaging of the world itself, of history itself."[21]

The great virtue of this rendering of radical theology is that it demonstrates the potential connection between the becoming-radical of theology as thought with religion as lived and practiced. Specifically, religion *yields* radical theology insofar as confessional theology "allows itself to yield to the insistence of the event, to the pressure the event puts on confessional theology."[22] The distinction, then, is not between faith and knowledge, as Kant and the postmodern fideist would have it, but between the first-order operation of religious beliefs and practices and the second-order reflection. In this case, though, because the radical theologian does not report back to any ecclesial authority—and hence radical theology is a secular theology—he reserves the right to ask any question, follow any lead, and risk the utmost apostasy.

To be clear, this makes radical theology parasitic, feeding off the stuff of religion while making no promises in exchange. Moreover, as a second-order reflection, radical theology does not simply reflect on (or feed off of) the lived practices and beliefs of religion but also reflects on the reflections offered up by confessional theologies. Caputo describes this as a double effect—a reflection that is admittedly a twisting, distorting, and subverting that effects both a displacement and an affirmation, an ironic distancing that reveals the historical contingencies of any and all faith communities, and an opening up to the event that insists on itself by the name of God. Thus, although radical theology is parasitic, it need not be conceived as a kind of vampirism. Instead, it can testify to the symbiosis of nature—a parasitic relationality that is a form of mutualism, cohabitation, and even co-creation. As Caputo puts it:

> While the work of radical theology is critical and subversive of what the actors embedded in first-order beliefs and practices are doing, its effect is not, at least not ultimately, negative. Nothing is worth our trouble if our only aim is to make trouble for it. . . . We see this when Kierkegaard's Johannes Climacus declines the compliment of "being" Christian and prefers to speak of "becoming" one, when Bonhoeffer speaks of religionless Christianity, and when Levinas speaks of loving the Torah more than God.[23]

So while acknowledging that this last point is one in need of much greater elaboration, I must also say that there is something to Caputo's unrelenting deconstructive vision that has led him to run Derrida, Vattimo, Catherine Keller, and Walter Benjamin together with St. Paul, a fortuitous linking that does not so much defend biblical religion to its cultured despisers as twist and turn the Bible to a surprising and forgotten revelation. This too is a viable religious vision. And, insofar as it is biblically faithful, it might also be a preferable one.

SEVEN

A Farewell to Radical Orthodoxy

In the last chapter I examined the radical theological appeal of the work of John Caputo regarding the nondebate in contemporary philosophical theology, and in this chapter I examine one particular debate that represents a false option. Specifically, I examine—from the edited exchange by Creston Davis, *The Monstrosity of Christ*—the debate between Slavoj Žižek and the British radical orthodox theologian John Milbank. We have already noted in previous chapters how Milbank's radical orthodoxy represents a theological alternative to the postmetaphysical approach to radical theology of those such as Caputo. My question in this chapter, which is more suggestive than fully developed, is not so much whether the radicalism of Milbank's radical orthodoxy is worthy of the name but more whether it is a radicalism that has any merit beyond that of putting up a good fight.

Moreover, we must ask the question of whether this skirmish—which, it should be noted, is yet another turf war being played out among white European males—has any broader significance. The question has a particular salience for this present work, considering my own stated intentions to open the legacy of radical theology beyond the presumed entitlement of Western man come-of-age after the death of God. A radical theology of the future must be deprovincialized; only then can it realize its dormant political, ontological, and cultural implications. And so it is that I wish to frame this debate over radical orthodoxy by revisiting the meaning of the designation of radical, which both radical orthodoxy and radical theology share. As I have already made clear, the meaning of radical I wish to affirm is that it must be more radical than rebellious, that it should be neither mere defiance nor the expression of an oedipal complex but instead a willingness to get at the roots of a discourse by thinking to its limits in such a way that it risks its utter dissolution while suffering change. The radicality of radical theology, so conceived, is more about identifying the provinciality and provenance of a certain lineage of thought than it is about self-styling. By this reading, then, radical orthodoxy, although extreme, fails to qualify as a truly radical theology. The failure of radical orthodoxy lies in its explicit disavowal of its own history, a disavowal that is as forgetful and disingenuous as it is imperialistic.

The Next Martin Luther

John Milbank was introduced in June 2000 to a broad American academic audience in a high-profile article written by Jeff Sharlet that appeared in *The Chronicle of Higher Education*. Sharlet introduced Milbank as the "earthly creator of Radical Orthodoxy" and speculated that Milbank's movement "may well become the biggest development in theology since Martin Luther nailed his 95 theses to the church door."[1] A year later, *Time Magazine* declared Milbank a bona fide "academic star" and identified him as one of its seven innovative thinkers for the new millennium, crediting him especially with clearing "a way for theologians to reclaim their place at the academic table, ending decades, if not centuries, of marginalization."[2]

Of course, those who know Milbank and his work should not be surprised at these exalted claims for his place in the history of Christian theology. For instance, in a formal session of the annual meeting of the American Academy of Religion, he once declared, "Martin Luther says unto you, justification by faith. But I say unto you, there is no justice without authority."[3] With his sudden adoption of King James English and his evocation of the familiar rhetorical structure of Jesus's own Sermon on the Mount, Milbank seemed to have taken the mantle of Martin Luther to heart.

This linking of Milbank with Luther goes to the heart of Milbank's—and by extension, radical orthodoxy's—evolving theological project. I think it also helps to establish the context for the theological debate between Milbank and Žižek on the "monstrosity of Christ." Put briefly, I could sum up what I mean by this link between Milbank and Luther with the reference points of history and the Protestant Reformation. And, my thesis for this present chapter is as follows: with his counternarrative trope of constructing an alternative history to modernity, Milbank has defined the school of radical orthodoxy according to the principal task of undoing the Protestant Reformation. So, if in fact radical orthodoxy proves to be the biggest development in theology since Martin Luther (a proposition of which I am highly skeptical, by the way), and if in fact Milbank has his way, we might as well pretend that the social, cultural, political, and religious torment that was the Protestant Reformation never happened at all and, by extension, that the Christian church might once again revel in the imperial glory of Christendom.

If this thesis strikes some as exaggerated, in my defense I must at the very least cite Milbank's stated goal of converting Žižek from the "Whiggish, Protestant" that Milbank reads him to be into the Catholic that he might become. Although the terms of their debate are established according to whether a paradoxical or dialectical perspective is best, these too are pitched with regard to the Protestant-Catholic divide. As Milbank tells it, it is Žižek's endorsement of a Hegelian dialectic that makes him all too Protestant. Further, "it is the dialectical perspective itself which engenders the nihilistic version of Christian universalism."[4] So, if, by Milbank's telling, dialectics are a "symptom" of an essentially modern, Protestant metanarrative, and if dialectics engender nihilism, then wouldn't we be correct to conclude that Protestantism is a form of nihilism? We might read Milbank's rejoinder to Žižek, therefore, not only as an ironic reading of Žižek—an effort to out-Žižek Žižek, if you will—but also as an effort to save Žižek from himself, to cure him of his ill-informed and superficial appropriation of Protestantism. As Milbank announces, "My case is that there is a different, latent Žižek: a Žižek who does not see Chesterton as sub-Hegel, but Hegel as sub-Chesterton. A Žižek therefore who has remained with paradox, or rather moved back into paradox from dialectics. And this remaining would be sufficient to engender a Catholic Žižek, a Žižek able fully to endorse a transcendent God, in whom creatures analogically participate."[5]

Milbank's repudiation of Protestantism is part and parcel of his rejection of history. As Milbank explains:

> The defense of paradox has to be conjoined with a refusal of the Protestant metanarrative in which Žižek is in thrall. In fact, at both the theoretical and the historical level the issue of Catholic versus Protestant is far more fundamental than the question of theism versus atheism—the latter is merely a subplot of the former conflict, which is today notably resurfacing. The key illusion of the Protestant metanarrative is that the mode in which modernity has occurred, and the stages that it has gone through, are the necessary and only possible modes and stages.[6]

This extended quote needs considerable unpacking. First, note how Milbank speaks of the intrareligious relations between Catholics and Protestants as a conflict in which Catholics are pitted against Protestants. Second, note the sly association of modern history with an illusion, as if our history is something from which we can pick and choose, or repudiate and reverse. I will take each of these observations up in turn.

First, the intimation of violence suggested by this quote has long been a source of concern for critics of radical orthodoxy. Sharlet was correct to point out in his aforementioned article on Milbank that "of the various strains of postliberal theology, Radical Orthodoxy is by far the most political." This is partly due to the Christian socialist background in Britain, but radical orthodoxy could even more be seen as a harbinger of the recent political turn in philosophical and theological circles. Certainly since the 9/11 attacks on New York City and Washington, DC, there has been a consuming interest in the relation between religion and politics and the specter of religious violence. This geopolitical reality reinforces electioneering strategies on the US domestic front, as George W. Bush was twice elected president largely due to the effective political mobilization of the religious Right. This political turn also reflects a generational change in the world of Continental philosophy, as leading French poststructuralist thinkers whose postpolitical identities were forged during the student protests of May 1968 have given way to outspoken critics who have been willing to venture forth with their own explicit political programs. The Continental philosophical thinkers of this new generation, led by Alain Badiou, Giorgio Agamben, and Antonio Negri, have been most critical of how easily classical modern liberalism mutates into, or can be conflated with, globalizing neoliberalism and, in a related fashion, how difficult it is for postmodern deconstruction to translate itself into a politics of collective action. As one scholar puts it, "The tragedy of the politics of subjectivity (at least the Derridean version thereof) is that it has no way of inserting the subject into the domain of the actually political."[7] Thus, this new generation of thinkers is offering up an alternative postmodernism that is deliberately more postliberal than poststructural and is therefore a repoliticization of cultural theory.

Both Žižek and Milbank belong within this general trajectory of the political turn, a point made at the very outset of their exchange in the introduction that sets the stage for the debate between these two towering figures. "In the pages that follow," the editor writes, "the orthodox Christian theologian John Milbank and the militant Marxist Slavoj Žižek engage one another around this revolutionary political problematic: How can the theological and the material unite to fund resistance to capitalist nihilism?"[8] But if it is a revolutionary political problematic that Milbank shares in common with Žižek and that distinguishes radical orthodoxy from the other variants of postliberal theology, then it is necessary to ask, as Sharlet did, what exactly does Milbank believe—or, more precisely, of what exactly would a radical orthodox politics consist? In addressing this question, Sharlet speculated then that "maybe orthodoxy sounds like theocracy. . . . More to the point, then, one wonders whether a Radical Orthodox world might resemble a premodern one, in which the church ruled, and heretics, instead of waxing philosophical in endowed chairs, were burned alive at the stake."

To be sure, to be political does not mean to be violent or to sanction political violence, but there is this nagging sense from Sharlet and repeated many times over that Milbank and the school of radical orthodox theology he represents are unapologetic Christian triumphalists. The question is whether this specter of violence is an inevitable consequence of its metaphysical predilection. That it is would certainly be the argument of a contemporary such as Vattimo, a postmetaphysical hermeneutic philosopher who has made the direct link between the history of metaphysics and violence. Indeed, Vattimo has argued that the very idea of metaphysics is a violent imposition.[9] In an earlier published review of the debate between Milbank and Žižek, Caputo asks a similar question: "Why not adopt the post-metaphysical idea that gives up searching for all such primordial underlying somethings or other?" The reason this postmetaphysical idea might be preferable, Caputo suggests, is that it would avoid the violence that is apparent throughout the book, both from Žižek, who, as Caputo writes, does not have "the slightest compunction about invoking violence," and from Milbank, who "batters our ears with a barrage of rhetorical violence, with the vintage violence of theological imperialism."[10] Like Vattimo, Caputo harbors a suspicion about metaphysics and concludes his review with the observation that "this polemic about the metaphysics of Christ" somehow squeezes out entirely the peaceful and peace-loving Jesus of the Sermon on the Mount.

Hardening the Death of God

Before we turn to the issue of Milbank's rejection of history, more must be said about this postmetaphysical theological challenge. But, incidentally, it is Žižek, not Milbank, who directly takes up this challenge. He does so by referencing Vattimo and Caputo specifically in a rebuttal of their respective postmetaphysical and deconstructive variants of postmodern theology—variants that Žižek labels as "soft" postmodern theology.[11] Žižek begins his rebuttal by pronouncing a changing of the guard from Derrida and Habermas to Agamben and Badiou or, in other words, from ethicopolitico philosophies of otherness to "its [contemporary theory's] theologico-political turn: a decidedly materialist focus on [a] theological topic . . . ; a radical political stance inclusive of a critical attitude toward democracy—to put it in a vicious way, democracy is not to come, but to go." This is to be "the first true taste of 'thought of the twenty-first century.'"[12] Then, after summarizing the common features in each of Caputo's and Vattimo's narrations of the so-called postmodern return of religion, Žižek goes on to insist on a theme familiar in his previous work on religion—namely, the subversive and perverse core of Christianity.[13]

For Žižek, Caputo and Vattimo pass too quickly and easily from the trauma of the death of God to the death of the death of God in the postmodern return of religion. In this (soft) reading, the death of God is rendered a happy event—a shedding of the moral-metaphysical God of ontotheology and a reawakening of genuinely biblical faith and a more authentic form of religiosity. But, on the contrary, "What dies on the Cross," Žižek insists, "is indeed God himself, not just his 'finite container,' a historically contingent name or form of God." When Žižek continues by saying that "the only way to redeem the subversive core of Christianity is therefore to return to death-of-God theology," he has Thomas J. J. Altizer's Hegelian variant of death-of-God theology specifically in mind.[14] Indeed, it is not an exaggeration to say that Žižek's reading of the death of God is entirely derivative of Altizer's, in which there is a total eclipse of God and dissolution of transcendence.[15]

As Altizer has recently written, "The apocalyptic transfiguration of the Godhead has been my deepest theological commitment as a radical theologian."[16] And so, in stark contrast to the postmetaphysical and largely cultural reading of the death of God offered by Caputo and Vattimo, Žižek concludes:

> It is thus not that death-of-God theology is a middle-of-the-road phenomenon, partially negating the classical onto-theology while remaining within its horizon, which is truly left behind only with postmodern deconstructive religion; it is rather that something traumatic erupts in death-of-God theology, something that is covered up by postmodern theology. We should go even further here: what if the entire history of Christianity, inclusive of (and especially) its Orthodox versions, is structured as a series of defenses against the traumatic apocalyptic core of incarnation/death/resurrection?[17]

In this passage, too, Žižek is repeating the themes long invoked by Altizer. Here it is the way in which a truly radical theology must necessarily express itself in terms of an assault on the history of the church. Here it is the ironic reversal, whether from Kierkegaard or Nietzsche, that it is only by an "attack upon Christendom" that the original way of Jesus may be restored. And so it is that Žižek-come-Altizer preaches the "good news" of Christian atheism.[18]

Although derivative, in this exchange Žižek still nevertheless shows himself as an adept theological thinker, which gives credence to his attempt at the revitalization of death-of-God theology through his seemingly oxymoronic atheistic theological materialism. His contribution to this debate is more theological than it is philosophical, anthropological, or even religious in that it is concerned with the being and nature of God by asking the core question of Christology. Indeed, along the way he even takes his materialists forerunners, Feuerbach and Marx, to task by identifying "the limit of the Feuerbaching-Marxian logic of dis-alienation."[19] Žižek thus not only rises to the postmetaphysical theological challenge but also provides the contours of what might be termed a new materialism. There is nothing in all of this that should lead one to think that Žižek is merely a Johnny-come-lately playing in the field of theologians or that his engagement with religion is merely an ironic strategy—or, in the words of Caputo, a "Trojan-horse theology."[20] Perhaps it is the case that Žižek could have come to his conclusions just as easily by Lacan or Hitchcock as by Christ, but there is no denying that when it comes to his analysis of the meaning of Christ's death on the cross, he has the power to evoke the original scandal of the gospel as well as, if not better than, any other contemporary thinker. Further, this reminder of the scandal of the gospel is an important and timely corrective to the triumphalistic tendencies of Christianity as well as to the facile, self-help, or fundamentalist tendencies of contemporary religion.

As Žižek writes, "Christ's death on the Cross thus means that we should imme-diately ditch the notion of God as a transcendent caretaker who guarantees the happy outcome of our acts, the guarantee of historical teleology—Christ's death on the Cross is the death of *this* God, it repeats Job's stance, it refuses any 'deeper meaning' that obfuscates the brutal reality of historical catastrophes." And on this point at least, Žižek stands together with Caputo and Vattimo and against Milbank in fully sharing the idea "of Christ as a weak God, a God reduced to a compassion-ate observer of human misery, unable to intervene or help."[21]

Radical Orthodoxy as Christianity Proper

The preceding discussion brings me back to the issue of history and to Mil-bank's counternarrative trope: where Žižek's atheistic theological materialism leads him to an embrace of the void and to the conclusion of the essential mean-inglessness of human history, Milbank's orthodox theological materialism leads him to a position he terms a "more Catholic historiography" that reads modern history as a "distortion." Although this modern history is "full of authentically Christian developments," Milbank admits that it has led to "horrendous distor-tions" because it has been allowed to occur "outside a proper Catholic aegis." Along the way, while defending a paternalism modified "with a greater humility and attentiveness to populist feedback," Milbank links Protestantism with athe-ism, calls capitalism "a mode of Protestant religion" that provides "theological legitimation of a new sort of 'amoral' economic practice," and ultimately finds in Protestant Christianity nothing but "totalitarian gloom." Correlatively, it is the "pre-Cartesian Catholic metaphysical vision" that truly makes possible the joy of sex and universal love. Further, "whereas Žižek's atheism achieves only a sad, re-signed materialism," Milbank claims it is his Catholic perspective that "achieves a materialism in a joyful, positive sense."[22]

It is hard to know whether or not to take this unrelenting denigration of Protestantism seriously. My main contention is that what it truly reveals is that Mil-bank does not take history seriously. His history operates as a kind of fabulation. He repeatedly accuses Žižek of buying into a Protestant narrative of progress and of treating history as a series of inevitable advances. Meanwhile, he makes much of his own version of an "alternative Trinitarian modernity" and a "more humanist Reformation" as the road not taken.[23] Admittedly, his vision is a beautiful and en-ticing one. His vision is of a world in which post-Reformation dogmatics and inter-religious violence would not have dominated early modern European life, of "less dualism of nature and grace in theory and of secular and sacred in practice—with the upshot that economic and political institutions might have remained more ec-clesiastically shaped, even though now more lay-directed."[24] But wishing it so does not make it so. Whether he is pretending we could have a humbler paternalism that is now attentive to populist feedback or a return to a church monopoly under a proper Catholic aegis that is now more lay directed, his vision is predicated on such a complete flight of fancy that it requires more than a leap of faith. Instead, it is a willful denial and denigration of history.

Our history may very well be a misbegotten path, but there is a great distance between the notion that the modern world is the historical triumph of the necessary outworking of a material logic and the notion that we may reverse or repudiate history at our whim. It is true that our history is full of latent possibilities and of roads not taken, but the way to build a different and better future does not come by way of denial. Beware of the return of the repressed.

Beyond the concern over defending the positive value of Protestantism, my real point of contention belongs on the theopolitical terrain. This is what it looks like in schematic form: (1) Milbank's disavowal and unrelenting denigration of Protestantism is achieved by way of, and is part and parcel with, his denial of history; (2) Milbank's fabulated history betrays a lingering Christian triumphalism in which an "ecclesiastically shaped, even though now more lay-directed" world of sacred harmony still nevertheless operates according to the principles of a church monopoly;[25] (3) no matter how much Milbank tries to temper the excesses of past church monopolies (for example, Milbank is even so bold as to defend a paternalism sufficiently modified "with a greater humility and attentiveness to populist feedback"[26]) by imaginatively reconstructing an alternative history ripe with alternative possibilities for a better future, this is nothing more than a theological flight of fancy; (4) wishing it so does not make it so; and (5) moreover, it is this wish itself that harbors within it a history of sacred violence that itself must be reckoned with and put to rest.

The Milbank Effect

The one element I would like to add to this multifaceted bone of contention is a seditious one. Although I affirm without condition Davis's articulation of the "revolutionary political problematic" shared by Milbank and Žižek and agree that it raises the question, "How can the theological and material unite to fund resistance to capitalist nihilism,"[27] following the technical definition that William James offers in "The Will to Believe," I am not persuaded that the choice between Milbank or Žižek leaves us with a "genuine option." This is the point Clayton Crockett makes when he writes, "We cannot (even if we desperately want to) simply choose Sunday over Saturday, paradox over dialectics, or even vice versa."[28] It is also the main critique offered up by Caputo when he asks, "What exactly is the compelling need we are under to agree with either one of these positions or to choose between them? Why do we have to love either one of these monsters? . . .

Why inscribe either absolute contradiction or absolute peace at the heart of things instead of ambience and ambiguity?"[29]

This is not to say that Milbank and Žižek do not present us with a choice. Indeed, Davis rightly frames the debate that exists between at least these two particular figures as a debate over paradox or dialectics offering up two differing Christological interpretations that give way to two opposing versions of materialism. One is a theological materialism in which the material world is seen as God's good creation anchored in the transcendent glory of God, and the other is a (atheistic) materialist materialism of radical contingency and total freedom. The exchange works by the terms it sets for itself. The stakes and urgency of their projects are clearly articulated. But what I do mean to suggest—where my sedition comes in—is my growing sense that the time has come for radical theology to lay down its arms against Milbank and the school of radical orthodoxy he has come to represent, not because his belligerence has become any more palpable but because his moment has passed.

Consider what has by now become common wisdom after the death of Osama bin Laden. When the nearly decade-long manhunt for bin Laden came to a conclusion with the Navy SEAL raid dubbed Operation Neptune Spear, he had already been swept to the sidelines of world events by the democratic uprisings that had ruptured the accepted order of the Arab world. First in Tunisia and then quickly thereafter in Egypt, the people's power had been shown in force. Leaderless, nonviolent, nonideological even, the protests in Tunisia and Egypt delivered more to their people in a short span, with the toppling of two hardened and ensconced dictatorial regimes in two successive months, than al-Qaeda or its affiliates ever did or ever could. As Jacques Derrida explained in his dialogue with Giovanna Borradori in the immediate aftermath of 9/11, in theoretical terms what made the "bin Laden effect" so unacceptable, beyond even its "cruelty, [its] disregard for human life, [its] disrespect for law [and] for women, [and its] use of what is worst in techno-capitalist modernity for the purpose of religious fanaticism," was that its actions "*open onto no future and, in my view, have no future.*"[30] So even as bin Laden's execution was celebrated on the streets of New York City, his death had long since been assured by the stillborn revolution he wrought.

Even though bin Laden so successfully fought the war of imagery against the United States, with his death there was a doubling down on his ignominy with the dissemination of the image of him with remote control in hand, watching the carefully crafted image of himself on television. Or there were the several outtakes of him with different shades of black dye in his beard delivering ominous messages of warning to the West. Which shades of black or gray look just right to project the appropriate image of austerity and vigor for a man holed up in a compound valued at three million dollars? Even worse, when bin Laden's final recorded message was released a couple of weeks after his death, he himself, as the purported leader of the radical edge of Islam, was seen to be playing catch-up to the revolutionary events of the so-called Arab Spring. He was brandishing his credentials on the backs of the movements of the very people who had rejected his promised means of deliverance—his was a voice from a dead man who, even while he had still been alive, had become the agent of his own irrelevance.

It is a stretch, perhaps, but I believe an instructive one, to compare the bin Laden effect with what might be termed the Milbank effect. If we recall the Sharlet profile on Milbank, we see that great promise and excitement was associated with the earliest days of radical orthodoxy. It was announced most clearly by Milbank himself in the introduction to his breakout book, *Theology and Social Theory.* Milbank defined the book's purpose as showing how Christian theology, properly understood, accomplishes a "demolition of modern, secular social theory."[31] But to accomplish this task Milbank believed it necessary for Christian theology to disavow and overcome its own pathos, or false humility, and reclaim its status as a metadiscourse. He insisted on Christian theology as the "ultimate organizing logic." Otherwise it ran the risk of falling prey to various forms of idolatry, making a God of modern secular reason. For Milbank, the stakes could not be any higher, for "only Christian theology now offers a discourse able to position and overcome nihilism itself."[32] By Milbank's reckoning, then, theologians will not reclaim simply any place at the academic table, but only the place at the head of the table. What makes theology theological is its authority "to position, qualify or criticize other discourses," willfully asserting its position as the queen of the sciences.[33] The logic of Christianity is thus undeconstructible because it is transcendent to and independent of secular reason.

If this was the promise, then the Milbank effect was the refashioning of what is essentially *an imperialistic Christian logic as the condition of peace.* But as Gavin Hyman has persuasively argued, this counternarrative trope is "characterized by an inescapable violence,"[34] which is particularly problematic for Milbank, considering his apologetic on behalf of Christianity—namely, that the logic of Christianity operates according to an ontology of peace rather than violence and thus tells the story much better than does secular reason. In Milbank's words, "Christianity . . . recognizes no original violence." On the contrary, the infinite is construed as "harmonic peace" founded in "the *sociality* of harmonious difference."[35] But whereas Milbank's claim is that the Christian story respects difference, others have charged that his theology rests on a subsumption of difference that actually obliterates difference altogether.[36] This is the concern expressed by Victor Taylor regarding Milbank's rendering of the materiality of Christ's body. By simultaneously being and belonging to a totality of materiality, Milbank's theological materialism "renders all difference as sameness," as "Christ/God becomes/is the 'set of all sets' as he dies *and* resurrects himself." This divine act of collecting and sorting not only preserves the "concept of the 'simple oneness' and ultimacy of God" but, by Taylor's analysis, actually *eradicates* "all difference in general, even different ideas." What Milbank calls "peace," therefore, Taylor rightfully describes as theological "hegemony," giving clarity to the Milbank effect as an offer of peace under the condition of a "difference-less totalitarianism."[37]

Returning to bin Laden, I want to point out that his subscription to a "maximalist" understanding of religion has been well chronicled. He believed that religion ought to permeate all aspects of human society.[38] He thus constructed his grievance against the West in religious terms, leaving no room left for neutrality, hesitation, or middle ground. Just as clear is that his radical militancy left him increasingly isolated from, and a source of embarrassment to, many of the Islamist leaders and ideologists with whom he had once had common cause. As early as 1996, when bin Laden left Sudan for Afghanistan, where he forged his partnership with the Taliban to foment a worldwide jihad against the West, signs of failure for the jihad extremists in places such as Bosnia, Algeria, and Egypt were already apparent, effectively bringing the global Islamist movement to a standstill. Gilles Kepel, the prominent French scholar of radical Islam, told this story even before the 9/11 attacks in his book, *Jihad: The Trial of Political Islam*. As Kepel put it, desperate terrorist acts have not and perhaps cannot ever "translate easily into political victory and legitimate power."[39]

Of course, bin Laden continued to steal headlines around the world, but, meanwhile, more and more Islamist leaders and groups were rejecting the violence by which bin Laden came to be defined. This was especially true after that violence, once projected outward against the West, became a plague on its own territories and populations because the jihadist ideology provided sanction to sectarian purges as rival factions sought to wrest political control from their political rivals. In the place of—or, more accurately, in the very midst of—this religious violence, there was what John Esposito has termed the Quiet Revolution, in which Islamic political movements came to power through ballots, not bullets.[40] These movements were most prominent in Turkey and Indonesia and are still hoped for in Tunisia in the wake of the Arab Spring. In the words of Kepel, after the jihadist militants of bin Laden and his ilk failed to deliver on their promises to the Muslim world, "Many Islamist leaders, ideologists, and intellectuals would advocate a clean break with armed struggle and seek ways of integrating the Muslim cultural heritage with democratic values, in opposition to the authoritarian behavior of the regimes."[41] So although the death of bin Laden was news, it must be noted that long before his death the Islamist coalition that he claimed to represent was already looking "for ways to escape the cul-de-sac into which they had been led."[42]

Like bin Laden, Milbank came to prominence at a particular moment in time when his defense of the singularity and exclusivity of Christian truth came to many as a welcome relief from the "current global tendencies toward increased mobility, indeterminacy, and hybridity" characteristic of most postmodernist discourses.[43] But given his radical posture against modern secular reason, his radical orthodoxy is defined not just as an antimodernist movement but as a kind of de-modernization. In light of this posture, the same analysis made by Antonio Negri and Michael Hardt of the current appeal of religious fundamentalisms can be applied to Milbank and radical orthodoxy as well—namely, that they are driven by a "powerful refusal of the contemporary historical passage in course." To say, then, as Hardt and Negri do, that they are best understood "not as a *pre*modern but as a *post*modern project"[44] is not simply to agree with Don Cupitt's critique that radical orthodoxy represents a "laundered facsimile of tradition"[45] but to believe that, as a distortion of a tradition and a denigration of history, it is a project without a future.

Milbank has always been up for a good debate, and he proves a worthy partner to the dazzling and dizzying mind of Žižek. Radical orthodoxy has always been up for a good fight as well. In his debate with Žižek, for instance, Milbank pits the Catholic against the Protestant metanarrative, which holds that Protestantism is good for nothing beyond "totalitarian gloom" (131). But such rhetorical excesses are so beyond the pale that to continue to fight back only legitimates the ridicule. Meanwhile, the march of history continues apace. We can no more deny it than we can escape it. The Milbank effect has run its course. Unless and until he recognizes the violence endemic to the exclusionary logic he continues to propound, the radical theology of the future may leave him and the radical orthodoxy he helped to create safely in the past.

EIGHT

God Is Green

Or, a New Theology of Indulgence

We all contribute to climate change, but none of us can individually be blamed for it. So we walk around with a free-floating sense of guilt that's unlikely to be lifted by the purchase of wind-power credits or halogen bulbs. Annina Rüst, a Swiss-born artist-inventor, wanted to help relieve these anxieties by giving people a tangible reminder of their own energy use, as well as an outlet for the feelings of complicity, shame and powerlessness that surround the question of global warming.

So she built a translucent leg band that keeps track of your electricity consumption. When it detects, via a special power monitor, that electric current levels have exceeded a certain threshold, the wireless device slowly drives six stainless-steel thorns into the flesh of your leg. "It's therapy for environmental guilt," says Rüst, who modeled her "personal techno-garter" on the spiked bands worn as a means of self-mortification by a monk in Dan Brown's novel "The Da Vinci Code."

—From *The New York Times Magazine*,
"The 8th Annual Year in Ideas" (12/14/08)

All those who believe themselves certain of their own salvation by means of letters of indulgence, will be eternally damned, together with their teachers.

—Martin Luther, Thesis 32 from the Ninety-Five Theses

In 1940, Dietrich Bonhoeffer spoke with Colonel Oster at the *Abwehr* meeting, during which he was enlisted in the plot against Adolf Hitler that would eventually lead to his imprisonment and execution. Shortly after this meeting, Bonhoeffer penned what remains one of the most scathing attacks against theoretical or systematic ethics. As he wrote in his unfinished book *Ethics* in the opening paragraph of the chapter "Ethics as Formation," ethical reasoning had become entirely superfluous, but not because of indifference and certainly not because of irrelevance. "On the contrary," Bonhoeffer wrote, "it arises from the fact that our period, more than any earlier period in the history of the west, is oppressed by a superabounding reality of concrete ethical problems."[1] In addition to exposing the failure of moral theorists, Bonhoeffer also exposes the ethical failings of so-called reasonable people, ethical purists—or, in his words, fanatics—who believe they "can oppose the power of evil with the purity of [their] will and of [their principle]." These are people such as the solitary individual of conscience who "fights a lonely battle against the overwhelming forces of inescapable situations which demand decisions," the person of duty who "will end by having to fulfil his obligation even to the devil," and the privately virtuous who "knows how to remain punctiliously within the permitted bounds which preserve him from involvement in conflict" and who thereby "must be blind and deaf to the wrongs which surround him."[2] Bonhoeffer saw each of these paths as false, or at least insufficient, to meet the challenge of his age, and, in what is perhaps the most recognized sentence from this fragmentary and unfinished work, he issues a clarion call: "Yet our business now is to replace our rusty swords with sharp ones."[3]

We have already seen how John Caputo cites Bonhoeffer's notion of a religionless Christianity for its subversive and affirmative potentiality. Caputo is not alone. Any lineage of radical theology necessarily includes Bonhoeffer, whether for his moral clarity, courage, and self-sacrifice and empathy or as a forerunner to the death-of-God theologians by his invocation of a "world come of age," in which the recourse to the hypothesis of God is no longer deemed necessary. At the same time, by identifying with Bonhoeffer, radical theology runs the risk of hagiography. At a minimum, we must acknowledge that a great gulf separates us from the ethical, political, and religious challenges Bonhoeffer faced, that the sharp swords forged in the crucible of the Nazi threat must be sharpened yet again, if not replaced altogether.

Here we stand yet again at such a moment of a widening economic inequality, a widespread political disillusionment, if not outright cynicism, and an unsustainably paced escalation of the global demand for energy that will only compound the environmental degradation already wrought. We stand intimately interconnected and interdependent with those around the world through the apparent triumph of global capital, but we have outmoded political institutions and ideas to rein in what the political theorist Benjamin Barber rightly identifies as "savage capitalism."[4] And our religion, long caught up either in engaging in the culture wars and the micropolitics of identity or in voluntarily confining itself to little more than self-help therapy, finds itself once again thrust into the public domain, forcing a fundamental theopolitical reevaluation of the basic modern liberal assumptions of the secular sphere as the naked public square.

This chapter marks a transition in the same spirit as Bonhoeffer's ethicotheological challenge born of political crisis. Specifically, I want to transition from what I have argued are the moribund (non)debates of the past to more pressing matters in contemporary culture, from what I consider the stillborn attempt at reactivating an explicit form of Christian imperialism via radical orthodoxy to the more modest effort at examining what radical theology might learn from and contribute to an engagement with the environment, race, and liberationist thought. This foray into cultural theology should not be thought of as an appendage to the book's primary effort to develop a radical theological method for change. On the contrary, this journey is the very means by which I am hoping not simply to demonstrate the contemporary relevance of radical theology but, more importantly, to reactivate and expand it. By directly engaging these matters of pressing contemporary concern, I am deliberately pushing the limits of radical theology to make the case that a radical theology of the future must become political and ontological in order for it to realize whatever cultural and ecclesiastical relevancy and impact it might once have believed its birthright.

That said, it would be a mistake to read this chapter as a practical theology. Although it is cultural, it is no less theoretical. Methodologically speaking, radical cultural theology is a work at theorizing otherwise. I want to show how cultural artifacts and events from history can serve as images of thought that evoke new associations and alternative assemblages. Demonstrating this is essential to developing a theological method for change because it changes both the parameters and direction of radical theology. Thus, my hope is that this foray into a cultural theology might help to both reactivate and deprovincialize radical theology. More specifically, I make the argument that radical theology can no longer afford the indulgence of its apocalyptical fantasies. The state of the world is too dire, the earth too fragile.

In this chapter I offer three snapshots from a generation past that at least partly fill in the lineage of radical theology by invoking voices and movements from that interim period between the first generation of death-of-God theologians Bonhoeffer helped to inspire and our present moment—or, better, our present crisis. In so doing, my aim is to raise the stakes of a radical theological method by way of a discussion on theology and energy. Although urgent and timely, the discussion is not a new one. It is marked by the very questions and issues with which we have been faced for some time, the very choices we have been asked to make but have long deferred, the very crisis that has been seen on the horizon and predicted by select lone voices and is now rapidly approaching. Perhaps now, with all of us increasingly feeling the oppression of the "superabounding reality of concrete ethical problems" we face, we stand poised to act and think differently.

In addition to the methodological implication already indicated, the other point I mean to convey in this particular exploration of theology and energy is that *for radical theology to be renewed, it must always be renewable*. That is to say, we must forego both the traditional theological fantasy of creation ex nihilo and the radical theological preoccupation with apocalypticism.[5] The earth does not have the luxury of starting over from scratch. Beyond the very real threat of nuclear annihilation that once rightly spooked the first generation of death-of-God theologians, we now know the end of the world as an environmental catastrophe of our own making. Our age is witnessing what Elizabeth Kolbert has explored in her Pulitzer Prize–winning book as the "sixth extinction," humanity's principal and most tragic legacy that threatens to render the earth uninhabitable for life as we know it.[6] We need more than the absolutism that apocalypticism provides, especially when considering the ways that end-of-the-world fantasies have been marshaled by the most conservative and evangelical forces to withstand or ignore the dire threat that climate change represents.[7] If nothing else, there should be concern that predicating the good news of religion on the world's end plays into the very political and economic machinations that ought to be resisted.

Renewal must not be bought at the price of death and destruction. On the contrary, the renewability I have in mind is one mired in the delicate equilibrium of nature, a world not only of evolution and mutation but also of extinction. So, instead of the fantasy of the phoenix rising from the ashes as an unscathed new creation, I choose Catherine Malabou's image of the salamander, one of nature's own signifying nature's capacity for self-renewal. I choose the image of a body that bears its scars but nevertheless goes on living.

God Is Red, Religion Is Green

In 1973, largely inspired by and in response to the previous year's debacle at the Bureau of Indian Affairs, when a group of Indian activists captured and destroyed parts of the federal building in Washington, DC, Vine Deloria Jr. published a book, *God Is Red: A Native View of Religion*, that would become one of the defining works of the American Indian movement. In this book, Deloria continues where he left off in his Indian Manifesto from 1969, *Custer Died for Your Sins*, by chronicling the cultural, political, and religious impasse that continues to exist between American Indians and non-Indians in the United States. As he wrote in *God Is Red*, "The impasse seems to be constant. Indians are unable to get non-Indians to accept them as contemporary beings."[8] Thus we can understand the significance of the 1972 violent protest by Native Americans, about which Deloria wrote, "Indians were no longer the silent peaceful individuals who refused to take dramatic steps to symbolize their grievances."[9] Instead, American Indian activists claimed their place on the larger stage of the civil rights movement. But, in borrowing from the playbook of other increasingly radicalized, militant civil rights groups from the late 1960s and early 1970s, the American Indian protesters "had become simply another protest group," which yet again confirmed for Deloria the "peculiar tragedy" not only of the Indian movement but also of the much broader history of relations between American Indians and non-Indians in the United States. Namely, this tragedy is that Native Americans have "never been able to influence the intellectual concepts by which Americans view the world."[10]

For Deloria, this irony of the American Indian movement was palpable. He was unclear what to make of the movement because it had expressed its grievances in the politics of identity that were characteristic of the civil rights era. Was it simply the final spasm of the revolutionary 1960s from a largely overlooked and forgotten minority group? Was their violent confrontation with the federal government a tactical advance in a broader social and political strategy or was it simply a sign of frustration and despair? After all, as Deloria asserts, "Few Indians ever accepted the premises of the Civil Rights movement" because the movement remained within the parameters of an essentially Euro-American Christian worldview.[11] Further, when we consider the American Indian movement in the broader context not only of the civil rights movement but also of the Vietnam War protests, the rise of the counterculture, and the beginnings of the environmentalist movement, "they can all be understood as desperate efforts of groups of people to flee the abstract and find authenticity, wherever it could be found," according to Deloria's analysis. And therein lies the irony, because it is at precisely this point, when the Western world seemed to be either caught up in its own violent upheaval or at the point of self-exhaustion, that "Indians [became] popular"—but only, Deloria argues, by becoming something they were not.[12]

The one sure sign of their sudden popularity was the money that flowed in from the mainline Protestant denominations. As Deloria writes, progressive-minded Protestants "were ecstatic when informed by Indians that they were guilty of America's sins against the Indians." By expressing their solidarity with the Native Americans, these well-intentioned WASPs could effectively "purchase indulgences for their sins by funding the Indian activists to do whatever they felt necessary to correct the situation."[13] Although Deloria was disgusted by the spectacle of once-proud American Indian activists becoming "little more than puppets dancing for liberal dollars," he was equally harsh in his assessment of the Christian churches who "bought and paid for the Indian movement and its climactic destruction of the Bureau of Indian Affairs."[14]

After all, the road to hell is paved with good intentions, and while the buying of indulgences might soothe the consciences of the damned, it does little to nothing to alter the intellectual categories or concepts by which the world is viewed. And, as we have already seen, bringing about such an alteration was Deloria's prime concern. Too often, rather than being the cause for a dramatic and fundamental shift in the intellectual conception of the world, the American turn toward the native was in fact an extension of the right to ownership and possession that had driven the American Indians from the land in the first place. For instance, in the chapter derisively titled "America Loves Indians . . . and All That," Deloria recounts repeated incidents of white Americans looting American Indian remains, collecting them as artifacts, and somehow thinking this act was an expression of the highest form of respect. The prerogative of American Manifest Destiny by which non-Indians took possession of the country's land takes the form of a plundering of the past in a misguided quest for authenticity, for now more than ever the American Indian "seemed to hold the key to survival."[15] America looked to its natives to save it from itself, but instead of allowing the Native American view of religion to call into question its basic orientation to reality, America instead, once again, co-opted its indigenous on its own terms. This time, however, it was not the land, but the very conception of land, that was at stake.

For Deloria, the appropriation of the Native American, although indulgent and misguided, nevertheless posed a fundamental choice. Whereas American Christians remained mired in their collective guilt, the native view of religion claimed by Deloria was oriented around ecology. As he writes, "The choice appears to be between conceiving of land as either a subject or an object." American Christianity "has avoided any religious consideration of ecological factors in favor of continuous efforts to realize the Kingdom of God on earth." And whether progressive or reactionary, liberal or conservative, when it comes to our religious understanding of the land, "neither left-wing nor right-wing Christianity appears to understand the nature of the ecological disaster facing us. Rather they both seem to vest their faith in the miraculous ability of science to solve the problem of the dissipation of limited resources."[16] This concern with ecology, which is fundamental to the native religious conception of the world, requires more than "the relatively simple admission of guilt before ecological gurus"; it involves a fundamental reorientation regarding the very locus of meaning.[17] In short, it is not forgiveness that is needed but restitution to the rightful "spiritual owners of the land," whereby the land is reconceptualized as inhabited—indeed, as living—space. More directly for our purposes, Deloria raises skepticism of those who would place too much faith in science and technology to solve the ecological disaster—and, by extension, the energy crisis—that we currently face. He suggests that such an approach would be yet another misguided effort to realize the Kingdom of God on earth.

Thus, in contrast to the death-of-God theologies that made their appearance in the United States a decade earlier, this sudden embrace of the American Indian

as the living alternative to all things Western led to Deloria's provocative proclamation that "God Is Red." As Deloria tells it, "Perhaps we have come to realize that
Western man cannot find his way in society either by demythologizing his condition as Kierkegaard, Nietzsche, and the social gospel people have attempted or
remythologizing it as Billy Graham and the Fundamentalists have tried to do. Perhaps an entirely new analysis of the nature of society must be undertaken, perhaps
a new understanding of the nature of religion must be found."[18]

We get an argument from Deloria, then, for a native approach to religion that
would bring matters of ecology, land, and space to the fore. Something other than,
something more fundamental than, the cycle of sin, penance, and redemption was
required—something more radical even than the seizing of a federal building in
militant protest. Deloria goes on to make the case that this conceptual revolution
would actually show religion to be more compatible with contemporary science
and technology. *When God is red, so the argument goes, the greening of religion is sure
to follow.* This approach has yielded much positive benefit, even within more traditional theological circles, for those who are increasingly concerned with, and
define themselves in terms of, ecotheology.[19] What is still needed, however, in addition to, but in no way in opposition to, these expressed concerns, is a focus on
energy. The chance remains, once again or perhaps for the first time, to finally recognize, even if far too late, the American Indian as our contemporary.

The (American) Gospel of Oil

In 1973, armed members of the American Indian movement and the Lakota
Nation made a final stand for native rights in a siege of the town of Wounded
Knee in South Dakota. The conflict, which lasted for seventy-one days, eventually
led to the arrest of twelve hundred people and effectively signaled the end of the
American Indian movement.

That same year, the Yom Kippur War began and ended, lasting a total of
only three weeks but having far-reaching implications, including the decision by
OPEC to restrict the flow of oil to all countries allied with Israel, which resulted
in the immediate spiking of oil prices by 200 percent. The effects of that war are
still felt today.

The fight over a promised land consolidated the power and influence of the
oil-producing states in the Middle East and beyond as it was realized that oil is
more than simply energy and a commodity. The *weaponization of oil* left all matters of energy inextricably entangled in discussions of power, money, and politics.

In reaction to the Arab oil embargo of 1973–74, the United States developed
the Strategic Petroleum Reserve (SPR) to provide an emergency stockpile of an
approximately two months' national supply of oil. This hoarding of energy, which
has now long substituted for a coherent national energy policy, was meant to

insulate the United States from global petro-politics and to stabilize the oil market. But as Lisa Margonelli, author of *Oil on the Brain*, explains, it is now "serving double duty as a defense and a target," further politicizing oil as a global commodity and perhaps even artificially inflating the price of oil by as much as 25 percent. "In a sense," Margonelli writes, "the SPR is a monument to the cataclysmic oil crisis of 1973. Like all monuments, it documents both the size of the shock and the sincerity of the emotion—700 million barrels! It's also become a bit of nostalgia, out of step with the world around it." Put succinctly, she says, "The SPR was cold war thinking translated to oil."[20]

As a monument to the long-term impact of the events of 1973–74, the SPR signified a last-gasp effort by a nation threatened with a crisis of identity. The same cultural malaise and sense of exhaustion that was described by Deloria has been captured by Margonelli as well. Americans had long come to define themselves by the sense of open space and endless expanse. The open road was the image not only of the Beat generation but also of the promise of an America with a sense of always oriented to the future. America's love affair with its cars, therefore, represents its perpetual capacity for reinvention and the potential to pick up and move somewhere different, someplace still to be discovered and yet to be tamed. "The whole definition of being American," Margonelli writes, "was that we drove our cars anywhere we wanted to." But "with the oil crisis, the long upward expansion of the US economy since World War II ended and started to reverse." The "oil shortage brought about a deep psychological insecurity" that, in the words of the U.S. comptroller general, gave Americans the "illusion of U.S. impotence."[21]

In this sense, much more than any economic or political impact it has had, the SPR proved to be a psychological cure to what was perceived to be merely a psychological problem. This psychological cure was remarkably similar to the way that the appropriation of the American Indian was a purchase of redemption for a nation exhausted by its own self-indulgence. After 1973, Americans needed to get their swagger back. The investment in the SPR was a *down payment for a generation's indulgence.* For an illustration, compare and contrast the characters of Travis Bickle in *Taxi Driver*, Martin Scorsese's masterpiece from 1976, and John Rambo in *First Blood*, Sylvester Stallone's 1982 rejoinder. Both Travis Bickle and John Rambo were Vietnam veterans who could not quite manage to assimilate themselves back into mainstream American society, both carried the American surrender in Vietnam with them as a personal trauma, and both externalized that internal self-loathing in a climactic act of violence. The difference is that Travis Bickle is an antihero whose bloodlust actually reveals his own death wish, whereas Rambo is a hero, who follows the script of the myth of redemptive violence when given the chance to make things right, thus restoring the American soldier to his proper heroic archetype. Or, contrast Jimmy Carter's sweater vest with Ronald Reagan's "morning in America." In each case, the reality of the vulnerability of the United States is replaced by a fiction, and the American dream is restored. I conclude this discussion of the SPR by returning to Margonelli. She ends her analysis of the SPR by writing that it "offers the illusion of safety but no real insurance. It is too small, too centralized in the Gulf Coast, and too vulnerable to be effective. Insulating the United States against oil shocks requires more work than just stockpiling."[22]

When it comes to America's energy policy, to say nothing of its view or fundamental conception of energy, we need much more than psychological reassurance. When we consider the long journey oil makes from around the world to fuel our cars, to heat our homes, and to be consumed as commercial products, we realize that it is much more than a financial commodity. The United States—indeed, the whole world in the age of globalization—depends on an entire culture of oil. Better still, as Kevin Phillips has shown in his book *American Theocracy*, the ascendancy of the United States as the world's lone superpower is predicated entirely on cheap and readily accessible oil. In short, the age of oil is the age of American supremacy, and, as Phillips adds, "Oil abundance has always been part of what America fights *for*, as well as *with*."[23] But with this great strength also comes great vulnerability, as Phillips explains when he says, "The politics of oil dependency in the U.S. is ingrained and possessive—a culture of red, white, and blue assumptions of entitlement, a foreign policy steeped in covert petroleum emphasis, and a machismo philosophy of invade-and-take-it." He thus describes the United States as a "vulnerable oil hegemon," liking the country to an imperial power whose best days are behind it, much like the Dutch when wind and water were the primary sources of energy and expansion and like the British in the age of coal.[24]

Thus, the persistence of the US culture of oil requires the passivity of the American citizen as consumer. Regardless of the posted price of a gallon of gas at the local station, there is a high price for oil that implicates the entirety of American foreign policy, the stranglehold of the military industrial complex, and our own peculiar brand of empire. From the depleted Black Giant of Texas to the geopolitics of petro-states such as Iran, Venezuela, and Russia; the maneuvering of a Nigerian warlord; and the rapidly expanding oil markets of China and India, our dependence on oil has global repercussions that are not just economic but also moral and religious. As Paul Roberts has written, "Our brilliant energy success comes at great cost—air pollution and toxic waste sites, blackouts and price spikes, fraud and corruption, and even war. The industrial-strength confidence that was a by-product of our global energy economy for most of the twentieth century has slowly been replaced by anxiety."[25]

What to do then? Margonelli's recommendation is for a cultural revolution in which we rethink our entire relation to energy, reconceptualize our space, and develop an ethic of conservation and efficiency rather than of consumption.[26] What is also needed, and this is where Phillips's analysis serves as a critical supplement and where the theoretical importance for radical theology comes to bear, is a *theo-political critique of the religiosity that is at the basis of America's culture of consumption*. In sum, as Americans "cling to and defend an ingrained fuel habit," we have been immersed in at least a forty years' war over Middle Eastern oil.[27] To explain this incredible shortsightedness, Phillips chronicles the political rise of the religious Right and the broad-based cultural fascination with apocalypticism. Put simply, as long as a sizable portion of the American population is convinced that the world will soon come to an end, there is no point in developing a coherent, long-term energy policy. This argument by Phillips is shared by the political philosopher Sheldon Wolin in his book *Democracy Incorporated*, in which he writes, "There is a timeless harmony between, on the one hand, the evangelical belief that this life is destined to pass away and, on the other, industrial practices that threaten to exhaust finite resources while polluting the earth and atmosphere."[28]

Phillips develops this argument further, pointing to the dangerous underside of a certain religious radicalism that must be distinguished from the lineage of radical theology. He writes, "To sketch the revival-prone sectarian and radical side of American religion: Its increasing presence is breeding a politics of cultural narrowness, moral and biblical bickering, revivalism in the White House, and international warfare to spread the gospel, fulfill the Book of Revelation, or both."[29] Although this American parochialism and fascination with the end-time might not be new, Phillips argues that it "take[s] on much greater importance now as Christian, Jewish, and Muslim holy lands occupy center stage in world politics and as sites of military confrontation."[30]

Taking his analysis even further, Phillips outlines the triple threat we currently face:

1. The increasing domination of US policy by the hunger for cheap oil in a world of dwindling supplies, which has led in turn to an obsession with projecting US power across the endlessly volatile Middle East.
2. The Republican Party seriously under the sway of Christians who believe in biblical inerrancy and a reading of scripture that inspires them to apocalyptic obsessions with that same part of the world.
3. The headlong growth of American debt of all kinds—household spending, a massive trade gap, and a federal deficit that leaves American policy susceptible to the foreigners who buy the securities that keep the US government afloat and who could sink it with the decision to stop buying.

The Transvaluation of God and Gold

Let us return to one more snapshot from the early 1970s. In 1971, in a policy measure that has come to be known as the Nixon Shock, President Richard Nixon unilaterally withdrew the United States from the Bretton Woods agreement and stopped the direct convertibility of the US dollar to gold. The Bretton Woods agreement had established the International Monetary Fund and the World Bank and had reestablished a modified version of the gold standard in an effort to bring stability to the global economy in the wake of World War II. Nixon felt forced into the decision to withdraw from the agreement by the realities of accelerated inflation caused by an escalating US trade deficit. Although the policy "closed the gold window" by making the US dollar inconvertible to gold, Nixon nevertheless tried to maintain a fixed exchange rate. But this quickly proved to be unfeasible, and by 1976, all of the world's major currencies were allowed to float, thus giving birth to the new global economic condition of high finance.

Phillips's articulation of the triple threat the United States currently faces makes clear the integral connection between energy, religion, and money. Likewise, Mark C. Taylor sees a broad cultural significance of the Nixon Shock. As Taylor writes in *Confidence Games*, "It is no exaggeration to insist that going off the gold standard was the economic equivalent of the death of God. God functions in religious systems like gold functions in economic systems: God and gold are believed to be firm foundations that provide a secure anchor for religious, moral, and economic values. When this foundation disappears, meaning and value become unmoored and once trustworthy symbols and signs float freely in turbulent currents that are constantly shifting."[31] One irony, as the *Wall Street Journal* pointed out on its January 2008 editorial page, is that although the US currency has been allowed to float, the price of oil and gold have run in almost perfect tandem since 2001.[32] For some this suggests that *oil has become the new gold standard*, replacing the American dollar as the true measure of value. If so, it conforms to Taylor's analysis, only with an added twist. If gold once functioned as a firm foundation by which to secure economic value, oil is a slippery and volatile sludge. Although the value of gold can be traced to its usefulness as coinage—and thus as the necessary third that makes possible the transformation from a basic barter economy—oil's value is in its convertibility to various petro-products. Therefore, oil is not only the fuel for the global economy but also its product of exchange.

If the collapse of the gold standard is equivalent to the death of God, then oil as the new gold standard can be likened to the postmodern return of religion. It suggests a world in which meaning and value have become unmoored, a world of infinite complexity and codependence in which the ecological, theological, and economic realities are all deeply intertwined, and a world with oil and gas pipelines crossing international borders and in which the international waters of the oil tankers' trade routes are policed almost exclusively by the American military. Meanwhile, the American government is effectively impotent at controlling, or even safely predicting, the price of a gallon of gasoline. It is a world in which business interests force cultures to collide and in which religions' claim for sacred space inevitably runs up against global capital's demand for open borders and the privatization of land. *It is a world in which the theological preoccupation with one's own private relation with God and the repeated cycle of sin and atonement no longer suffice as an adequate religious orientation for our time.* Taylor describes it as a "world without redemption." We might just as well call it a world at war, the inescapable consequence of the pegging of all value to that which is explosively volatile, that which is toxic, that which is at or near its peak, and thus that which is bound to disappoint.

In his book *Religion and Capitalism*, British philosopher of religion Philip Goodchild asks the question, what is the price of piety, especially considering how money has become our new God. I answer this question by offering up the image of the oil gusher as a representation of the postmodern return of religion. An oil gusher, which has been cinematically portrayed in such movie classics as *Giant* and, more recently, *There Will Be Blood,* is an uncapped oil well connected to a deep reservoir of oil under intense pressure. When unleashed, the oil can shoot two hundred feet or higher into the air. The gusher includes not only the oil but the sand, mud, rocks, and water as well. It could be considered an image of plenty, of sudden and ever-renewing wealth, but an oil gusher is to be avoided at all costs, an *image of waste rather than wealth*, a dangerous explosion that hardened oil wildcatters know has the power to kill. They can be, and are, effectively managed by current subterranean drilling techniques, but they still stand as a visual reminder of the volatility of—indeed, the very explosive potential of—a global consumer economy bankrolled by cheap oil.

The perils of the petro-states for geopolitics are well documented. Around the globe, there is seemingly a direct relation between vast mineral resources, political corruption, and the stratification of society. The easy money associated with oil means there is little demand for transparency or accountability from the people. With the vast transfer of wealth from the oil-importing states to the oil-exporting states has come the inordinate influence of Iran and Saudi Arabia in fueling radical Islam. Also, as Phillips makes clear, it has led to the inordinate influence of southern evangelicals on American politics. Perhaps we have done everything in our power to keep this volatile mix in check, or safely beneath the surface. Perhaps at least a half century's worth of realpolitik has provided for the ready supply of oil that our way of life demands. Perhaps we might continue to pay down the price of these indulgences so that our way of life and very mindset might remain undisturbed, unsullied by the despoiled and tarred landscape we have left behind. Or perhaps instead the gusher is about to blow, in what is bound to be a wasteful and destructive orgy of violence.

There is only so long the well can remain tapped, only so long before our endless consumption consumes us, only so long before our purchase of indulgences comes due at the day of reckoning. If God is green, the choice still remains. Will it be a token gesture toward our collective ecological guilt, a realization of how money stands in for God after the death of God, or, indeed, the spiritual and theological reformation long sought?

As radical theology seeks to renew itself by digging beneath the surface of its own discourse and by asking questions of its own provenance, my wish is that it not only discern, interrogate, and indict the toxicity of a late-capital consumer culture predicated on cheap and ready oil but also find common cause with those environmental activists and ecotheologians who for well over a generation have forged a path of solidarity and resistance. *Where radical theology once bore the signature of theological apocalypticism, may we now understand that our world is too fragile to engage in such death-ridden fantasies.* On this point, the lineage of radical theology has been guilty of a fundamentalism of its own. Like the conservative evangelical variant of fundamentalism that it resolutely rejects, the fundamentalism of radical theology is one that betrays a perverted fantasy with death and destruction, making a fetish out of the world's end.

The radical theology of the future must be one that changes from being apocalyptic to being counterapocalyptic, from being the harbinger of the sudden overturning suggested by the etymology of catastrophe to being a catalyst for the alteration of the habits, dispositions, and modes of thought necessary to sustain the world we risk losing. I suggested earlier that the appropriate image of thought for this radical theology of the future would be that of the salamander. Malabou contrasts the salamander with the phoenix as a way of explaining her differences with Hegel—or, more precisely, the differences between the concept of plasticity and the operations of the Hegelian dialectic. Although the salamander does not possess the mythic lore and dramatic glory of the phoenix in its triumphant rise from the ashes, the salamander has the benefit of nature's reality. It is the earth's own bruised and scarred creation. It suffers loss but goes on living—a stubborn life that resists death by way of regeneration.

Beyond death and resurrection, and before we are faced with the irredeemable crisis of the world's end—which we know means first the loss of certain worlds (and not others) and represents first a threat to certain people (and not others)—may the image of the salamander provide us with the affirmation of life as we know it, which has always been the existential claim staked by radical theology, old and new. Only now, that existential claim is paired with the vast ecological crisis before us, meaning that we need more than merely a psychological cure. It is in this framework that this book has argued for the political becoming of radical theology. The cycle of guilt and indulgence has left us wanting the world's end, desperate for an apocalyptical solution. For radical theology to be renewed, it must resist. And in that resistance, it must find a life worth living fit for the world's survival.

NINE

A Rhapsody on Race, Repetition, and Time

Repetition changes nothing in the object repeated, but does change something in the mind which contemplates it.

—Gilles Deleuze

I don't believe Louis Armstrong was a real human being. He was sent here by God to make people happy.

—Phoebe Jacobs

So if oil represents a volatile mix of money, ecology, and geopolitics, what of race? The image from the last chapter of the oil gusher as a representation of the postmodern return of religion may also apply to the theopolitical consideration of race. Who can forget Spike Lee's 1989 masterpiece, *Do the Right Thing*? Scorching heat, misplaced ethnic pride, police brutality, and simmering racial tensions all combined in a toxic blend bound to explode in a blind, destructive rage. Lee discussed how the great challenge in making the film was that he wanted the viewer to really feel the suffocating heat of the city that historically correlated with a rise in domestic abuse and homicides. As a commentary on race relations in the United States, the film suggests that all it would take is a small spark for the simmering cauldron of pride, resentment, and hostility to explode.

Another interesting statement on race relations can be found in Adam Mansbach's deeply subversive novel, *Angry Black White Boy* (2005). The main character is Macon Detornay, a misguided, white suburbanite searching for a more authentic identity, which is fulfilled by way of his hyperidentification with hip-hop. He represents the embodiment of white guilt with a self-loathing that becomes complete when he launches the "Race Traitor Project." As the celebrity spokesperson for the evils of whiteness, he plans a Day of Apology in New York City. After the day blows up into a race riot of epic proportions, Detornay escapes to Alabama and then has the opportunity to prove his racial bona fides through an act of ritual violence. After refusing, his own death wish is fulfilled when the gun is turned against him and he becomes a martyr for a cause that he hardly understands. For Detornay, racial identity was merely an act of theater, and solidarity was nothing but a pose. By playing the game of racial reconciliation, he became a star while real lives, relationships, and jobs hung in the balance. At least in Mansbach's rendering, there is safety in invisibility and a relative peace in anonymity. His message is the same as that of Lee: beware of the volatile and violent sludge that simmers beneath the surface.

And so in this final chapter I recognize the need to proceed with extreme caution and a deliberate humility. What, after all, does radical theology have to do with critical race theory? The answer heretofore has been very little or nothing at all. But this book's purpose is to suggest, if not completely chart, a different future—not just to identify and rehabilitate radical theology but to change it. Throughout this book I have suggested a series of important shifts for the future of radical theology—from a theological turn to a theological becoming, from overcoming to changing ontotheology, from transcendence to transformation, from messianism to metamorphosis, and from apocalypticism to counterapocalypticism. It should be clear by now that each of these shifts is of a sort, that a strict logic of immanence is at work. This was the message of Gabriel Vahanian when he described utopic biblical hope in terms of changing the world, not changing worlds. It was also the critique I opened up with in the introduction when I compared radical theology with T. E. Lawrence. I have argued that radical theology must be alert to its own will-to-self-actualization that is the presumed entitlement of Western man come of age after the death of God, with the lesson that radical theology must be more radical than rebellious.

Catherine Malabou's concept of plasticity proves decisive in making this lesson clear. By rejecting Derrida's messianism and reclaiming Hegel's dialectic, Malabou runs the risk of a closed ontology that operates as a totality. The fear is that by admitting nothing outside, there is no hope or even prospect for change, that without the possibility of the encounter with a radical alterity, we remain stuck with the (self-)same, a nightmarish repetition without change and without hope. It is for this reason that John Caputo has accused Malabou's plasticity of not being plastic enough. The difference between the two thinkers hinges on the possibility of the impossible. Caputo distinguishes between what he calls the "future impossible" and the "absolute impossible," with the former operating as a continuation of the same and the latter coming as a surprise.[1] When he defines deconstruction in terms of it being driven by a hope for the impossible, he is holding out hope for the absolute impossible, whereby change happens by virtue of the encounter with the unexpected, the unpredictable, or the incalculable. We need the tension between the conditioned and the unconditional because without it we would be closed in by the claustrophobia of a totalizing immanence. Malabou, by contrast, sees this tension as a gesture of transcendence and charges it with exoticism. In her book *The Future of Hegel*, she provides an alternative, nonmessianic, immanent view of the future that turns on the phrase "to see what is coming."

The script might very well be set, but this does not foreclose the possibility for an infinite variability, for improvisation, and even for a resistance that still operates within the bounds of nature and in relation to the structures of power. Thus, one might read Malabou as a kind of mash-up of Deleuze and Foucault by way of Hegel and Heidegger.

The importance of this notion of resistance for the present chapter is twofold. First, I am upholding Malabou's ontology as a viable depiction of how change happens. As I have already shown, this ontology bypasses—or, better, subtracts itself from—the logic of identity and difference by its refusal of the priority of the ontological difference. It is not difference that produces change but vice versa. The upshot is that we do not need a God to save us; rather, we possess the latent potential for resistance within our own nature. Second, Malabou's depiction of resistance bespeaks not only a radical freedom but also a radical vulnerability. By virtue of our materiality, we are pressed, marked, and bound from all sides. Although we might wish for an escape—for an otherworldly redemption or for the rupture that comes from the inbreaking of transcendence or end-of-the-world apocalypticism—there is no exit, no exchanging this world for another. And yet, we are not confined to fatalism, to the quiet acceptance of the world as a continuation of the same, for we can see in what is coming a different future—many different futures, in fact, to the point of a seemingly infinite array of possible configurations and reconfigurations. The radical theology of the future I am suggesting thus begins to resemble that of process thought, only here by way of Malabou rather than Whitehead.

But, as in the previous chapter, I also want to uphold the methodological point I have sought to make with regard to radical theology—namely, that for radical theology to fulfill its own ontological and political becoming, it must be more than ideational. What is at stake is more significant than is the choosing of sides. When I stated that radical theology is as much a methodology as it is a sensibility, this mode of resisting racial oppression is where the proof is revealed. The foray into cultural theology is a methodological choice that demonstrates the degree to which a radical theological sensibility can provide a meaningful and relevant reading of our times. In Charles Winquist's words, the test of its critical engagement is that it must be "real and important."

And so it is that I present what follows as a meditation on time that offers a commentary on our times. Specifically, I look to the great jazzman Louis Armstrong as the paragon of a certain kind of resistance that holds out for an alternative mode of deliverance. This chapter is thus also a meditation on immanence—not just in terms of finite vicissitudes but in terms of very real constraints and in terms of a permanent passing away, of a repetition of death and denigration to the point of infinity.

If there is redemption in this tale, it is only of the transient kind. If there is transcendence, it is always mediated and bound by immanence. If there is hope, it is found in joy. And if there is resistance (and I am certain that there is), then it comes masked in the most abhorrent form of racial denigration.

A Beatitude in the Making

It has been called "the creative process incarnate," a means to give us a "painless way to assess ourselves," to say nothing of its celebration of life, virtuosity, sexuality, and syncretism. It is said that its name originated from the jasmine perfume worn by the New Orleans prostitutes who frequented the bars and clubs where its music was first heard—indeed, where the very music was invented. It was born out of a combination of other musical forms—ragtime, the blues, and Black spiritual gospel singing. It was also born out of distinct musical locales—Africa, the Caribbean, and Europe all at once. It achieved the Americanization of culture called for nearly a century prior in Ralph Waldo Emerson's famous speech from 1837, "The American Scholar," but it did not achieve this as Emerson had imagined it.[2] If jazz was America's gift to the music of the world and thus was an essential component in America's "intellectual declaration of independence,"[3] then it was an Americanization of culture that was just as much an Africanizing of American culture. In other words, the story of jazz, at least of its origins, is the story of race in America. And, not surprisingly, if it is a story of race in America, then it is also a story of disavowal, of an almost literal shunning that leaves jazz—and its first and most enduring genius, ambassador, and star, Louis Armstrong—as a bastard child.

In historical and political terms, the birth of jazz and the legal codification of Jim Crow segregation laws throughout the American South were concomitant. The landmark US Supreme Court decision Plessy v. Ferguson, which endorsed the doctrine of separate but equal, was handed down in 1896. Over half a century before Rosa Parks, Homer Plessy had deliberately engaged in an act of civil disobedience to challenge the 1890 Louisiana law enacted that required all those classified as black to sit in the "colored" train car.[4] Plessy, who was a light-skinned New Orleans mulatto, born a free person, one-eighth black and seven-eighths white, had been chosen by the New Orleans Committee of Citizens for this act of civil disobedience. After his case failed to overturn the law of this early form of racial apartheid, it had the effect of remapping the social landscape, in New Orleans particularly. In a city known for its longstanding mixing of races and cultures there was now an emerging racial consciousness and culture of strict segregation. One benefit, however, was that the elite, classically trained, Creole musicians who had once been welcomed in the European-style dance halls were now forced to join together with their fellow blacks if they wanted to continue their livelihood at all.

These elite musicians brought their technical virtuosity with them and thereby contributed to the birth of a new music.

By 1918, although jazz had not yet become a national obsession, it had become firmly established in New Orleans. Strange, then, that on the eve of the decade that would famously be celebrated by F. Scott Fitzgerald as "the jazz age," the New Orleans newspaper of note, *The Times-Picayune*, published its editorial denouncing all things jazz.[5] The editorial begins with the impossible question, "Why is the jass music, and therefore, the jass band?" So as not to grant jazz the dignity of the rose in bloom that does not ask why, the question is followed by another: "As well ask why is the dime novel or the grease-dripping doughnut?" The answer to both sets of questions is that they are "manifestations of a low streak in man's tastes that has not yet come out in civilization's wash." They are the "indecent story,. . . the improper anecdote" better left "behind closed doors and drawn curtains." The editorial goes on to assert that jazz subverts the line of separation between music and nonmusic, belonging neither to "the great assembly hall of melody" nor to the "inner sanctuaries of harmony." Instead, it emanates from the basement apartment, "a kind of servants' hall of rhythms" where those who "love to fairly wallow in noise" belong.

The racial and sexual overtones in this editorial should be clear enough. Jazz is associated with the base, the low, and the unrefined. Although it is granted that this new music might have an "intoxicating effect," that effect was considered no different from that brought on by "crude colors and strong perfumes, the sight of flesh or the sadic pleasure in blood." In an apt cultural and religious observation, Wynton Marsalis is spot-on when he notes that jazz was born in New Orleans for a reason. New Orleans was not, and never had been, a Puritan colony. As Marsalis tells it, its French creole culture was a hotbed of sexual activity. And the music of jazz, like the city itself, "didn't hide what went on under the sheets."[6] It is for this reason that the *Times-Picayune* declared jazz the music of the night that belongs behind closed doors, an "atrocity in polite society." All the same, it was New Orleans's own. Thus, the editorial's denunciation was most complete when it stated, "We do not recognize the honor of parenthood," and that New Orleanians must "make it a point of civic honor to suppress it."

No doubt, nearly all great art, art forms, and artists have at one time or another been shunned and suppressed. But there is still something special about the particular story of the origins of jazz. The *Times-Picayune* was not mistaken in its assessment of the revolutionary possibilities of jazz. At least at one point in time, jazz had the effect of turning the world upside down. By giving voice to the shunned and forgotten and the repressed and suppressed, by its radical act of subversion that set musical theory and popular culture on their heads, by its musical anarchy and the earliest jazz musicians who would be denounced and disowned as "musical anarchists," jazz was a beatitude in the making. And no one embodies this story better than Louis Armstrong.

Making Time

Jazz was born of New Orleans, in a city that once disavowed its parentage. As New Orleans forsook its creole heritage and conformed to the Jim Crow South—in which all legal, political, cultural, and economic pressure was brought down such that the color barrier between white and black was rarely, and never legally, breached—jazz was patched together like a dreamwork. Calling jazz a return of the repressed is correct but misleading. Rather, racial segregation was the degradation of the master-slave dynamic reinscribed in social legislation. But jazz moved beyond tragedy and trauma to joy and affirmation. As is commonly said of the blues, there is a great difference between "having the blues" and "playing the blues." Jazz plays the blues. Moreover, by looking to Louis Armstrong in particular, jazz instantiates a *repetition* of the blues—but in true Deleuzian fashion, it is not a repetition of the same but of difference. It is this repetition, even more than jazz's much-discussed syncopation, that gives jazz its swing and makes its contribution to the invention of modern time especially distinct.

Listeners recalled Armstrong belting out as many as two hundred fifty high Cs in a row during early 1930s marathon performances of "Shine." The feat was less a case of virtuosity than it was of showmanship, but Armstrong was nevertheless honing an act and a sound that would become the canon from which future jazz greats would learn and against which they would eventually rebel. For those who came after him, it was clear that as Armstrong squeezed out that one additional high C note, it exacted a great price, even though it thrilled his audience. He was known to blow his horn until his lip would literally burst open. He was ever the showman, a willing accomplice in his own exploitation, and his was an act of self-sacrifice that led his critics to say he lacked self-dignity.

But setting the psychosocial aside for a moment, consider the feat afresh. What exactly makes the repetition of a note musical? What is it that elevates musical repetition to an expression of solitary genius? When learning to play the horn, one often seeks to hit a note clear and true. There is a qualitative leap from the playing of that solitary note to the audacious, time-bending act of repetition reveled in by Armstrong and his adoring fans. And, to be clear, when Armstrong repeats his succession of high Cs, he sustains listeners' attention not by bending the notes or making the notes growl, sing, or talk. It is just the one, single note followed by another, albeit with impeccable timing. It is one note after another to the point that the listener cannot tell when, or even whether, it will end.

The repetition for which Armstrong would become famous can be heard on one of his earliest recordings, the 1924 rendition of "Shanghai Shuffle." As

Armstrong biographer Terry Teachout puts it, this is where Armstrong truly announces himself on record when he "crashes out of the starting gate with a syn-
copated phrase that leads into a blistering-hot chorus in which he pulls one of his
favorite musical tricks out of his hat for the first time on record: He plays eigh-
teen Cs in a row, avoiding monotony by varying the accentuation of each one."
Teachout adds, "To modern ears his solo contains no surprises, for the rhythmic
language that he was forging . . . was to become the lingua franca of jazz."[7] The
miracle of Armstrong's playing was that it demonstrated how music could make
time by creating suspense. Time was effectively suspended by the seemingly endless repetition of that single, pure, and piercing note. For this reason, observers
have called jazz "the ultimate temporal art form."[8] It is the essence of swing, the
simplicity of hitting the right note at the right time, even if in this case it means
the repetition of one note over and over again to the point that the musicality tran-
scends to pure artistry, pure genius.

Armstrong pulls the same trick out of his hat in the performance of "Shine"
contained in the short-film version of *A Rhapsody in Black and Blue* (1932).[9] That
Teachout calls such repetition a "musical trick" is not without significance. Ob-
viously, Armstrong never considered himself beneath the crowd-pleasing tricks
of the trade, many of which he learned at the hand of his surrogate father, King
Oliver. Indeed, the contemporary viewer must almost turn a blind eye to the over-
the-top racist theatrics, costumes, and caricatures from *A Rhapsody in Black and
Blue* to even hear the music.[10] The ten-minute Paramount Pictures film begins
with Armstrong playing the role of the lazy, shifty, ne'er-do-well husband who
wants only to sit idly and listen to his jazz records, while his wife, looking the part
of a mammy, beats him senseless over the head to get him to do his household
chores. But as soon as his wife leaves the room, Armstrong drifts off to sleep to
the sounds of his own horn blowing. The next scene cuts to Armstrong in a dream
sequence. Decked out in full jungle regalia, he emerges from the midst of a soap-
sudded floor and begins to play his trumpet and sing for the African jungle king
of "Jazzmania." The music soars. The rhythm pounds. Armstrong's voice groans
and growls. It is bestial.

Dressed in leopard skin with his torso exposed, Armstrong looks strong and
youthful but also captive. Looking back, it is evident that this supposed dream was
a national nightmare, a repetition of minstrelsy that, almost up until the time of
jazz's ascendency, had been America's most popular form of entertainment. As
in the minstrel show, Armstrong played the part of the lazy, buffoonish, joyous,
and musical Negro. Also as in the minstrel show, Armstrong's culture was lam-
pooned and his race ridiculed, if not entirely effaced. It took Ralph Ellison to capture the heartbreak. In the prologue to his immortal novel from 1952, *Invisible
Man*, Ellison wrote in reference to Armstrong's "Black and Blue" (first recorded in

1929), an almost incomprehensible expression of racial subjugation and degradation that Armstrong somehow made into a mainstream hit decades before such
public proclamations of black pride were acceptable. Ellison—or, more appropri-
ately, Ellison's narrator, the invisible man—waxes poetic about Armstrong's ability
to bend "that military instrument into a beam of lyrical sound." But, as always,
the sound, even if it is a transcendent sound, tells only part of the story. The invisible man confesses that he likes Armstrong "because he's made poetry out of
being invisible." And, he adds, "I think it must be because he's unaware that he *is*
invisible."[11] Ellison manages to paint Armstrong, even with his leopard-skin jungle
suit, his unmistakable voice, and his virtuosity on the trumpet, in blackface with
the suggestion that he somehow manages to hide in plain sight.

Others were not so kind. For instance, both Dizzy Gillespie and Miles Davis,
Armstrong's two greatest jazz successors on trumpet, admitted a certain queasi-
ness at what Gillespie described as Armstrong's willingness to engage in "Uncle
Tom–like subservience."[12] It was a charge and a criticism that would stick with
Armstrong throughout his career. Even today, for many, those crowd-pleasing an-
tics and his insistence on making music that gave pleasure render him unacceptable to the contemporary ethos of race politics and out of step with the later
revolutions in jazz, such as the frenzied bebop led by the likes of Gillespie, Charlie
Parker, and Thelonious Monk and the cool, modal jazz made famous by Dave Br-
ubeck, Miles Davis, and John Coltrane. The running criticism was that Armstrong
sacrificed his musical genius at the altar of popular tastes. As one whose preening
before sold-out white audiences made him unacceptable, Miles Davis said it best
and, along the way, put Gillespie in the same boat:

> I always hated the way they used to laugh and grin for the audiences.
> I know why they did it—to make money and because they were en-
> tertainers as well as trumpet players. They had families to feed. Plus
> they both liked acting the clown; it's just the way Dizzy and Satch
> were. I don't have nothing against them doing it if they want to. But
> *I* didn't like it and didn't *have* to like it. I come from a different social
> and class background than both of them, and I'm from the Midwest,
> while both of them are from the South. So we look at white people a
> little differently. . . . I felt that I could be about just playing my horn—
> the only thing I wanted to do. I didn't look at myself as an entertainer
> like they both did.[13]

Ellison, however, was not so quick to condemn. His depiction of racial identity was full of ambiguity, of inner tensions and contradictions. Therefore, it
should not be taken as an early expression of political correctness. As Teachout
puts it, in Armstrong's "Black and Blue," Ellison ultimately saw "an anthem whose

stark honesty points to the possibility of deliverance."[14] But for my purposes here, it is the connection Ellison makes between invisibility and time that is of most interest. As Ellison's narrator tells it, by virtue of his invisibility, he is not lulled into "the swift and imperceptible flowing of time." Instead, he is more "aware of its nodes, those points where time stands still or from which it leaps ahead." Then comes the most suggestive claim of all: "That's what you hear vaguely in Louis' [Armstrong's] music."[15]

Phenomenology of Time

What is time? More specifically, what does it mean to say that jazz contributes to the making of modern time? Theologians, most famously St. Augustine, have long been interested in the concept of time. One senses Augustine's angst when he details in Book X of his *Confessions* how the pondering of time confronts one with the inevitable, but no less paradoxical, conclusion that time does not exist. By contemplating time, one is confronted with the nothingness of existence, an irreparable gap between thought and experience. After all, what do we really *know* of time? The past is past, meaning that it is no longer. It is lodged only in our memory, which is fleeting and unreliable. The future is not yet, just fancied in our imagination as anticipation, hope, or perhaps dread. And the present is ephemeral, a persistent passing away without any duration. By the time we think the present moment, the moment is gone.

To make sense of this paradox, Augustine uses narrative as a recourse. Here, context is everything, because Augustine's contemplation of the paradox of time takes place within his larger story of conversion. Thus, it figures as a paradox employed on behalf of a theological confession (and, not without significance, on behalf of the church). Augustine's restless heart and aimless wanderings parallel the mind's contemplation of time. Left to our own devices, we are left wanting in a state of perplexity and forced to confront the nothingness of our existence. Augustine paints himself as a foolish, ignorant, and arrogant rogue, captive to a restless heart and a sinful will. He detests his inability to control his sexual appetite and prays to be cured of his lust. But, as he famously added, he just did not want to be cured too quickly. He tells the story of the time he and his friends stole pears just for the perverse pleasure of stealing. The pears were left uneaten. Pure waste.

Likewise, consider the history of philosophy. The ancient ethical maxim handed down from Socrates by way of Plato was that "to know the good was to do the good." For Augustine, however, the self was not so simple. It did not always follow that actions took their lead from the mind, that the body's desires could so easily be aligned with the head's reason. It is here that an emerging Christian anthropology makes its unique contribution to the history of Western thought. For Augustine, harking back to St. Paul, the self is a divided, conflicted self. Moreover, no accounting of the self is complete that does not acknowledge the role played by the will. The will, so conceived, is the necessary third that stands between the mind and the body. By Augustine's reckoning, then, Christian theology corrects and completes ancient wisdom.

Returning to the paradox of time, I have said that this is a paradox *employed*. If there is no past time or future time, and the moment of the now is always passing away—in other words, if time does not exist, and if as a concept it cannot be explained—then what prevents us from abandoning all hope for reason, and what saves us from despair? Here is where Augustine pulls out his trump card. Although the concept of time is beyond human reasoning, although time as a concept is utterly incomprehensible to the human mind, time exists in the mind of God. Because God is eternal and omniscient, he was *before* time and exists *outside* of time. The best analogy for understanding this confessional claim on the part of Augustine is found in the very structure of his own narrative. His *Confessions* tells the complete story of his sin and ignorance, his death, and his rebirth as a new creation in Christ. It is only in knowing how the story ends that Augustine's early years of turmoil can begin to make sense. As the narrator of his own story, Augustine exhibits the capacity to stand outside himself. *Confessions* thereby creates the genre of the autobiography. Many interpreters have gone even further, however, and claimed that Augustine is the creator of the Western concept of the self.

A cross-religious comparison would be instructive. From a strictly phenomenological perspective, there is nothing separating Augustine's view on time from the Buddhist concept of *anicca*, or impermanence, one of the three marks of existence. All of life is experienced as flux. The problem of existence is that we seek to arrest the flux. We grasp, refusing to accept the flow of time. We are ignorant, denying the inevitability of death and decay. But whereas classic Buddhist thought follows this logic all the way through to the point that it connects the concept of *anicca* with the concept of the *anatta*, or the nonself, Augustine begins from the point of himself as a mystery to himself, only to end with a fully narrated story of a self-journey from God and returning to God. He ends with an illuminated and knowing self, thanks to the self-disclosure of God. It is knowledge of God that anchors self-knowledge. And it is knowledge of God that turns the paradox of time from being a mystery to becoming a testimony to the greatness of God.

Jazzmania

The Trappist monk Thomas Merton—whose spiritual autobiography, *The Seven Storey Mountain*, can be read as a contemporary repetition of Augustine's *Confessions* and who was an early admirer of death-of-God theology[16]—once said that what he saw in Louis Armstrong was Zen. Merton never elaborates on this point, although he was known to be a lover of jazz music as well as a great modernizer of the Catholic church and one of the twentieth century's greatest champions of interreligious study and dialogue. What Merton learned from his study and practice of Zen Buddhism was the contemplative practice of mindfulness. Specifically, he learned to be mindful of the passing of each and every present moment of time. For Merton, this brought with it an acute awareness of certain problems within the Western metaphysical tradition that were characterized by a tendency to valorize the mastery of the self. When Merton applied this psychological realization to certain cultural analyses, he came to believe this emphasis on mastery was the root cause of the technoscientific mindset by which the modern, scientific world lorded over the natural world. With the Atomic Age grappling with the horrors of the Holocaust and Hiroshima, Merton increasingly sought refuge in the contemplative practices from the East.

Yet those who know Merton and his work know that he was always a man chafing against himself. So even as he deepened his knowledge of the Zen and Taoist traditions, traveled to the East as a pilgrim, and lived with and had extensive correspondences with monks from various other spiritual traditions, he remained to the end a man of the modern world. He was an American at that, having spent almost his entire adult life in rural Kentucky. He knew that, for many, the United States as a nation, and even more as an idea, was synonymous with modernity, for both good and bad reasons. So perhaps on one level when Merton expressed that Armstrong "was Zen," he saw in Armstrong a neglected, obscured, or hidden resource within America's own tradition, or at least a cultural resource that had grown up within close proximity to him.

Armstrong would thus represent the creative possibilities of dwelling in the void, of an artist making his own time and finding his own sound, of an emerging art form that is an assemblage of inherited styles and traditions that makes possible a repetition with difference. The subversive nature of this new sound must be noted. Even as Paul Whiteman, the self-declared king of jazz, remained the most popular jazz musician throughout the United States during the late 1920s, Armstrong, who was entering into what jazz critics universally regard as his prime years, was forming an alliance with Earl Hines and Zutty Singleton. Together, the three were declared the Unholy Three. Their collaboration, forged on the road with little commercial success, became the basis of Armstrong's recordings, including the 1928 classic "West End Blues," with the Hot Five. The work they left behind has been called the "Old Testament of classic jazz."[17] From the margins to the canon, the soundtrack and cultural landscape of America was being upended.

Put philosophically, if jazz is the long-awaited "intellectual declaration of independence for the United States," then jazz is the *becoming of America*. And, as the "ultimate temporal art form," jazz is made by its making of modern time. Just as the automobile and, before that, the railroad remade the American landscape with their embodiment of freedom, possibility, and speed, so too was jazz an American dream. Full of nervous, frenzied energy, an improvisational art that allowed the musicians to make it up as they went along, it was a music that matched a people, as the nation put its stamp on what became known as the American century. Add race to the mix, and this "becoming of America" is a *becoming black and blue*— a story at once of economic, political, and cultural ascendency and, at the same time, of racial division and subjugation.

This was what was meant earlier by the observation that this Americanization of music was simultaneously an Africanization of American culture, a cultural transformation that was not welcomed by all. This was true not only in the United States but also in other parts of the world. For instance, it is sometimes thought that famed black jazz artists were welcomed with open arms throughout Europe. If that was the case in later years when jazz musicians self-consciously aspired to artistic status and cultural significance, it was not Armstrong's experience. Stories are told of mass exoduses from the audiences during his first trip to Europe in 1932. Armstrong would later recall how he endured tomatoes being thrown at him from English audiences. Newspaper accounts of his shows spoke of the "barbaric" nature of his "stage mannerisms." It was said that he looked and behaved "like an untrained gorilla." But even so, in the midst of the contempt for Armstrong's musicality, singing, and unrefined nature came the unwitting association that cuts to the heart of Armstrong's enduring significance: "[Armstrong's] savage growling is as far removed from English as we speak or sing it—and as modern— as James Joyce."[18]

Armstrong's was a modern voice and a modern sound that ran as deep and was as offensive as the glossolalia that was an essential ingredient in the Pentecostal wildfire spreading throughout the modern church at the same time. Both were beyond representation. Without meaning. Without authority. Effaced. No wonder Merton identified Armstrong as Zen. As ultramodern, Armstrong's jazz music might also be compared with that other modern marvel that became a standard of popular culture—cinema. When the earliest film critics and theorists sought to identify the essence of cinema's appeal, they looked to its most basic components. Cinema is *moving* pictures. By capturing movement on film, cinema was thought to have the unique capacity to capture—and eventually to manipulate and distort— time. Cinema did not simply capture a moment in time but also captured time's duration. By its succession of still images, it made pictures move.

Great early filmmakers such as D. W. Griffith made maximum use of this possibility to manipulate time through an innovative technique called "parallel editing," by which the viewer could seemingly escape the space-time continuum. Using this technique, which has since become commonplace, Griffith was able to construct a complex narrative and build suspense simply by cutting from scene to scene and thereby allowing the viewer to follow the simultaneous action of two or three places at the same time. For instance, in the climactic scene from *The Birth of a Nation* (1915), we see a group of women and children holed up with several former Union and Confederate soldiers on the outskirts of town. As the shack that serves as their fortress is being torn down by the angry mob of freed blacks, we see the white townspeople dressed in the Ku Klux Klan (KKK) white robes and masks riding to their rescue with the sounds of Wagner's "Ride of the Valkyries" roaring to a crescendo in the background. The moment before their rescue, the elderly father raises a knife in his hand, preparing to kill his daughter rather than allow her to be taken by the mob of black aggressors. Before the father follows through on the sacrifice, his hand is stayed, as was Abraham's before him, by the timely arrival of the heroic KKK. Throughout the scene, Griffith has switched back and forth between the interior scenes of the fear and desperation of those trapped in the shack, the wild aggression of the black mob outside, and the valiant rescue of the white knights of the KKK, all in "real time."

Now we return to the short Paramount Pictures film from 1932, *A Rhapsody in Black and Blue*. This film was to serve as a vehicle for Armstrong's stardom, staged theatrics that were nothing more than a ruse for him to play his trumpet before a mass audience. In other words, it was not high art but a pure marketing promotion. But because the film came only a few years after the smashing box-office success of Griffith's white supremacist tirade *The Birth of a Nation*, the overt racism contained in *A Rhapsody in Black and Blue* cannot be overstated. It was a repetition of the minstrel show. But although minstrelsy remains an affront because of its lampooning and exploitation of African American culture, it must also be said that the shows provided a platform for African American performers. The real difference between Griffith's *The Birth of a Nation*, which had white actors painted in blackface to advance its revisionist ideology of white supremacy, and *A Rhapsody in Black and Blue* is most apparent when Griffith brings in an image of a risen, triumphant Christ at the film's conclusion to sanction and bless the restoration of the natural order accomplished by the heroic KKK. By contrast, there is no external authorization in *A Rhapsody in Black and Blue*, only the beatitude of Armstrong's music portrayed as a radical interiority, a dream within a dream. Griffith aspires to create the grand historical narrative making a claim to authority; the short film featuring Armstrong takes place in a time beyond time and in a purely imagined space.

Thus, we might say that *The Birth of a Nation* stands to *A Rhapsody in Black and Blue* as Augustine's magisterial church orthodoxy does to Merton's Zen. Armstrong repeats the degrading racial stereotypes from the inherited tradition, but he gets the last laugh when his sound is the sound that would become the new lingua franca of American music. This is not the exchange of one authority for another or a reinscription of a grand narrative of deliverance; rather, it is much simpler and more ephemeral. Watching and hearing Armstrong in *A Rhapsody in Black and Blue* is like encountering a koan. All sense eludes us when matching the mockery of racial identity with a solitary genius whose tricks of the trade work like a magician casting a spell over time itself.

To explain, there comes a point at the conclusion of *A Rhapsody in Black and Blue* at which image and sound come together to reveal the time-bending nature of modern cinema and music. After Armstrong completes his first musical number, "I'll Be Glad When You're Dead You Rascal You," the king of Jazzmania demands of his royal stooge that he have Armstrong play one more tune. Armstrong gladly acquiesces and launches into a rendition of "Shine." When Armstrong hits the high C note at the end of the song and repeats the note clear and true again and again, the African drumbeat simultaneously pounds harder, louder, and faster, and at that precise point, the picture on the screen begins to spin around and around. By this matching of image and sound, the film takes the viewer into the dream within a dream. We know that some time has elapsed in this dizzying display because when the spinning stops, the king of Jazzmania has gone from bobbing his head to the rhythm to nodding off (although the music—specifically, the repetition of that single note—plays on). How long exactly has this repetition taken? How many high Cs has Armstrong hit in succession? Time somehow has been suspended and expanded in an almost infinite duration.

We return to this jungle dream sequence in the land of Jazzmania when the spinning stops, and we discover that Armstrong's audience has fallen asleep in the interim. All that is left now is the music. Armstrong is no longer playing for the pleasure of this caricature of an African king but for himself, to himself, in a state of dreamlike wonder. It is pure immanence, a realization of Deleuze's attempt to think difference apart from representational identity in *Difference and Repetition*, an eternal return in which the "returning is the becoming-identical of becoming itself."[19] It is with an appreciation of this musical time-bending display that the words to the song Armstrong sings can be heard anew. They are the words of a performer, no doubt, but when that performer reaches such dizzying heights of musical genius and virtuosity, the words become something more. They are the story of one extraordinary man, to be sure. But they also might be the story of jazz as that most distinct of American art forms and of music as the possibility for deliverance and the capacity to transcend.

> Oh chocolate drop, that's me
> 'Cause, my hair is curly
> Just because my teeth are pearly
> Just because I always wear a smile

Like to dress up in the latest style
'Cause I'm glad I'm livin'
Take troubles all with a smile
Just because my color shade
Is different maybe
That's why they call me "Shine"

Becoming Black and Blue

Jazzmania reveals the desire for escape as a dream. That is not to say that the dream is without any merit or any consequence. On the contrary, it is in the dream within the dream that time is suspended in an infinite duration of pure immanence. And it is there that the primordial nature of resistance is on full display.

This form of resistance is an indication of what I mean when I say that radical theology must be more radical than rebellious. Indeed, Armstrong teaches us something of the true nature of resistance. Resistance is not reactive, but creative, generative of a counterpower, to be sure, but no less constituent. Radical theology might learn from this form of resistance that no matter how much we might wish the world away, the point of theology is not to dissolve or exchange the world as presently constituted. It does not necessarily bring the aggressor to heel. It does not automatically overturn systems of oppression. It does not offer a redemption that is once and for all. But it does find a life in joy, and joy in life, even as it is bruised and bloodied to the point of being black and blue. It is a transcendence in immanence, a holiness in the muck, a theology that goes by different names with a sensibility, a sound, and a feel that we might rightly identify as radical.

Theses on a Radical Theology of the Future

Return with me to the scene of the crime as laid out in the introduction. I have insisted throughout on a theological method that is neither reformational nor conservative but instead transformational and radical. I have also claimed that this radical theology has a recognizable lineage and sensibility that makes it an identifiable tradition of thought that can be invoked and whose limits can be pressed. I cited T. E. Lawrence as a cautionary tale not so much for his perceived blasphemous conceit or even the naiveté of his neocolonial designs but as an example of a man in whom the modern West's obsession with freedom, autonomy, and rebellion was revealed as framed vainglory. No sooner is rebellion marshalled (and martialized) and independence won than the map is redrawn, triumph is turned to disillusionment, and the exoticized other is made into a mirror of one's own self-loathing and despair.

Consider the following incident as related by the noted T. E. Lawrence biographer Scott Anderson. Anderson regarded Lawrence as "one of the most enigmatic and controversial figures of the twentieth century." He tells the story of Lawrence as "the young, bashful Oxford scholar who rode into battle at the head of an Arab army and changed history."[1] But it is the incident of October 30, 1918, that really captures the enigma and ambivalence of the man. It was on this date that Lawrence was summoned to Buckingham Palace, where the king and queen were prepared to make him a Knight Commander of the Order of the British Empire in a private investiture service. This would have fulfilled an ambition that Lawrence had had since he was a young boy. Shockingly, however, Lawrence refused the honor.

Perhaps it is too much of a stretch, but consider the following parallel. Gabriel Vahanian's *The Death of God*, the first book in death-of-God theology, was published in 1957. In that same year, the evangelist Billy Graham held a mission in New York City's Madison Square Garden, where he filled the arena every night from May 15 to September 1. The mission was labeled the New York Crusade, and over the course of its sixteen-week duration, more than two million people attended. The success of the crusade solidified Graham's national profile as the voice of American evangelicalism.

Less than a decade after the publication of *The Death of God*, *Time* magazine published its famous cover story on the death-of-God movement. When published, it was the best-selling issue in the magazine's history. Yet only three years later, the cover read, "Is God Coming Back to Life?" In a letter from the publisher, *Time* editors wrote:

> On April 8, 1966, *Time's* cover posed the question "Is God Dead?" The story discussed the emergence and growing voice of the "God is dead" school of theologians. It proved to be one of the most provocative articles the magazine has ever run, and for months the arguments and addenda kept coming in from concerned readers.
>
> Recently, the death-of-God theologians have fallen silent, while ministers of all denominations have embarked on new, dynamic ways of bringing the divine back into daily existence. Hence *Time's* follow-up cover story, "Is God Coming Back to Life?"[2]

If the death-of-God theologians fell silent, Graham's fame only grew. He would become the spiritual advisor to a nearly fifty-year succession of US presidents, beginning with Dwight Eisenhower and ending with George W. Bush. At the same time, the born-again movement he represented went from the margins to the mainstream of American society and culture and from being piously indifferent to politics to becoming a successful vehicle for political mobilization.

From this parallel, it seems evident that radical death-of-God theology's time was short and its impact slight. The standard reading by scholars is that it was too academic and never truly reflective of people's sense of religiosity. While the death-of-God theologians were garnering the headlines, evangelicalism was building itself as a movement that included a distinct ecclesiology and politics. And because radical theology never established itself in any institutional form beyond that of academia—and even there, its proponents were generally solitary voices functioning as *agents provocateurs*—its ability to carry forward its legacy has been mitigated. Thus, one cannot help but wonder at the parallel between Lawrence returning from the battlefield triumphant as the general of an Arab army but nevertheless disillusioned and the long, fallow period of relative obscurity for radical theology. It is not that the original death-of-God theologians stopped teaching and writing, but that increasingly the movement they started has come to be regarded as a flash in the pan, a framed vainglory in which the post-Christian man announced a world come of age after the death of God only to witness not simply the return of religion but also the growth of fundamentalisms, the success of evangelical electioneering, and a violent clash of civilizations along religious identitarian lines.

It should be clear from the pages of this book that I do not subscribe to this standard narrative. Radical theology is certainly alive, with an identifiable lineage and as a discernible tradition of thought, but it never died in the first place. The mistake is to read radical theology exclusively in terms of the death-of-God movement. In the introduction, I defined radical theology as a postliberal tradition of thought that emerged out of the death-of God-movement of the 1960s. But although radical theology emerged out of the death-of-God movement, it is not bound by that movement. What remains for me in the conclusion is to specify the ways in which I have sought both to mine and to push against the limits of the tradition in order to envision a radical theology of the future that might think what radical theology has heretofore left unthought.

1. Radical theology is postsecular, with a difference

Within the broad field of religious studies, there has been a reconsideration of the basic secularist assumption that has been operative throughout much of the history of the academic study of religion—namely, the assumption that the more modern we become, the less religious we would become. The so-called secularization thesis was brought to question by scholars of religion long before the events of 9/11. After 9/11, however, these academic discussions became part of a much larger and more public dialogue, leading some, such as the American conservative political columnist David Brooks, to describe themselves as "recovering secularists." As Brooks wrote in a column for the *Atlantic Monthly* in March 2003, the secularization thesis has proven to be "yesterday's incorrect vision of the future."[3]

This secularist assumption is a remnant of the ambiguous legacy of the Enlightenment. As the historian of religion Jonathan Z. Smith once wrote, *"The academic study of religion is a child of the Enlightenment."*[4] As a product of the Enlightenment, the very concept of religion conjures up an intellectual tradition that not only has domesticated religion by delimiting it in the sphere of secular reason alone but also has passed down its attitude of skepticism, if not outright hostility, toward faith as a lesser form of knowledge and toward religion as exclusively a matter of either superstition or dogma.

The anthropologist of religion Talal Asad, who is equally interested in the construction of religion as an academic category, has shown how, in conjunction with the Enlightenment rationalist project outlined by Smith, there are the political consequences of the colonial subjugation by the West of other cultures and religions. For Asad, the political promise held out by the West for emancipation carries with it the religiocultural significance of normalizing secularization as the proper mode by which religion ought to be practiced. Specifically, secularization is the liberal strategy of containment, in which religion is treated exclusively as a private matter of individual conscience. When applied to the academic study of religion, this has all too often resulted in undue priority being placed on belief over ritual and in a treatment of religion as an "essentially cognitive" matter made up of a "set of propositions." This reduction of religion to individual belief not only shows how religion has become increasingly marginalized in the modern world but also betrays the covert theological bias that continues to exist within the field of the study of religion—namely, that the academic treatment of religious belief "is a modern, privatized Christian one."[5] As Asad writes, "This modest view of religion (which would have horrified the early Christian Fathers or medieval churchmen) is a product of the only legitimate space allowed to Christianity by post-Enlightenment society, the right to individual *belief*."[6]

It is true, as Asad and others such as Jacques Derrida and Jonathan Z. Smith have pointed out, that the terms "religion" and "secular" are not "translatable," that they have a Latin root and carry with them a history in which they have been forcibly imposed. This becomes most apparent when we consider the assumptions made about the connection—or lack thereof—between religion and politics. For Asad, behind the Western mandate of the separation of Church and State rests a twin assumption that associates modernization with secularization and also treats religion as an exclusively private, individual affair of personal conscience. As he writes, "This is at once part of a strategy (for secular liberals) of the confinement, and (for liberal Christians) of the defense, of religion." He goes on to say that "this separation of religion from power is a modern Western norm, the product of a unique post-Reformation history. The attempt to understand Muslim traditions by insisting [for instance] that in them religion and politics are coupled must, in my view, lead to failure."[7]

Meanwhile, it has become increasingly apparent to many that the private is not without public consequence and that, in spite of the efforts at separating religion from politics, the religious is always already a political affair. This was the subject of Derrida's essay on religion titled "Faith and Knowledge: Two Sources of 'Religion' at the Limits of Reason Alone," an essay oftentimes credited with bringing the current global resurgence of religion to the attention of philosophers. With this current interest in the political dimension of religion and with studies supporting a certain resurgence of religion on an individual level as well as the public visibility of religion within the political realm, it is clear now, as Peter Berger once cautioned, that "those who neglect religion in their analyses of contemporary affairs do so at great peril."[8] Berger, who was a one-time advocate of the secularization thesis, notes that we have moved from a secular age to a postsecular world in which it can no longer be safely assumed that the public is best served by keeping religion private.

It is ultimately Vattimo who is most helpful in showing how radical theology is a postsecular theology. For Vattimo, secularization is a process of *desacralization* that establishes the contemporary cultural conditions in which today's religions might have meaning. This belief is in accordance with his reading of the history of philosophy as the weakening of being. In this sense, the postmodern return of religion is very much a postsecular religiosity because there is no longer a unified religious authority—in short, religious authority has been relativized. But although Vattimo has frequently explored the significance of this so-called return of religion, he is careful not to confuse it with what others have called "desecularization." For instance, when asked whether the return of religion disproves the secularization thesis, Vattimo answered frankly, "I don't know what a desecularized world would be."[9] That is because, as he expressed earlier in that same conversation, whatever the nature of this resurgence of religion, it is "a religiosity that lives only as a consequence of secularization."[10]

Thus, we can say with Vattimo that *the postsecular is not a repudiation or reversal of secularization but is its historical and cultural consequence, which requires us to take note of the enduring existence of the religious.* In the words of Hans Joas, "'Postsecular' . . . doesn't express a sudden increase in religiosity, after its epochal decrease, but rather a change in mindset of those who, previously, felt justified in considering religions to be moribund."[11] Along with this changed mindset, however, comes a changed public perception about religion together with a revised politics about the proper role of religion within the public sphere. This is an argument put forward by de Vries when he associates the postsecular with the opportunity to rethink the role of religion within the public sphere or to rethink the proper relation between religion and politics and between the private and the public. As de Vries writes, "In such a reading, what undergoes transformation is less the nature of the secular state, let alone its constitutional arrangements guaranteeing, say, a separation between church and state, but rather the state's 'secularist self-understanding.'"[12]

In summary, then, for those whom secularization meant a diminishment of religious belief or the fading away of religion from the public's consciousness, clearly David Brooks's quip is correct: that was yesterday's incorrect vision of the future. But for others for whom secularization refers to the altered epistemological, cultural, and political terrain on which religion is practiced, believed, and studied, these remain live questions that must be pursued, even in the midst of today's postsecular world. Therefore, when I posit that radical theology is postsecular, this should *not* be construed as a theology of secularism. That is to say, it does not forecast the demise or insignificance of religion. Likewise, its aim is not to dismantle old beliefs and to advocate unbelief as the enlightened option. On the contrary, the radical theologian may think theologically but nondogmatically, which is much more in line with how Ivan Strenski conceives the scholar of religion who "thinks religion" as neither an attacker nor a defender but rather as a critic.[13]

Also, a radical theology, which is situated in a pluralistic society with a diversity of beliefs, is not beholden to the secularization thesis. The term *secular* indicates radical theology's autonomy from religious control and the sense that even though radical theology does not speak in an official capacity on behalf of the positive religions or the historical faith communities, there is still the need to reflect on the meaning of a society's sense of ultimacy. It is secular in the sense that it is worldly.

If the saeculum is the shared world that provides the common ground on which distinctions between the sacred and the profane are made, then a radical theology is also an act of profanation by its effect of desacralizing. This act of profanation is similar to what Sam Gill says of the impact Jonathan Z. Smith has had on shaping the field of religious studies. As Gill writes, "Smith's approach can only be recognized as an act of profanation."[14] In saying this, Gill is contrasting Smith's approach to that of Mircea Eliade, who, as an early comparative religion scholar, sought to bring some objectivity to the comparative study of religion with his focus on the various manifestations of the sacred in what he called "hierophanies." Although Eliade's religious categories were meant to be "nontheological and religiously neutral terms," in the words of Gill, they in fact stemmed "from an essentialist presumption that [did] little more than disguise their theological character." Smith's approach, however, "proceeds from no essential structures that define religion, but rather from the conviction that religion is a mode of creating meaning."[15] This is why the study of religion requires the profanation of the religious, because instead of simply accepting the inherited meanings associated with a particular religious phenomenon or as told by religious authorities, scholars must accept their outsider status, which, by virtue of this altered perspective, allows for the generation of new and different meanings. In the words of Gill, "The academic study of religion demands the removal of the sacred from the temple, or at least the examination of the temple and what takes place inside the temple from the perspective of the world outside."[16]

As historians of religion have acknowledged their outsider status, so too has radical theology accepted its outsider status. *Whereas the history of religions removes the sacred from the temple, radical theology is removed from the church.* Indeed, radical theology faces a double exile. Not only is it a *re-placed theology* that has been displaced from its original home within an ecclesiastical context in service to the church, but it also defines itself as a nondogmatic practice. This means that it purposely does not advance a particular confessional perspective and that it is independent of, and not answerable to, religious authority. Nevertheless, there remains a certain suspicion, if not hostility, to the very idea of doing or even studying theology within an academic context. For instance, countless genealogies of the academic field of religious studies have suggested that making religious studies a legitimate and respectable member of the academy requires purging it of its theological residue.[17] Thus, in a state of double exile, radical theology is simultaneously a profanation of ecclesiastical, confessional theologies and a profanation of religious studies as it is currently constituted.

In sum, to say that radical theology is postsecular is to acknowledge the secularizing effect on what it means to think theologically—that is to say, *the ways in which theology has been desacralized and profaned.* As we have learned from Feuerbach, theology is in and of the world. And, as we must still learn, theology must be made *for* the world. Thus, radical theology takes its lead from Tillich's theology of culture. But unlike with Tillich's theology of culture, which transformed the formal nature of theology while keeping its essential truths intact, with a radical theology both the means and content of theological thinking are fundamentally altered, or at least called into question.

2. Radical theology is postliberal, with a difference

As I already indicated in the introduction, the difference here must be specified in two different registers. First, by using the term *postliberal* I do not mean to conjoin radical theology with the postliberal, neo-Barthian school of theology associated with Frei, Lindbeck, Hauerwas, and others. Radical theology is neither neotraditional nor confessional. Indeed, this is the main point of differentiation for John Caputo's radical theology—namely, the distinction between confessional theology and a circumfessional theology, the former of which actually *exists* as the concrete expression of existing religious communities and the latter of which *insists* as a demand of thought responsive to the event harbored within the name of God. As Caputo explains, "I start with confessional theology while trying to expose it, to expose myself, to its own excess, to hold us all open to the event." It is therefore a theology under erasure, or, as it is otherwise known, a "weak theology."[18]

Second, by labeling radical theology as postliberal I do not mean that it is a repudiation of liberal theology; instead, I mean to mark a particular lineage of thought that grows out of the liberal tradition but nevertheless can and should be distinguished from it. Radical theology's history is a relatively brief one, beginning in the post–World War II years in a time of considerable angst and upheaval. Essentially simultaneous with the Non-Aligned Movement that was committed to the political task of decolonization that functioned as an *external* dismantling of Western hegemony, death-of-God theology developed as an *internal* movement within the West, functioning as an immanent critique. For some, this was equivalent to a post-Christian era, as the moral-metaphysical God of the West had been revealed as a false idol bequeathing a legacy of xenophobia, misogyny, and genocidal violence.[19] For others, the death of God was taken less as a cultural moment in time and more as a metaphysical truth and was thus announced as the "gospel of Christian atheism."[20]

At its most basic, radical theology was born from Dietrich Bonhoeffer's prison-cell writings, in which he issued the challenge to live in a world without the working hypothesis of God.[21] This is the world come of age and represents a distinctly postliberal sensibility in that, like Barth before him, Bonhoeffer totally repudiated the cultural form of religion that was the great achievement of the likes of Kant, Hegel, and Schleiermacher in their efforts to salvage religion from the Enlightenment critiques. Bonhoeffer's call for a religion-less Christianity set the template for radical theology's self-distancing from religion. From this perspective, it is easy to see the continuity between Bonhoeffer and Caputo, whose reading of Derrida's "religion without religion" represents just a variation on a theme.

Finally, I have also introduced another meaning for the term *postliberal* on which I have to insist in this conclusion. I must shift registers a bit now and explain that, by the term *liberal,* I am less concerned here with the tradition of liberal theology per se than I am with modern liberalism writ large. The work of Paul Kahn has been instructive on this point. Recall from the introduction when I was making the distinction between the legal and the political the point from Kahn that, strictly speaking, there is no liberal concept of the political. It is thus that I want to think what radical theology has heretofore left unthought.

My critique of radical theology—or, better, my effort at pushing its limits— has not been that it has somehow been complicit with regimes of power. I say this in spite of the fact that it has operated almost entirely within the provenance of a largely Western and Christian discourse and that it has largely neglected the potential alliances between feminist, liberationist, and process thinkers. Instead, my critique is that it has been ineffectual. This critique is consistent with the standard academic narrative of the movement, but with a difference. There is little debate over the fact that radical theology has been marginalized and obscured. But what I want to suggest is that it is possible to make a virtue out of this necessity. This is the importance of the rhetorical strategy adopted by Charles Winquist when he identifies theology as a minor intensive use of a major discourse. If we push Winquist even further, we see that this rhetorical strategy must be identified as a point of resistance. This is neither a form of play for personal edification nor the soteriological drama in another register but a *political act of creative destruction. It is postliberal in that it rejects the modern liberal separation of powers that renders religion merely a cultural artifact or a matter of individual personal conscience. In short, radical theology is postliberal insofar as it is a political theology.*

3. Radical theology is a political theology, or a liberation theology, with a difference

The critique of radical theology that I have developed most thoroughly is that it has been insufficiently political and, further, that there is no truly radical political theology. This concern has been mitigated in recent years by those who self-identify with the radical theological lineage and by the widespread theoretical attention to political theology generally and to the legacy of Carl Schmitt more specifically.[22] In the pages of this book I have engaged the difficult passage from the ethical to the political in the work of Levinas and the political becoming of hermeneutics in the work of Vattimo and Zabala, and I have done so at least partly to suggest models and resources for radical theology's own political becoming.

But by far the most effective and far-ranging theopolitical intervention has been that of liberation theology. It has been certain feminist theologians and queer theorists, moreover, who have best worked at the crossroads of radical theology and liberation theology. Although the lineage of radical theologians I have invoked throughout has largely neglected liberationist thought, pioneering figures such as Mary Daly, Rosemary Radford Ruether, and Catherine Keller have long drunk from both wells. Consider especially Ruether's work from 1970, *The Radical Kingdom*, in which she affirms and unleashes the revolutionary ideology that runs from the Radical Reformation through the death-of-God, civil rights, Black Power, and anarchist movements of the twentieth century.[23] Make no mistake, Ruether shows by her probing critique of all forms of hierarchy, patriarchy, and violence that this is feminist theology that is a radical theology. Moreover, this radical feminist theology demonstrates not only the possibility but also the efficacy of a radical political theology.

Likewise, the work of Marcella Althaus-Reid has invoked the roots of liberation theology as a dynamic theology that once embraced the hermeneutics of suspicion. But when it comes to issues of sexuality and family norms, liberation theology has been seized by a kind of orthodoxy. Interestingly, according to Althaus-Reid, this heterosexual norm is not a reflection of the views or priorities of the base ecclesial communities—the urban poor and those who have been excluded from Church discourses for centuries—but is instead a product of academic colonization on the part of Euro-American scholars. She claims that a "kind of closet Liberation Theology developed at the fringes of the churches that has been closer to popular Latin American spirituality and culture than the orthodox liberationist discourses."[24] This closet theology is a radical theology of kenosis—so radical, in fact, that in addition to being emptied of "ideological methodologies" and having its message fundamentally altered, it runs the risk of its own death.[25] What Althaus-Reid shows is a liberation theology that puts (its own) difference at the center of its critique and renewal. Thus it is a liberation theology with a difference.

When I cite Malabou as a principal resource for a radical theology of the future, I want to suggest that the repercussions of her thought for this variant of liberation theology can be real and provocative. We see her, for instance, achieving

a rehabilitation of the word *essence* in her discussion of gender and sexuality. It is
a critique, albeit a sympathetic one, of the social constructivism of queer theory
in which the ties between biology and identity have been absolutely severed. It is
a refusal of the distinctions between mind and brain that rests in her fundamental ontology of change.

What I have tried to argue is that Malabou represents a new and different kind
of radicality by her insistence that there is something more fundamental than identity and difference. This means, by her reckoning, that revolutionary, emancipa-
tory change is achieved not by a politics of identity but first and more basically by
the recognition that *before the difference of identity comes the change of being*—being
qua change, the change that happens by which each and every being always and already becomes different from itself. Always differing. This is a different difference
than that of Derridean différance, because it is a difference predicated on change.
For Malabou, difference does not operate as a transcendental concept, not even
as a quasi-transcendental concept. Instead, it is derived, produced. *Difference is displaced by change.* The really real is change, by virtue of which difference happens.

Likewise, it is a different difference than that which has animated the politics
of identity, and it is also different from Althaus-Reid's indecent theology. This puts
the moral, political, theological, and philosophical critiques of essence into critical
relief. As I have asked, what is it about essence, after all, to which we rightly object?
When employed in discussions of sexuality and gender or with race, *the problem
with talk of essence is that it implies, is associated with, and is employed toward the end of
a fixed essence, a naturalization of social norms, an ideological construction that then provides the rationalization of and script for continuing prejudice and oppression.* But what
if, in contrast to this fixed view, essence is thought of in plastic terms? The differences would be no less real—not even less material or biological—even while being recognized as a product of our own making. Difference has a history, a heritage
even. Differences matter. And while real, biological, and material, that need not
imply that we are stuck in or with these differences, captive to this history, with an
endless perpetuation of the same. Because just as change comes before difference,
change never stops. It is without beginning or end, a metabolic ontology that just
might be the basis of a new and different liberationist thinking.

This is the radical political theology I have in mind. Its merit, as I see it, is a
more robust political ontology. This would be a political becoming of radical theology that does not eschew ontology for its tendency to totalize or essentialize
but instead recognizes in being the very nature of change and resistance. It would
therefore be a revolution for both radical theology and liberation theology alike.

4. Radical theology is ontotheological, with a difference

At least since his short instructional text, *Philosophy and Theology*, Caputo has
sought to bring philosophy and theology together. He advises thinking of the two

as "different *acts* or modes of thinking, as two different dimensions of a whole human life" that can happily and productively coexist. Holding the two together yields thinking believers, or believing thinkers, people "of learning and of faith."[26] As discussed in chapters 4, 5, and 6, this mixing of discourses has been more the exception than the rule at least since the time of Heidegger and his highly influential critique of the so-called problem of ontotheology. For the most part, philosophers and theologians following in the wake of Heidegger have wittingly or unwittingly accepted his prescriptive analysis that philosophy and theology make two, along with the consequent assertions that there can be no Christian philosophy or philosophical theology, or that to write a theology, the word *being* should not appear.

And so, returning to Caputo, we are presented with what he has identified as two types of postmodern philosophy of religion, one that takes its lead from Kant and the other from Hegel. Kant conceived of religion as the unthought and the unthinkable, factually unknown and structurally unknowable. He salvages religion from the modern Enlightenment critique of it as dogmatic, superstitious, and irrational, but at a high price—namely, he cuts faith off from reason and thus separates theology from philosophy. At the same time, Kant reduces religion to morality, the only manifestation of religious life that safely abides within the confines of reason alone. Hegel, though, thinks the two together. In Caputo's words, "The truth needs philosophy but philosophy needs religion."[27] Rather than locating faith outside the bounds of reason and correlatively reducing religion to morality, religion is seen as a *Vorstellung*, or a figurative presentation of truth found, for instance, in the Christian stories of the incarnation, crucifixion, and resurrection of Christ. This is the prerational stuff of religious life that nourishes theological thinking. It is for this reason that Caputo credits Hegel with effectively inventing radical theology. Hegel has moved beyond the rationalism of Kant's delimitation of religion within the limits of reason and, at the same time, has rejected the otherworldliness, "mythic supernaturalism," or "two-worlds dualism" of classical orthodoxy. As Caputo writes, "Hegel has undermined the subordination of reason to revelation, of philosophy to revealed theology, and in the process made the contents of revelation part of the business of philosophy."[28]

I do not want to diminish the significance of this breaching of the divide between philosophy and theology. The insistence on treating philosophy and theology as two separate and distinct discourses has been one of the most unfortunate consequences of the identification and analysis of the problem of ontotheology. But as I have also tried to demonstrate, thinking philosophy and theology together gets us only part way to the more fundamental task, which is the rethinking of the ontotheological condition itself. While much of contemporary philosophical theology has been preoccupied, if not consumed, with the task of overcoming ontotheology, *theology might become more radical by thinking ontotheology otherwise, by embracing rather than resisting the ontotheological dimension of thought.* This is where

Malabou's work figures in. By providing an alternative conception of being, she allows for the rethinking of the once-eschewed identification of God with being.

As I have argued, the problem of ontotheology belies a quest for purity. In place of this quest for purity I have suggested miscegenation and metamorphosis as two images of the reject that might help to reclaim the ontotheological condition of thought. Ontotheology is a mixed discourse. It recognizes the ethicopolitical significance of thinking on the border. Thinking ontotheologically is a rejected way of thinking that nevertheless gives birth not so much to something new as to something old, something impure. *A miscegenated form of thought does not reject the reject but instead rejects the misguided quest for purity in the task of overcoming.*

Likewise, with metamorphosis the traditional reading of the problem of ontotheology is concerned with how it establishes an artificial limit—from the beginning to end and from the ground up, the identification of God with being is complete, a totalizing gesture that renders human history as irrelevant, if not dead on arrival. God is established as the eternal norm from which there can be no deviation. Ontotheology, then, is the ultimate alienation. Liberation is predicated on an impossible infinitude, (because) change is considered a violation of the natural order. It is also a fundamental self-contradiction—radical immanence betrays a secret desire for transcendence, (because) the being of God is a God *beyond* being. But, what if, as Malabou insists, there can be "radical transformation without exoticism?" If God is plastic, then not only is God change but God makes change and God changes. So given, the cause for concern that identifies ontotheology as a problem is eliminated. Metamorphosis does not represent the absurdist tragedy suggested by Kafka but is the secret agent by which we might come to know better the nature of reality, the immanent possibility for change, and the power of resistance.

By embracing the ontotheological condition of thought—which in this case means accepting miscegenation and metamorphosis as appropriate figures of theological thought—radical theology might get beyond questions of identity (and difference) or the territorial disputes so endemic to the academic industrial complex. Purity emits the stench of otherworldliness. The quest for purity that characterizes so many efforts at overcoming ontotheology is also haunted by the specter of God as the graven image of white male normativity. This is the stillborn, moral-metaphysical God who is dead. Exposing the idolatry inherent in this form of ontotheology has heretofore been the critical task of radical, death-of-God theology.

Miscegenation and metamorphosis are bolder still, affirming the divine in the impure, the polluted, the reject, and the flux. Beyond and before the pearly gates is the dirt and dirtiness of material flesh.

From dust to dust, and so it is with God.

5. Insofar as God exists, God is plastic

In my book *In Search of a Non-Dogmatic Theology* I made the case that by virtue of phenomenology's efforts to think to the other, one can now think theologically without God. That is to say, once one comes to accept that "every other is totally other," *one no longer needs the concept of God in order to think transcendence.* This suggests a transition from a vertical to a horizontal transcendence in which the impassable distance of the other is now displayed along a plane of immanence experienced in terms of a radical alterity. But this begs the question: if we can now think theologically with or without God, and we can now see a substitutability between phenomenology and theology when it comes to the structure of thought thinking to the other, then why do we need theology at all? With the demonstration of (radical) theology's compatibility with contemporary (Continental) philosophy, has theology been rendered merely a gloss? Does theology have any value and viability of its own?

The key difference between this book and that one is that here I have affirmed radical theology as an identifiable lineage and a discernible tradition of thought, whereas in the earlier work that lineage and tradition were merely assumed. And so it is that certain hard-earned insights key to the radical becoming of theology have been left unremarked. Return to the legacy of Bonhoeffer, for instance. I have said that radical theology was born from his prison-cell writings, in which he issued the challenge to live in a world without the working hypothesis of God. This was a moral, political, and existential challenge that emerged out of crisis. But what must be noted also is that it was biblically inspired. Bonhoeffer was a post-liberal theologian insofar as he accepted the argument from Karl Barth regarding the primacy of revelation for his epistemology of faith. And so it was accepted that the Word of God was revealed within the words of scripture. It is in scripture that we find a robust concept of faith that stands at odds with the modern liberal practice and cultural artifact of religion. It is there that we find Jesus's preaching that primarily consisted of references to the Kingdom of God. Jesus provided us with neither a concept of God nor clarity with regard to God's being or personhood; instead, when God was spoken, he was spoken of as an addressee, and when the Kingdom of God was explained, Jesus told deeply subversive parables that belied his status as a Jewish peasant and could have foretold his death as an anti-imperialist political revolutionary. This Bonhoefferian legacy may be affirmed anew and should make clear that radical theology is neither antitheological nor anti-Christian. On the contrary, the lineage of *radical theology, especially when joining forces with process and various forms of liberationist thought, provides at least one way of doing Christian theology otherwise.*

Likewise, although I have argued here that the radical Tillich was the onto-theological Tillich, what we might also uphold in the contemporary relevance of the lineage of radical theology is Tillich's nontheism. He cuts through the debates over the existence or nonexistence of God. An engagement with Tillich's thought displays the shallowness of the so-called new atheists in that their view of religion is entirely one-sided without the profound reckoning with the ambiguities of faith so characteristic of Tillich's existentialism. It is Tillich who writes the script of the death of God as a kind of crucible through which contemporary theological thinking must pass in order to be relevant and credible. As I indicated earlier, this script is not without its own problems, which are akin to the distinction Derrida once made between negative theology and deconstruction—namely, to the extent that Tillich affirms the God beyond God, his thinking belies a quest for purity and his death-of-God critique remains entirely within the provenance of a metaphysics of presence. This is why his separate claim regarding God as being itself is worth thinking anew.

Of course, the hermeneutics of suspicion is also an indispensable resource within the radical theological lineage. For instance, we might consider the significance of Ludwig Feuerbach with regard to the meaning of Tillich's identification of God with being itself. It is Feuerbach who calls into question the very condition of possibility for thinking theologically. If all talk of God is really talk of humanity, then what are we to make of the claims of the being of God? The Feuerbachian challenge remains, in the sense of the difficulty, if not impossibility, of closing or erasing the gap between the (human) experience of thinking about God and (still-human) thoughts about God as Godself. Some might argue along with Barth that revelation provides its own epistemological grounds, but, even so, the claims derived still rest in an interpretative process that cannot escape the circle of human experience and categories of understanding. There is no thinking of God's essence that is unmediated. The question that remains is whether this projection is necessarily alienating.

Caputo comes to this Feuerbachian insight by way of his radical hermeneutics, in which he demonstrates the full reach of deconstruction when he tells us that everything that has been constructed can be deconstructed. This includes the concept of God, a mediated historical construct that belongs in different ways to the particular historic faiths. As Caputo's deconstructive phenomenology of religion (without religion) develops into his (weak) theology, he makes certain claims not only about the affirmative religious passion that drives deconstruction but also about what it is we affirm when we speak about God. As this develops, we get a more explicit identification with theological thinking as well as a more explicitly radical theology. We hear how the desire for God outlives the death of God. We learn how the strong, moral-metaphysical, sovereign God must be replaced with a profession of the weakness of God, who offers no easy guarantees, no assurances. This weak God does not lord over history divvying out rewards and punishments, an orchestrator of divine violence, but is a suffering God whose will relies entirely on humanity. In this way, the Kingdom of God resembles less a realm of sovereign rule and more a sacred anarchy, with an indeterminacy that evokes the radical implications of process thought. We learn the difference between the name of God and the event of God, with the two standing together as a call and response. Finally, we are told that God does not exist; rather, God persists and insists. And so, by virtue of the event of truth contained within the name of God, whatever it is we affirm when we speak of God becomes another placeholder for the undeconstructible.

To conclude, I believe we may push this further as well. It is time that radical theology give consideration to the thought that God is plastic. Whereas Caputo leads us to the same place as Tillich with regard to nontheism, insofar as he professes the nonexistence of God, as we have already seen with Malabou, she insists that there is nothing that is undeconstructible. On the contrary, the undeconstructible is just another placeholder for transcendence or for the immaterial. Just as she rejects the split between nature and culture in her rehabilitation of essence, the concept of plasticity might effectively deconstruct the distinction between the conditioned and the unconditional operative in Caputo's thought. To combat the naturalization of social norms that has been the ideological basis for patriarchy and white supremacy, Malabou has resisted the temptation to read this as merely a cultural byproduct that would suggest the immateriality or irrelevance of nature. As I have already shown, her ontology of change is the key to this intervention on her behalf. That is to say, as long as one understands that it is not just beings that change, but being itself that changes, the talk of essence need not imply a fixed nature—biology is not destiny. What is does not necessarily fix what will be. In short, change is not predicated on otherness or transcendence, but difference happens as a result of change, which is being's ownmost possibility. This is what Malabou means when she speaks of change *without exoticism*.

This metabolic ontology applies also to the existence and nature of God. One motif that has run throughout the history of death-of-God theology has been the proclamation of the death of God as a crucible in an iconoclastic spirit. This important critique has revealed the normative concept of God as an idol. But another motif, which goes even further, has been the insistence that the death of God refers not just to the historical and culturally conditioned concept of God but to God's very being and nature. This is what Žižek means when he seeks to "harden" the death of God in contrast to what he labels the "soft" postmodern theology of Caputo and Vattimo. And this is the point at which radical death-of-God theology is correctly identified with atheism. It is Altizer more than any other who has sounded this theme, and it is what he means when he refers to the "apocalyptic transfiguration of the Godhead."

At the same time, when the development of an ontology based on the concept of plasticity teaches us that the nature of being is to change, what does this mean for radical theology? It means that on a basic level we may affirm the testimony of a God who not only gives form but receives form. This is a way of speaking that gives expression to the world's formation through the limits and possibilities of nature and of nature's capacity for generation and evolution. It also acknowledges the ways we have altered nature through language and technology and that, by virtue of our interdependency, nature is always already culture. This latter notion is captured by the language of entwinement, or, from quantum mechanics, entanglement—a recognition of an agency inherent to all things, a new materialism by which matter is not rendered as inert mass but instead as a notion of matter that matters. Put theologically, it must be said that the God who forms the world is informed by it. This would not be a pure projection in that God becomes whatever we want God to be or simply that we make God what we will. In Malabou's words, that would be a plasticity without the genius—that is to say, a plasticity defined in terms of flexibility only and without the power to resist.

So to say that God is plastic is also to say that God resists, even to the point of death and beyond. This suggests an alternative reading of the postsecular. It is not so much that postmodernism establishes the cultural and epistemological conditions of possibility for the return of religion in its pure fideistic form. And it is not as the *Time* magazine cover story from 1969 suggests triumphantly, that after radical death-of-God theology had its brief moment, God has somehow come back to life, resplendent, triumphant, and unchanged. This belies plasticity in the same way that regeneration must be distinguished from resurrection, or the salamander from the phoenix. What we might say instead is that *God resists death*. To confess God as plastic is to identify God not only with the being that is change but also with the life that resists death. It is not a life after death but a life before—that is, the constituent power or ontological basis of the life that goes on living in the midst of being bruised and bloodied and scarred. Or, more radical still, the plastic God is a God whose death is revealed in the innumerable deaths of God's good creation. In other words, *every death is meaningful*. The death of God is no more or less significant than the innocent civilians counted as collateral damage in today's wars, than the death of the elderly Alzheimer's patient who has forgotten her name, than the malnourished child starving to death. To me, this is the great challenge of James Cone's *The Cross and the Lynching Tree*—namely, that from the black liberationist perspective, the more one appreciates and understands the significance of Christ's death, the more one recognizes God in the lynchee, and thus the more one rejects and resists the violent normalcy of human civilization.

So, to be clear, *the radical theology I have in mind does not bespeak the nonexistence of God but rather the plasticity of God.* The unconditional is not determined in the sense that it is fixed, but it is determined in the sense that it is plastic. Plasticity plumbs the depths and scales the heights to the point at which even the affirmation of the God beyond God is now subject to the radical death-of-God critique. God changes. The God who was, is no longer. Yet, still we may see the God who is coming. Malabou's rendering of Hegel affirms not only the way in which the essential becomes accidental but also the way in which the accidental becomes essential. It goes beyond merely the cultural critique of religion and the positive reaffirmation of religion characteristic of postsecular discourses. And so we are able once again to affirm the existence of God insofar as God is plastic. God remains not just as a word for desire or the event of truth harbored within the name but as the ever-changing ground of being—indeed, as being itself through which we have the power not just to reenvision the world but to change it.

And so it is that the radical theology of the future that emerged out of the death-of-God movement is no longer bound to it, no longer bounded by it. The death of God marks a moment. It marks a moment not just as a passing fad but as a realization by which we can better understand the nature of being as change. It marks a moment that remains as the inception of a lineage that lives on by its insurrectionary potential. And so it is that radical theology might be liberated— beyond its fixation on death, beyond its end-world apocalypticism—such that its dormant political and ontological implications might finally be realized.

This book has been an effort toward that end. It emerges out of the radical theological lineage. It employs radical theology as a methodology. It shares with radical theology a sensibility. At the same time, it reads the tradition against itself by introducing new voices and placing the ontological, political, and cultural in the foreground. From transcendence and reformation to transformation and creativity, from the apocalyptic to the counterapocalyptic, from death to life, and from resurrection to regeneration, the shifting contours are set for the renewal, rehabilitation, and reactivation of a radical theology of the future.

NOTES

Introduction

1. See Scott Anderson, *Lawrence in Arabia: War, Deceit, Imperial Folly and the Making of the Modern Middle East* (New York: Doubleday, 2013).

2. Jonathan Rose, *The Literary Churchill: Author, Reader, Actor* (New Haven, CT: Yale University Press, 2014), p. 170.

3. Charles E. Winquist, *Desiring Theology* (Chicago: University of Chicago Press, 1995), pp. ix, x.

4. Ibid., p. xi.

5. Gilles Deleuze, *The Logic of Sense*, trans. Mark Lester (New York: Columbia University Press, 1990), p. 281.

6. Charles E. Winquist, *The Surface of the Deep* (Aurora, CO: The Davies Group, 2003), p. 271.

7. See Friedrich Nietzsche, *Writings from the Late Notebooks*, ed. Rüdiger Bittner (Cambridge, UK: Cambridge University Press, 2003), esp. p. 139.

8. Most significantly, see Peter Rollins, *Insurrection: To Believe Is Human, to Doubt, Divine* (New York: Howard Books, 2011).

9. John D. Caputo, *The Insistence of God: A Theology of Perhaps* (Bloomington: Indiana University Press, 2013).

10. See Slavoj Žižek and John Milbank, *The Monstrosity of Christ: Paradox or Dialectic?* (Cambridge, MA: MIT Press, 2009), pp. 256–260.

11. Mark C. Taylor, *Erring: A Postmodern A/theology* (Chicago: University of Chicago Press, 1984), p. 6. Italics his.

12. Most especially, see John D. Caputo, *The Prayers and Tears of Jacques Derrida: Religion without Religion* (Bloomington: Indiana University Press, 1997).

13. For his radicalization of hermeneutics, see John D. Caputo, *Radical Hermeneutics: Repetition, Deconstruction, and the Hermeneutic Project* (Bloomington: Indiana University Press, 1987); and John D. Caputo, *More Radical Hermeneutics: On Not Knowing Who We Are* (Bloomington: Indiana University Press, 2000). For his radicalization of theology, see Caputo, *The Insistence of God*.

14. The school of postliberal theology has come to be defined and accepted as a neo-Barthian movement under the direction of and inspired by the Yale theologians Hans Frei and George Lindbeck. This school of postliberal theology has adopted a critical posture toward the tradition of modern liberal theology by announcing itself as a point of radical departure from that tradition. As such, it has found sympathy with certain schools of progressive evangelicalism, although other forms of postliberalism might be imagined. The

difference depends on the meaning of the term *post-*. John B. Cobb and Bernard Eugene Meland, for instance, once suggested a postliberal theology of their own that would have been less a departure from modern liberalism and more a moving through and beyond liberalism. For a more thorough discussion of this subject, see Gary Dorrien on the "postliberal challenge," in *The Making of American Liberal Theology: Crisis, Irony, and Postmodernity, 1950–2005* (Louisville, KY: Westminster John Knox Press, 2006), pp. 530–534.

15. Gary Dorrien, *The Making of American Liberal Theology: Imagining Progressive Religion, 1805–1900* (Louisville, KY: Westminster John Knox Press, 2001), p. xv.

16. Ibid., p. xxiii.

17. Dorrien, *The Making of American Liberal Theology, 1950–2005*, p. 1.

18. See Gabriel Vahanian, *The Death of God: The Culture of Our Post-Christian Era* (New York: George Braziller, 1957).

19. See Richard L. Rubenstein, *After Auschwitz: History, Theology, and Contemporary Judaism*, 2nd ed. (Baltimore: Johns Hopkins University Press, 1996); and Morris Berman, *The Twilight of American Culture* (New York: W. W. Norton, 2000).

20. Taylor, *Erring*.

21. Thomas J. J. Altizer, *The Gospel of Christian Atheism* (Philadelphia: Westminster Press, 1961); Carl A. Raschke, *The End of Theology* (Aurora, CO: The Davies Group, 2000).

22. See Jeffrey W. Robbins, *In Search of a Non-Dogmatic Theology* (Aurora, CO: The Davies Group, 2003).

23. Paul Kahn, *Sacred Violence: Torture, Terror, and Sovereignty* (Ann Arbor: University of Michigan Press, 2008), p 135.

24. Ibid., pp. 135–136.

25. See Jeffrey W. Robbins, *Radical Democracy and Political Theology* (New York: Columbia University Press, 2011).

26. Kahn, *Sacred Violence*, p. 139.

27. Ibid., pp. 138, 139.

28. Dorrien, *The Making of American Liberal Theology, 1950–2005*, p. 1.

1. The Theological Becoming of Phenomenology

1. See Mark Lilla, *The Stillborn God: Religion, Politics and the Modern West* (New York: Vintage, 2008).

2. Ludwig Wittgenstein, *Tractatus Logico-Philosophicus*, trans. D. F. Pears and B. F. McGuinness (New York: Routledge, 1974), p. 5.

3. Dominique Janicaud, "The Theological Turn of French Phenomenology," in *Phenomenology and the "Theological Turn": The French Debate* (New York: Fordham University Press, 2000).

4. Ibid., p. 99.

5. Ibid., p. 96.

6. Ibid., p. 27.

7. For instance, see Jacques Derrida, "Violence and Metaphysics," in which he writes that "Levinas resigns himself to betraying his own intention in his philosophical discourse." In *Writing and Difference*, trans. Alan Bass (London: Routledge, 1978), p. 151.

8. Janicaud, "The Theological Turn," pp. 37–38.

9. Ibid., p. 42.

10. Ibid., p. 99.

11. See Thomas J. J. Altizer, *The New Gospel of Christian Atheism* (Aurora, CO: The Davies Group, 2002).

12. See Jacques Derrida, *The Gift of Death*, trans. David Willis (Chicago: University of Chicago Press, 1995), esp. chap. 4, pp. 82–115.

13. The idea that Heidegger and Barth are two sides of the same coin is developed in chapter 1 of my *Between Faith and Thought: An Essay on the Ontotheological Condition* (Charlottesville: University of Virginia Press, 2003), pp. 13–39.

14. For instance, David Tracy writes that Barth is Marion's "natural ally in Protestant theology." Foreword to *God without Being: Hors-Texte*, by Jean-Luc Marion, trans. Thomas Carlson (Chicago: University of Chicago Press, 1991), p. xii.

15. See Steven G. Smith, *The Argument to the Other: Reason beyond Reason in the Thought of Karl Barth and Emmanuel Levinas* (Chico: Scholars Press, 1983). See also Graham Ward, *Barth, Derrida, and the Language of Theology* (Cambridge, UK: Cambridge University Press, 1995).

16. See Ward, *Barth, Derrida, and the Language of Theology.*

17. Taylor, *Erring*, p. 6.

18. Ibid., pp. 5–6.

19. See John Robinson, *Honest to God* (Philadelphia: Westminster, 1963).

20. As Clayton Crockett writes, "I am suggesting that we . . . think of religion as the breakdown of these autonomous spheres of culture, not in the sense of the dissolution of such spheres, but in their 'depth' or 'higher form,' that is, where they fold back upon themselves in their attempt to represent the cultural or psychological dynamics that make them possible in the first place. In this sense, theology can be defined as the thinking of this sublime religiosity, that is, the reflection which pursues or traces the folds to their very 'breaking-point.'" *A Theology of the Sublime* (London: Routledge, 2001), p. 105.

21. See Winquist, *Desiring Theology*, pp. xi, 134.

22. Hent de Vries, *Philosophy and the Turn to Religion* (Baltimore: Johns Hopkins University Press, 1999), pp. 2–3.

23. Ibid., p. 3.

24. Ibid., p. 9.

25. Ibid., p. 18.

26. Gianni Vattimo, *After Christianity*, trans. Luca D'Isanto (New York: Columbia University Press, 2002), p. 16.

27. Ibid., pp. 18–19.

28. Janicaud, "The Theological Turn," p. 99.

29. See Marion, *God without Being*; Robert Scharlemann, "The Being of God When God Is Not Being God," in *Deconstruction and Theology* (New York: Crossroad, 1982); Vattimo, *After Christianity*; and Richard Kearney, *The God Who May Be: A Hermeneutics of Religion* (Bloomington: Indiana University Press, 2001).

30. Janicaud, "The Theological Turn," p. 103.

2. From the Ethical to the Political

1. Jacques Derrida, *Adieu: To Emmanuel Levinas*, trans. Pascale-Anne Brault and Michael Naas (Stanford, CA: Stanford University Press, 1999), p. 4.

2. Simon Critchley, *The Ethics of Deconstruction: Derrida and Levinas* (Oxford, UK: Blackwell Publishers, 1992), p. 3.

3. Ibid., p. 2.

4. See John D. Caputo, *Against Ethics: Contributions to a Poetics of Obligation with Constant Reference to Deconstruction* (Bloomington: Indiana University Press, 1993).

5. As Edith Wyschogrod writes, "A postmodern ethics? Is this not a contradiction in terms? If postmodernism is a critical expression describing the subversion of philosophical language, a 'mutant of Western humanism,' then how can one hope for an ethics when the conditions of meaning are themselves under attack?" *Saints and Postmodernism: Revisioning Moral Philosophy* (Chicago: University of Chicago Press, 1990), p. xiii.

6. Roger Burggraeve, *The Wisdom of Love in the Service of Love: Emmanuel Levinas on Justice, Peace, and Human Rights*, trans. Jeffrey Bloechl (Milwaukee: Marquette University Press, 2002), p. 28.

7. For example, see Leonardo Messinese, *The Problem of God in Modern Philosophy*, trans. Philip Larrey (Aurora, CO: The Davies Group, 2005).

8. John D. Caputo, *On Religion* (New York: Routledge, 2001), p. 46.

9. Emmanuel Levinas, "God and Philosophy," in *Of God Who Comes to Mind*, trans. Bettina Bergo (Stanford, CA: Stanford University Press, 1998), pp. 62–63.

10. Ibid., p. 64.

11. Ibid.

12. Ibid., p. 66.

13. Ibid., p. 65.

14. Ibid., p. 67.

15. Ibid., p. 69.

16. Ibid., pp. 69–70.

17. From "'Only a God Can Save Us': *Der Spiegel's* Interview with Martin Heidegger (1966)," in *The Heidegger Controversy: A Critical Reader*, ed. Richard Wolin (Cambridge, MA: MIT Press, 1998), p. 107.

18. Emmanuel Levinas, "Signature," *Research in Phenomenology* 8 (1978): p. 177.

19. Emmanuel Levinas, *Otherwise Than Being, or Beyond Essence* (Pittsburgh: Duquesne University Press, 1998), p. 161.

20. Ibid., p. 157.

21. Ibid.

22. Derrida, *Adieu*, p. 99.

23. As Levinas writes, "Then ethical language succeeds in expressing the paradox in which phenomenology finds itself abruptly thrown. For ethics, beyond the political, is found at the level of this reverting. Starting with the approach, the description finds the neighbor bearing the trace of a withdrawal that orders it as a face." *Otherwise Than Being*, p. 121.

24. Derrida, *Adieu*, p. 76.

25. Ibid., p. 71.

26. Kenneth Surin, "Rewriting the Ontological Script of Liberation: On the Question of Finding a New Kind of Political Subject," in *Theology and the Political: The New Debate,* ed. Creston Davis, John Milbank, and Slavoj Žižek (Durham, NC: Duke University Press, 2005), p. 255.

27. Winquist, *Desiring Theology,* p. 141.

28. Emmanuel Levinas, "The Rights of Man and the Rights of the Other," in *Outside the Subject,* trans. Michael B. Smith (Stanford, CA: Stanford University Press, 1994), pp. 122–123.

29. Ibid., pp. 124–125.

30. Ibid., p. 125.

31. Levinas, "Signature," p. 177.

32. For instance, see Adriaan Peperzak, *To the Other: An Introduction to the Philosophy of Emmanuel Levinas* (West Lafayette, IN: Purdue University Press, 1993), esp. pp. 4–7.

33. Catherine Malabou, *Plasticity at the Dusk of Writing: Dialectic, Destruction, Deconstruction,* trans. Carolyn Shread (New York: Columbia University Press, 2010), p. 40.

34. Ibid., pp. 40–41.

35. Ibid., p. 42.

36. Ibid., p. 43.

37. Judith Butler, *Parting Ways: Jewishness and the Critique of Zionism* (New York: Columbia University Press, 2012), pp. 9–10.

38. Ibid., pp. 12–13.

39. Ibid., p. 23.

40. Ibid.

41. Ibid., p. 21.

42. James H. Cone, *The Cross and the Lynching Tree* (New York: Orbis Books, 2011), p. 56.

43. Butler, *Parting Ways,* p. 23.

44. Ibid., p. 13.

45. Charles W. Mills, *The Racial Contract* (Ithaca, NY: Cornell University Press, 1997), p. 1.

46. Ibid., pp. 18–19.

47. Ibid., p. 94.

3. The Political Becoming of Hermeneutics

1. Mark Lilla, *The Reckless Mind: Intellectuals in Politics* (New York: New York Review Books, 2001), p. 216.

2. Gianni Vattimo and Santiago Zabala, *Hermeneutic Communism: From Heidegger to Marx* (New York: Columbia University Press, 2011).

3. Walter Mignolo, *The Darker Side of Western Modernity: Global Futures, Decolonial Options* (Durham, NC: Duke University Press, 2011), p. 55.

4. Ibid., p. 57.

5. Quoted in Richard Wolin, ed., *The Heidegger Controversy: A Critical Reader* (Cambridge, MA: MIT Press, 1998), p. 4.

6. Ibid., p. 2.

7. John D. Caputo, *Demythologizing Heidegger* (Bloomington: Indiana University Press, 1993), p. 3.

8. Catherine Malabou, *The Heidegger Change: On the Fantastic in Philosophy*, ed. Peter Skafish (Albany, NY: SUNY Press, 2004), pp. 2–3.

9. Ibid., p. 7.

10. Ibid., pp. 139, 270.

11. Ibid., p. 278. Italics hers.

12. Ibid., p. 286.

13. Vattimo and Zabala, *Hermeneutic Communism*, pp. 2–3.

14. Ibid., p. 1.

15. Ibid., p. 4.

16. Ibid., p. 50.

17. Ibid., p. 4.

18. Ibid., p. 5.

19. See Robbins, *Radical Democracy and Political Theology*.

20. See Vattimo and Zabala, *Hermeneutic Communism*, pp. 76–77.

21. Mignolo, *The Darker Side of Western Modernity*, p. xvi.

22. Ibid.

23. Ibid., p. xviii.

24. Vattimo and Zabala, *Hermeneutic Communism*, p. 122.

25. Ibid., p. 129.

26. Vattimo and Zabala, *Hermeneutic Communism*, p. 122.

27. Ibid., pp. 110, 111.

28. Ibid., p. 111.

29. Mignolo, *The Darker Side of Western Modernity*, p. xxxi.

30. It is worth noting here how Zabala himself has acknowledged that the term *communism* is not native to the South American political movements and figures that he and Vattimo have together cited. For instance, in an interview with Silvia Mazzini, he admitted that it is true that Chavez does not call himself a communist but instead uses the term "socialism for the twenty-first century." See "Chavez Is Still a Model for Obama: Interview with Santiago Zabala," *Al Jazeera*, November 11, 2012, http://www.aljazeera.com/indepth/opinion/2012/11/2012118121638309403.html.

31. For instance, see Ola Sigurdson, *Theology and Marxism in Eagleton and Žižek: A Conspiracy of Hope* (New York: Palgrave Macmillan, 2012).

32. Terry Eagleton, *The Illusions of Postmodernism* (London: Blackwell, 1996), p. 9.

33. Ibid., p. 14.

34. Ibid., pp. 21–23.

35. Ibid., p. 132.

36. Surin, "Rewriting the Ontological Script of Liberation," pp. 240–266.

37. Ibid., pp. 252–253.

38. Ibid., p. 255.

39. Ibid., p. 257.

4. Changing Ontotheology

1. Most especially, see John Thatanamil, "Tillich and the Postmodern," in *The Cambridge Companion to Paul Tillich*, ed. Russell Re Manning (Cambridge, UK: Cambridge University Press, 2008), pp. 288–302. See also J. Blake Huggins, "Tillich and Ontotheology: On the Fidelity of Betrayal," *Bulletin of the North American Paul Tillich Society* 38, no. 3 (Summer 2012): pp. 27–36.

2. Thatanamil, "Tillich and the Postmodern," p. 290.

3. See Jacques Derrida, "How to Avoid Speaking: Denials," in *Derrida and Negative Theology*, eds. Harold Coward and Toby Foshay (Albany, NY: SUNY Press, 1992).

4. John D. Caputo, *The Prayers and Tears of Jacques Derrida: Religion without Religion* (Bloomington: Indiana University Press, 1997), p. 46.

5. See Martin Heidegger, "Phenomenology and Theology," in *The Piety of Thinking* (Bloomington: Indiana University Press, 1977), p. 6.

6. For instance, in *The Piety of Thinking*, Heidegger writes, "We understand each other better when each speaks in his own language."

7. Heidegger, *The Piety of Thinking*, p. 21.

8. This is the basic point of my book *Between Faith and Thought: An Essay on the Ontotheological Condition* (Charlottesville: University of Virginia Press, 2003).

9. See Robbins, *Between Faith and Thought*, pp. 24–28.

10. See Bernd Jaspert and Geoffrey W. Bromiley, eds., *Karl Barth–Rudolf Bultmann: Letters, 1922–1966* (Grand Rapids, MI: Eerdmans, 1981), p. 41.

11. See Heidegger, *The Piety of Thinking*, pp. 59–71.

12. Mary Ann Stenger and Ronald H. Stone, *Dialogues of Paul Tillich* (Macon, GA: Mercer University Press, 2002), p. 188.

13. Cone, *The Cross and the Lynching Tree*, p. 30.

14. Ibid., p. 32.

15. Ibid., pp. 56, 60.

16. See J. Kameron Carter, *Race: A Theological Account* (Oxford, UK: Oxford University Press, 2008), p. 188.

17. James H. Cone, *Black Theology of Liberation: Twentieth Anniversary Edition*, (Maryknoll, NY: Orbis Books, 2001), p. xix. Italics his.

18. Carter, *Race*, p. 183.

19. Ibid., pp. 188, 187.

20. Ibid., p. 4.

21. Thatanamil, "Tillich and the Postmodern," p. 292.

22. Ibid.

23. Ibid., p. 293.

24. Ibid., p. 299.

25. For instance, see the doctoral dissertation by Christopher D. Rodkey, *In the Horizon of the Infinite: Paul Tillich and the Dialectic of the Sacred* (Madison, NJ: Drew University, 2008). See also Richard Grigg, *Gods after God: An Introduction to Contemporary Radical Theologies* (Albany, NY: SUNY Press, 2006).

26. For instance, see the blog post by Peter Rollins, "Dawkins, Dennett and Hitchens: The New Theists?" *The Huffington Post* (blog), March 10, 2013, http://www.huffingtonpost .com/peter-rollins/dawkins-dennett-and-hitch_b_2830963.html. See also Jeffrey W. Robbins and Christopher D. Rodkey, "Beating 'God' to Death: Radical Theology and the New Atheism," in *Religion and the New Atheism: A Critical Appraisal*, ed. Amarnath Amarasingam (Boston: Brill, 2010): pp. 25–36.

27. For an example of how Tillich has been situated within the history of the developing field of religious studies, see Walter H. Capps, *Religious Studies: The Making of a Discipline* (Minneapolis: Fortress Press, 1995), esp. pp. 30–35. For a discussion of the notion of "secular theology" and its place within the academic study of religion, see two special issues of *The Council of Societies for the Study of Religion Bulletin* 37, nos. 2 and 3 (April and September 2008).

28. For instance, see John Thatanamil, *The Immanent Divine: God, Creation, and the Human Predicament* (Minneapolis: Fortress Press, 2006). See also Capps, *Religious Studies*, pp. 289–296.

29. Robert P. Scharlemann is the exception to this rule. See especially his *Religion and Reflection: Essays on Paul Tillich's Theology* (Berlin: LIT Verlag, 2005).

30. Carter, *Race*, p. 3.

31. Ibid., p. 30.

32. Ibid.

33. John D. Caputo, *"Voir Venir:* How Far Plasticity Can Be Stretched," *theory@buffalo* 16 (2012): p. 116.

34. Catherine Malabou, *The Future of Hegel* (New York: Routledge, 2005), p. 134.

35. Ibid., p. 155.

36. Ibid., p. 145.

37. Thatanamil, "Tillich and the Postmodern," p. 290.

38. See Robbins, *Between Faith and Thought*.

39. Caputo, *Demythologizing Heidegger*, p. 28.

40. Ibid., p. 116.

41. Ibid., p. 6.

42. See Malabou, *Plasticity at the Dusk of Writing*, pp. 17–29.

43. Ibid., p. 44.

44. Ibid.

45. Carter, *Race*, p. 188.

5. The Hermeneutics of the Kingdom of God

1. See John D. Caputo and Gianni Vattimo, *After the Death of God*, ed. Jeffrey W. Robbins (New York: Columbia University Press, 2007).

2. Taylor, *Erring*, p. 6. Taylor is echoing a claim first made by Carl A. Raschke that deconstruction is, in final analysis, the death of God put into writing. *Deconstruction and Theology* (New York: Crossroad, 1982), p. 3.

3. See Paul Ricouer, *Freud and Philosophy: An Essay on Interpretation*, trans. Denis Savage (New Haven, CT: Yale University Press, 1970), pp. 32–36.

4. In Jacques Derrida and Gianni Vattimo, eds., *Religion*, (Palo Alto, CA: Stanford University Press, 1998). For more on the philosophical treatment of this postmodern return of religion, see Hent de Vries, *Philosophy and the Turn to Religion* (Baltimore: Johns Hopkins University Press, 1999); and Dominique Janicaud et al., *Phenomenology and the "Theological Turn": The French Debate* (New York: Fordham University Press, 2000).

5. For an elaboration on this observation, see Clayton Crockett and Jeffrey W. Robbins, *Religion, Politics and the Earth: The New Materialism* (New York: Palgrave Macmillan, 2012), pp. 17–36.

6. Van Harvey, *Feuerbach and the Interpretation of Religion* (Cambridge, UK: Cambridge University Press, 1995).

7. Tyler Roberts, *Contesting Spirit: Nietzsche, Affirmation, Religion* (Princeton, NJ: Princeton University Press, 1998).

8. James DiCenso, *The Other Freud: Religion, Culture and Psychoanalysis* (New York: Routledge, 1999).

9. Caputo, *Prayers and Tears*, p. 14.

10. John D. Caputo, *On Religion* (New York: Routledge, 2001), pp. 56–66; and Caputo and Vattimo, *After the Death of God*, pp. 66–70, 144–150.

11. De Vries, *Philosophy and the Turn to Religion*, p. 9.

12. John D. Caputo, *The Weakness of God: A Theology of the Event* (Bloomington: Indiana University Press, 2006), p. 1.

13. Karl Barth, *The Word of God and the Word of Man*, trans. Douglas Horton (Gloucester, MA: Peter Smith, 1978), p. 186. Emphasis in the original.

14. See Caputo and Vattimo, *After the Death of God*, p. 135; and "Loosening Philosophy's Tongue: A Conversation with Jack Caputo," *The Journal for Cultural and Religious Theory* 3, no. 2 (April 2002), http://www.jcrt.org/archives/03.2/index.html?page=caputo_raschke.shtml.

15. John D. Caputo, *What Would Jesus Deconstruct? The Good News of Postmodernity for the Church* (Grand Rapids, MI: Baker Academic, 2007).

16. Ibid., p. 7.

17. Ibid., p. 19.

18. Ibid., pp. 24, 26.

19. Ibid., p. 29.

20. Ibid., p. 30.

21. Ibid., p. 121.

22. Ibid., p. 96.

23. Ibid., p. 103.

24. Ibid., p. 94.

25. Ibid., p. 87.

26. Ibid., p. 95.

27. Ibid., p. 81.

28. George Yancy, introduction to *Christology and Whiteness: What Would Jesus Do?*, ed. George Yancy (New York: Routledge, 2012), p. 4.

29. Ibid., p. 5.

30. Ibid., p. 12.

31. Ibid.

32. Karen Teel, "What Jesus Wouldn't Do: A White Theologian Engages Whiteness," in *Christology and Whiteness: What Would Jesus Do?*, ed. George Yancy (New York: Routledge, 2012), p. 25.

33. Ibid. Italics hers.

34. Caputo, *What Would Jesus Deconstruct?*, pp. 81, 82.

35. Ibid., p. 110.

36. Ibid., p. 111.

37. See Jean-Luc Nancy, *Dis-Enclosure: The Deconstruction of Christianity* (New York: Fordham University Press, 2007).

38. See Rudolf Bultmann, *New Testament and Mythology* (Minneapolis: Augsburg Fortress, 1984).

39. Caputo, *What Would Jesus Deconstruct?*, pp. 26–27.

40. Ibid., p. 137.

41. Ibid.

42. Caputo, *The Weakness of God*, p. 14.

43. Ibid.

44. Ibid., p. 13.

45. See Caputo's differentiation of the name and the event in *The Weakness of God*, pp. 2–7.

46. See Caputo, *The Weakness of God*, pp. 23–41. For a critical exposition of the theo-political implications of this suggestion, see Clayton Crockett, *Radical Political Theology: Religion and Politics After Liberalism* (New York: Columbia University Press, 2011), pp. 43–59.

47. For instance, see John D. Caputo, *Against Ethics: Contributions to a Poetics of Obligation with Constant Reference to Deconstruction* (Bloomington: Indiana University Press, 1993).

48. Caputo, *Weakness of God*, p. 96.

49. Ibid. Italics in the original.

50. See John Dominic Crossan, *Jesus: A Revolutionary Biography* (San Francisco: HarperSanFrancisco, 1994).

51. See John Dominic Crossan, *God and Empire: Jesus against Rome, Then and Now* (New York: HarperOne, 2007).

52. See John Dominic Crossan, *The Greatest Prayer: Rediscovering the Revolutionary Message of the Lord's Prayer* (New York: HarperOne, 2011).

53. See John D. Caputo, *The Insistence of God: A Theology of Perhaps* (Bloomington: Indiana University Press, 2013).

6. The Radical Becoming of Theology

1. Christopher Ben Simpson, *Religion, Metaphysics, and the Postmodern: William Desmond and John D. Caputo* (Bloomington: Indiana University Press, 2009).

2. For instance, see John D. Caputo, "Love Among the Deconstructibles: A Response to Gregg Lambert," *Journal for Cultural and Religious Theory* 5, no. 2 (April 2004): 37–57; John D. Caputo, "The Return of Anti-Religion: From Radical Atheism to Radical The-

ology," *Journal for Cultural and Religious Theory* 11, no. 2 (Spring 2011): 32–125; and John D. Caputo, *Reexamining Deconstruction and Determinate Religion: Toward a Religion with Religion*, eds. J. Aaron Simmons and Stephen Minister (Pittsburgh: Duquesne University Press, 2012).

3. Gavin Hyman, *The Predicament of Postmodern Theology: Radical Orthodoxy or Nihilist Textualism?* (Louisville, KY: Westminster John Knox Press, 2001), p. 2.

4. Ibid., pp. 2, 4.

5. Slavoj Žižek and John Milbank, *The Monstrosity of Christ: Paradox or Dialectic?*, ed. Creston Davis (Cambridge, MA: MIT Press, 2009); John Milbank, Slavoj Žižek, and Creston Davis, *Paul's New Moment: Continental Philosophy and the Future of Christian Theology* (Grand Rapids, MI: Brazos Press, 2010); Marko Zlomislic and Neal DeRoo, eds., *Cross and Khora: Deconstruction and Christianity in the Work of John D. Caputo* (Eugene, OR: Pickwick Publications, 2010); Caputo and Vattimo, *After the Death of God*; and Gianni Vattimo and Rene Girard, *Christianity, Truth and Weakening Faith: A Dialogue*, ed. Pierpaolo Antonello (New York: Columbia University Press, 2010).

6. Simpson, *Religion, Metaphysics, and the Postmodern*, p. 1.

7. Ibid., p. 3.

8. Ibid., p. 4.

9. Ibid., p. 21.

10. Ibid., p. 49.

11. Ibid., pp. 49, 50.

12. See John D. Caputo, "Loosening Philosophy's Tongue: A Conversation with Jack Caputo," *Journal for Cultural and Religious Theory* 3, no. 2 (Fall 2002).

13. Caputo and Vattimo, *After the Death of God*, p. 139.

14. See Mother Teresa, *Come Be My Light: The Private Writings of the Saint of Calcutta*, ed. Brian Kolodiejchuk (New York: Doubleday, 2007).

15. Simpson, *Religion, Metaphysics, and the Postmodern*, p. 53.

16. Caputo, *The Insistence of God*, p. 63.

17. Ibid., pp. 100, 103.

18. For more on this observation regarding the disassociation of faith from both knowledge and culture, see Oliver Roy, *Holy Ignorance: When Religion and Culture Part Ways* (New York: Columbia University Press, 2010); and Stephen Prothero, *Religious Literacy: What Every American Needs to Know—and Doesn't* (New York: HarperOne, 2008).

19. Caputo, *The Insistence of God*, p. 67.

20. Ibid., pp. 87, 92–95.

21. Ibid., p. 93.

22. Ibid., p. 68.

23. Ibid., p. 81.

7. A Farewell to Radical Orthodoxy

1. Jeff Sharlet, "Theologians Seek to Claim the World with God and Postmodernism," *The Chronicle of Higher Education* 46, no. 42 (June 23, 2000): p. A20.

2. See David Van Biema, "Thinkers: God as Postmodern," *Time*, December 17, 2001, http://www.time.com/time/magazine/article/0,9171,1001474,00.html#ixzz0y7OF5c76.

3. These comments were made at the 2008 Annual Meeting of the American Academy of Religion held in Chicago and sponsored by The Centre of Theology and Philosophy. The theme was "The Return of Metaphysics: A Dialogue on the Occasion of the Publication of *Belief and Metaphysics.*"

4. Žižek and Milbank, *The Monstrosity of Christ*, p. 112.

5. Ibid., p. 113.

6. Ibid., p. 114.

7. Surin, "Rewriting the Ontological Script of Liberation," p. 255.

8. Žižek and Milbank, *The Monstrosity of Christ*, p. 4.

9. See Caputo and Vattimo, *After the Death of God*, p. 93.

10. See John D. Caputo, review of *The Monstrosity of Christ: Paradox or Dialectic?* In *Notre Dame Philosophical Reviews* (2009): http://ndpr.nd.edu/review.cfm?id=17605.

11. Žižek and Milbank, *The Monstrosity of Christ*, p. 260.

12. Ibid., p. 255.

13. For instance, see Slavoj Žižek, *The Puppet and the Dwarf: The Perverse Core of Christianity* (Cambridge, MA: MIT Press, 2003).

14. Ibid., pp. 257, 260.

15. This point is publically acknowledged by Žižek at a Wildcard Meeting with Altizer at the 2009 Annual Meeting of the American Academy of Religion, "Whither the 'Death of God': A Continuing Currency?"

16. Thomas J. J. Altizer, *The Call to Radical Theology*, ed. Lissa McCullough (Albany, NY: SUNY Press, 2012), p. 133.

17. Žižek and Milbank, *The Monstrosity of Christ*, p. 260.

18. See Thomas J. J. Altizer's classic text in radical theology, *The Gospel of Christian Atheism* (New York: Collins, 1967).

19. Žižek and Milbank, *The Monstrosity of Christ*, p. 75.

20. This is an important part of Caputo's critique of Žižek. For instance, toward the conclusion of his review of this volume in *Notre Dame Philosophical Reviews*, Caputo writes, "We all know that Žižek can very well make his main case with no mention of Christ at all, that he can use the seminars of Lacan, the films of Alfred Hitchcock or the novels of Stephen King just as well. His whole point, as he says elsewhere, is subversive: to build a Trojan-horse theology, to slop the nose of a more radical materialism under the Pauline tent of theology in order to announce the death of God." Review of *The Monstrosity of Christ*.

21. Žižek and Milbank, *The Monstrosity of Christ*, p. 55.

22. Ibid., pp. 116, 117, 125, 127, 129, 131.

23. Ibid., pp. 115, 192.

24. Ibid., p. 115.

25. Ibid.

26. Ibid., p. 127.

27. Ibid., p. 4.

28. Clayton Crockett, "The Monstrosity of the Other," *Journal for Cultural and Religious Theory* 11, no. 2 (Spring 2011): p. 27, http://www.jcrt.org/archives/11.2/crockett.pdf.

29. See Caputo, Review of *The Monstrosity of Christ*.

30. Giovanna Borradori, *Philosophy in a Time of Terror: Dialogues with Jurgen Habermas and Jacques Derrida* (Chicago: University of Chicago Press, 2003), p. 113. Italics from the original.

31. John Milbank, *Theology and Social Theory: Beyond Secular Reason* (Oxford, UK: Blackwell, 1990), p. 1.

32. Ibid., p. 6.

33. Ibid., p. 1.

34. See Hyman, *The Predicament of Postmodern Theology*, pp. 73–77.

35. Milbank, *Theology and Social Theory*, p. 5.

36. For instance, see Hyman, *The Predicament of Postmodern Theology*, p. 74.

37. See Victor Taylor, "Absolute Christ of 'WDCD?': The Question of Christian Materiality in *The Monstrosity of Christ: Paradox of Dialectic*," *Journal for Cultural and Religious Theory* 11, no. 2 (Spring 2011), http://www.jcrt.org/archives/11.2/taylor.pdf.

38. See especially Bruce Lincoln, *Holy Terrors: Thinking about Religion after September 11* (Chicago: University of Chicago Press, 2003).

39. Gilles Kepel, *Jihad: The Trial of Political Islam*, trans. Anthony F. Roberts (Cambridge, MA: Harvard University Press, 2002), p. 19.

40. See John L. Esposito, *Islam: The Straight Path*, 4th ed. (Oxford, UK: Oxford University Press, 2011), pp. 233–235.

41. Kepel, *Jihad*, p. 13.

42. Ibid.

43. Michael Hardt and Antonio Negri, *Empire* (Cambridge, MA: Harvard University Press, 2000), p. 150.

44. Ibid., p. 149.

45. As quoted in Hyman, *The Predicament of Postmodern Theology*, p. 74.

8. God Is Green

1. Dietrich Bonhoeffer, *Ethics* (New York: Simon and Schuster, 1995), p. 66.

2. Ibid., pp. 66–67.

3. Ibid., p. 70.

4. See Benjamin Barber, *Jihad vs. McWorld: Terrorism's Challenge to Democracy* (New York: Ballantine, 1996).

5. It should be noted that on both of these fronts—foregoing the theological fantasy of creation ex nihilo and the preoccupation with apocalypticism—Catherine Keller has led the way. She has consistently done pioneering theological work that is radical in the very best sense of the term by providing a constructive and creative theo-poetic synthesis of feminist, process, deconstructive, and environmental thought. In particular, she has successfully deconstructed the presumed biblical warrant for the doctrine of creation ex nihilo in her book, *The Face of the Deep: A Theology of Becoming* (New York: Routledge, 2002). She has also provided an explicitly counterapocalyptic theology in her book *Apocalypse Now and Then: A Feminist Guide to the End of the World* (Boston: Beacon, 1997).

6. See Elizabeth Kolbert, *The Sixth Extinction: An Unnatural History* (New York: Picador, 2015).

7. See Kevin Phillips, *American Theocracy: The Perils and Politics of Radical Religion, Oil and Borrowed Money in the 21st Century* (New York: Penguin, 2007).

8. Vine Deloria Jr., *God Is Red* (New York: Grosset and Dunlap, 1973), p. 56.

9. Ibid., p. 6.

10. Ibid., pp. 6, 38.

11. Ibid., p. 59. Incidentally, this reading of the 1960s counterculture is shared by Mark C. Taylor in his book *After God*. As Taylor writes, "Protests to the contrary notwithstanding, the counterculture was a *religious* movement. The culture wars and religious wars of the past two decades have demonized the sixties as a decadent period when individuals and society lost their way by slipping into the morass of relativism, which, critics argue, inevitably leads to nihilism. But this is a naïve and simplistic view. . . . The religious language of redemption and salvation was translated into the language of personal fulfillment and social liberation. Though the terms changed, the questions remained the same as have been asked throughout the history of Christianity: Is liberation primarily personal or social? In other words, must one change consciousness to change society or change society to change consciousness?" *After God* (Chicago: The University of Chicago Press, 2007), pp. 249, 251.

12. Deloria Jr., *God Is Red*, p. 64.

13. Ibid., pp. 58–59.

14. Ibid., pp. 59, 65.

15. Ibid., p. 64.

16. Ibid., pp. 70, 72.

17. Ibid., p. 74.

18. Ibid., pp. 68–69.

19. For instance, see Bill McKibben, *The End of Nature* (New York: Random House, 2006); Denis Edwards, *Ecology at the Heart of Faith* (Maryknoll, NY: Orbis Books, 2006); Sallie McFague, *A New Climate for Theology: God, the World, and Global Warming* (Minneapolis: Fortress Press, 2008); and Leah Schade, *Creation-Crisis Preaching: Ecology, Theology and the Pulpit* (St. Louis: Chalice Press, 2015).

20. Lisa Margonelli, *Oil on the Brain: Adventures from the Pump to the Pipeline* (New York: Nan A. Talese, 2007), pp. 103, 104.

21. Ibid., p. 104.

22. Ibid., p. 115.

23. Phillips, *American Theocracy*, p. 3. Italics his.

24. Ibid., p. 12, 33.

25. Paul Roberts, *The End of Oil: On the Edge of a Perilous New World* (New York: Houghton Mifflin, 2004), p. 3.

26. This distinction between conservation and efficiency is an important one as evidenced by a cover story from *Time* magazine that makes the case that if the United States develops better energy efficiency, little or nothing needs to be changed in our ingrained habits or way of life. Conservation, however, requires sacrifice. See "Wasting our Watts," *Time*, January 12, 2009, pp. 32–36.

27. Phillips, *American Theocracy*, p. 54.

28. Sheldon S. Wolin, *Democracy Incorporated: Managed Democracy and the Specter of Inverted Totalitarianism* (Princeton, NJ: Princeton University Press, 2008), p. 128. Incidentally, Toby Hemenway makes the converse argument—namely, that just as the Right has its cult of the apocalypse in the form of the *Left Behind* series, so too does the Left in the form of the peak oil movement. As Hemenway writes, "I now believe that Peak Oil catastrophism is largely a manifestation of our primary cultural myth: that all things end with suffering, death, and then resurrection. Belief in apocalypse is programmed into western civilization. Given our heritage, "the end is nigh" is the nearly unavoidable personal and collective response to times of uncertainty and rapid change. Apocalypticism is at the core of the Judeo-Christian social mythology, and it influences our beliefs far more deeply than we are conscious of." See http://www.patternliteracy.com/doomer.html.

29. Phillips, *American Theocracy*, p. 121.

30. Ibid., p. 103.

31. Mark C. Taylor, *Confidence Games: Money and Markets in a World without Redemption* (Chicago: University of Chicago Press, 2004), p. 6

32. Editorial, *Wall Street Journal*, January 4, 2008, http://online.wsj.com/article/SB119941453085566759.html.

9. A Rhapsody on Race, Repetition, and Time

1. Caputo, *On Religion*, p. 9.

2. Ralph Waldo Emerson, "The American Scholar" (speech, Phi Beta Kappa Society, Cambridge, MA, August 31, 1837), http://www.emersoncentral.com/amscholar.htm.

3. This was the assessment made by Oliver Wendell Holmes upon hearing the speech. See Susan Cheever, *American Bloomsbury: Louisa May Alcott, Ralph Waldo Emerson, Margaret Fuller, Nathaniel Hawthorne, and Henry David Thoreau; Their Lives, Their Loves, Their Work* (Detroit: Thorndike Press, 2006), p. 80.

4. Beginning in 1876 and accelerating after Reconstruction came to a formal close in 1877, former Confederate states throughout the American South passed legislation and amended constitutions in order to mandate de jure racial segregation. Beginning in 1890 this was extended to voting rights, with most African Americans being effectively disenfranchised through various measures such as poll taxes and literacy tests.

5. Editorial, *Times-Picayune, June 20, 1918*, http://nonotes.wordpress.com/2006/04/22/jass-its-musical-value-is-nil-and-its-possibilities-of-harm-are-great/.

6. As told in *Jazz: A Film by Ken Burns*, PBS Paramount, 2001. Transcript available at http://www.pbs.org/jazz/about/pdfs/MarsalisW.pdf.

7. Terry Teachout, *Pops: A Life of Louis Armstrong* (New York: Mariner Books, 2010), p. 85.

8. As quoted from Matt Glaser in *Jazz: A Film by Ken Burns*.

9. This 1932 film can be viewed on YouTube at http://www.youtube.com/watch?v=aUcQESVYlec.

10. As pointed out to me by Mike Grimshaw, this jarring visualization of Armstrong's music can be seen as an important precursor to what has since become commonplace in

today's video age wherein there is a tension between watching and listening to popular music. The music video was launched as a platform for dissemination and as a means to brandish the musical performer as a star. But what happens when the image overtakes the sound? Or, perhaps more precisely, must we then conclude that in fact the medium is the message?

11. Ralph Ellison, *The Invisible Man* (New York: The Modern Library, 1994), pp. 7–8.

12. See Teachout, *Pops*, pp. 6, 305–306.

13. As quoted in Teachout, *Pops*, pp. 305–306.

14. Ibid., p. 139.

15. Ellison, *The Invisible Man*, p. 8.

16. It is interesting to note how Merton's engagement with the death-of-God movement was paired with his political writings on Vietnam and the civil rights and Black Power movements. It seemed that by virtue of his attempt to conceive of a theology of resistance, he was of the first to recognize the fuller political significance of radical theology. See Thomas Merton, *Faith and Violence: Christian Teaching and Christian Practice* (Notre Dame, IN: University of Notre Dame Press, 1968).

17. See Teachout, *Pops*, p. 91.

18. As quoted in Teachout, *Pops*, pp. 186–187.

19. Gilles Deleuze, *Difference and Repetition*, trans. Paul Patton (New York: Continuum, 2004), p. 41.

Conclusion

1. Scott Anderson, *Lawrence in Arabia: War, Deceit, Imperial Folly and the Making of the Modern Middle East* (New York: Knopf Doubleday, 2013), Kindle edition, location 123, 126.

2. "A Letter from the Publisher," *Time*, December 26, 1969, http://content.time .com/time/magazine/article/0,9171,941765,00.html.

3. David Brooks, "Kicking the Secularist Habit: A Six-Step Program," *Atlantic Monthly*, March 2003, http://www.theatlantic.com/magazine/archive/2003/03/kicking -the-secularist-habit/302680/.

4. Jonathan Z. Smith, *Imagining Religion: From Babylon to Jonestown* (Chicago: University of Chicago Press, 1982), p. 104. Italics his.

5. Talal Asad, *Genealogies of Religion: Discipline and Reasons of Power in Christianity and Islam* (Baltimore: Johns Hopkins University Press, 1993), p. 47.

6. Ibid., p. 45. Italics his.

7. Ibid., p. 28.

8. Peter Berger, "The Desecularization of the World: A Global Overview," in *The Desecularization of the World: Resurgent Religion and World Politics* (Grand Rapids, MI: William B. Eerdmans, 1999), p. 18.

9. Gianni Vattimo, "A Prayer for Silence: Dialogue with Gianni Vattimo," in *After the Death of God*, ed. Jeffrey W. Robbins (New York: Columbia University Press, 2007), p. 98.

10. Ibid., p. 95.

11. As quoted in Hent de Vries and Lawrence Sullivan, *Political Theologies: Public Religions in a Post-Secular World* (New York: Fordham University Press, 2006), pp. 2–3.

12. Ibid., p. 3.

13. See Ivan Strenski, *Thinking about Religion: An Historical Introduction to Theories of Religion* (Oxford, UK: Blackwell, 2006).

14. Sam Gill, "Territory," in *Critical Terms for Religious Studies*, ed. Mark C. Taylor (Chicago: University of Chicago Press, 1998), p. 306.

15. Ibid., pp. 304, 306.

16. Ibid., p. 306.

17. For instance, see Walter H. Capps, *Religious Studies: The Making of a Discipline* (Minneapolis: Fortress Press, 1995).

18. Caputo, *The Insistence of God*, p. 60.

19. Most notably, see Vahanian, *The Death of God*; and Richard Rubenstein, *After Auschwitz: History, Theology and Contemporary Judaism*, 2nd ed. (Baltimore: Johns Hopkins University Press, 1992).

20. Most notably, see Thomas J. J. Altizer, *The Gospel of Christian Atheism* (Philadelphia: Westminster Press, 1966).

21. See Dietrich Bonhoeffer, *The Letters and Papers from Prison*, ed. Eberhard Bethge (New York: Macmillan Publishing, 1971).

22. See especially Crockett, *Radical Political Theology*. See also Hent de Vries and Lawrence E. Sullivan, eds., *Political Theologies: Public Religions in a Post-Secular World* (New York: Fordham University Press, 2006); Creston Davis, John Milbank, and Slavoj Žižek, eds., *Theology and the Political: The New Debate* (Durham, NC: Duke University Press, 2005); and Clayton Crockett, ed., *Religion and Violence in a Secular World: Toward a New Political Theology* (Charlottesville: University of Virginia Press, 2006).

23. See Rosemary Radford Ruether, *The Radical Kingdom: The Western Experience of Messianic Hope* (New York: Harper and Row, 1970).

24. Marcella Althaus-Reid, *Liberation Theology and Sexuality* (Burlington, VT: Ashgate, 2006), p. 2.

25. See Marcella Althaus-Reid, *From Feminist Theology to Indecent Theology* (London: SCM Press, 2004), p. 72.

26. John D. Caputo, *Philosophy and Theology* (Nashville: Abingdon Press, 2006), p. 6.

27. Caputo, *The Insistence of God*.

28. Ibid.

INDEX

JEFFREY W. ROBBINS is chair and professor of religion and philosophy at Lebanon Valley College, where he also serves as the director of the American Studies program and the Undergraduate Research Symposium and as the faculty mentor for the Allwein Scholars Program. He is a fellow of the Westar Institute, where he actively participates in the ongoing seminar on "God and the Human Future," and is an affiliated faculty member of the Global Center for Advanced Studies. He is the author or editor of seven books, including most recently *Radical Democracy and Political Theology* (2011), the co-authored book *Religion, Politics and the Earth: The New Materialism* (2012), and the co-edited volume *The Future of Continental Philosophy of Religion* (2014). He is also a contributing editor of the *Journal for Cultural and Religious Theory*.

CPSIA information can be obtained at www.ICGtesting.com
Printed in the USA
BVOW01*1237230816

459895BV00006B/42/P